MOZAMBIQUE

MOZAMBIQUE

UN Peacekeeping in Action
1992–94

RICHARD SYNGE

UNITED STATES INSTITUTE OF PEACE PRESS
Washington, D.C.

The views expressed in this book are those of the author alone. They do not necessarily reflect views of the United States Institute of Peace.

United States Institute of Peace
1550 M Street NW
Washington, DC 20005

First published 1997

Printed in the United States of America

The paper used in this publication meets the minimum requirements of American National Standard for Information Sciences—Permanence of Paper for Printed Library Materials, ANSI Z39.48-1984.

Library of Congress Cataloging-in-Publication Data
Synge, Richard
    Mozambique: UN peacekeeping in action, 1992–94 / Richard Synge.
        p.   cm.
    Includes bibliographical references and index.
    ISBN 1-878379-70-4. — ISBN 1-878379-69-0 (pbk.)
    1. United Nations—Mozambique.   2. Mozambique—Politics and government—1975– I. Title
DT3389.S96 1997
327.1'7'09679—dc21   97-17773
                                                                          CIP

In *Mozambique: UN Peacekeeping in Action, 1992–94*, Synge takes up Mozambique's story where Cameron Hume left off. Synge follows the peace process in Mozambique from the signing of the 1992 accords between the Frelimo government and the Renamo rebels, through the creation of the UN operation (ONUMOZ) and the endeavors of its military and civilian components, to the expiration of ONUMOZ's mandate in December 1994, on the same day that Mozambique's newly elected president was inaugurated. Synge focuses on how ONUMOZ dealt with the obstacles it confronted as it sought to organize itself, assemble and demobilize the opposing forces, remove landmines, repatriate refugees, and prepare for Mozambique's first-ever democratic elections. Taken as a whole, the operation was clearly a success. As Synge says, ONUMOZ "helped to steer a large, war-torn country firmly in the direction of peace. Thus the principal purpose of the UN mandate was achieved."

Given that UN peacekeepers are frequently criticized as ineffectual and that their real achievements are often ignored, Synge's conclusion is important—and should give pause to those who would write off as futile any efforts to assist African nations to restore their internal stability.

No less important, however, are Synge's conclusions about why ONUMOZ succeeded to the extent that it did, and about where and why it failed. With access to confidential UN files and key individuals, Synge has been able to go behind the scenes of the operation and make informed, balanced, and candid judgments about the strengths and weaknesses of the machinery and personnel involved. He also factors in the impact of external circumstances; the pros and cons of contributions from key third-party states, multilateral organizations, and NGOs; and the attitudes and actions of the Mozambican parties and people themselves.

In other words, while this portrait of *UN Peacekeeping in Action* serves to caution against undue pessimism, it also provides a reality check for those inclined to respond to African conflicts by routinely urging the dispatch of a large-scale, multifaceted UN mission. ONUMOZ was by no means a flawless operation. Overambitious mandates, bureaucratic inefficiencies, interorganizational rivalries, scandalous behavior, questionable priorities—the list of impediments and missteps is quite long. Furthermore, as this book makes clear, even the best-conducted elements of the UN operation depended for their effectiveness on matters beyond their control: the engagement of powerful states determined to see an end to Mozambique's war; propitious regional circumstances; and the overwhelming support for peace from the Mozambican people.

CONTENTS

FOREWORD

With the end of the Cold War, the competition between the superpowers for African proxies and client states also ended. Accordingly, the leading members of the international community have had much less reason than before to intervene in African conflicts. Even when the international community has found sufficient motive and resources to intervene, the intervention has very often failed to yield the desired results, with the UN operation in Somalia being the most notable example.

There are, indeed, reasons to be pessimistic when assessing the prospects for helping to bring peace and stability to Africa. But, as Richard Synge convincingly demonstrates in this important book, there are concrete grounds for optimism as well. "Since 1990 and the end of the Cold War," he notes, "successful mediation has produced promising long-term solutions for Namibia, South Africa, Ethiopia, Eritrea, and Mozambique, all of which suffered conflicts deemed 'ripe for resolution' as long ago as 1984."

Mediation in the case of Mozambique—a subject examined in another book from the United States Institute of Peace Press, Cameron Hume's *Ending Mozambique's War*—involved a variety of international actors spending two years to help the warring parties forge the October 1992 General Peace Agreement. That agreement was a significant achievement in itself, but its sheer complexity and its inadequate attention to logistical realities and organizational requirements meant that the task of translating the agreement into practice would be far from easy or straightforward.

For those readers who believe that intervention is not always doomed to failure, who are rightly wary of entanglement but who also recognize the price of disengagement, who judge the case for intervention on the merits and circumstances of the situation at hand—for such readers Richard Synge provides a wealth of dispassionate analysis, measured judgment, and instructive lessons for future practice.

In seeking to contribute to informed discussion of complex, policy-relevant issues, *Mozambique: UN Peacekeeping in Action* is an important addition to the work of the United States Institute of Peace. Through its Grant Program, the Institute funded much of the research for this book. A good deal of other work relevant to conflict and intervention in Africa has also been supported by the Institute through its Grant Program, the Jennings Randolph fellowship program, and other activities. Much of this work has been published by the Institute's Press. Aside from Cameron Hume's *Ending Mozambique's War,* recent Institute books include John Hirsch and Robert Oakley's reflections on *Somalia and Operation Restore Hope;* UN special representative Mohamed Sahnoun's analysis of earlier international intervention in the same country, *Somalia: The Missed Opportunities;* Peter Gastrow's analysis of South Africa's National Peace Accord, *Bargaining for Peace;* Pierre du Toit's examination of *State Building and Democracy in Southern Africa;* David Smock's edited volume on foreign intervention throughout Africa, *Making War and Waging Peace;* Fen Hampson's study of the implementation of five peace settlements, *Nurturing Peace;* and a volume edited by David Smock and Chester Crocker, *African Conflict Resolution: The U.S. Role in Peacemaking.*

Other Institute publications include two Special Reports, *Zaire's Crises of War and Governance* and *Dealing with War Crimes and Genocide in Rwanda;* and a number of issues in our Peaceworks series, among them J. C. Willame et al., *Zaire: Predicament and Prospects,* David Smock, *Humanitarian Assistance in Africa* and *Creative Approaches to Managing Conflict in Africa,* Denis Mclean, *Peace Operations and Common Sense,* Michael Hardesty and Jason Ellis, *Training for Peace Operations,* and Roxanne Sismanidis, *Police Functions in Peace Operations.*

To this considerable body of work, Richard Synge's *Mozambique: UN Peacekeeping in Action* makes a significant contribution. The Institute trusts that the reader will find much that is challenging within this revealing study of the realities of peacekeeping in Africa.

Richard H. Solomon, President
United States Institute of Peace

ACKNOWLEDGMENTS

The research for this book was greatly facilitated by a grant from the United States Institute of Peace, as well as by the sustained support of the Catholic Institute for International Relations in London and the African Studies Centre of the University of Cambridge. At these institutions I owe special thanks to David Smock, Nigel Quinney, Steve Kibble, and Keith Hart for their interest and encouragement. Among the specialists on Mozambique who provided valuable advice and assistance, I must especially mention Alex Vines, Andrea Bartoli, Michèle de Rosset, Lucila Romero, Margaret Hall, Joe Hanlon, Moises Venancio, and Jose Soares. I was also greatly helped at different stages of the research and writing by Roy Laishley, Salim Lone, Richard Amdur, Anjeli Peck, Antonio Donini, Norah Niland, Jose Campino, Nick van Hear, Ken Wilson, Miguel de Brito, João-Paulo Coelho, Sam Barnes, Tim Born, Paul Fauvet, Philip Machon, Caroline Toulemonde, Ton Pardoel, Sue Willett, and Agostinho Zacarias, and I thank them all. Last but not least, I thank my family for their patience and understanding.

ABBREVIATIONS

Note: An asterisk indicates abbreviation of Portuguese wording.

Adimemo*	Handicapped Veterans' Association of Mozambique
ADP	Accelerated Demining Program
Amodeg*	Mozambican Demobilized Soldiers' Association
AWEPA	Association of West European Parliamentarians for Southern Africa
CCF*	Cease-Fire Commission
CCFADM*	Commission for the Joint Armed Forces for the Defense of Mozambique
CCPPCCN*	Coordinating Council for Prevention and Combat of Natural Disasters
CENE*	National Executive Committee for the Emergency
CHAP	Consolidated Humanitarian Assistance Program
Civpol	UN Civilian Police
CNAT*	National Commission for Territorial Administration
CNE*	National Elections Commission
COMINFO*	National Information Commission
COMPOL*	National Police Affairs Commission
CORE*	Reintegration Commission
CSC*	Supervision and Control Commission
DHA	United Nations Department of Humanitarian Affairs
DPCCN*	Department for the Prevention and Combat of Natural Disasters
DPKO	United Nations Department of Peacekeeping Operations

FADM*	Armed Forces for the Defense of Mozambique
FAM*	Mozambique Armed Forces
GPA	General Peace Agreement
GNU	Government of National Unity
GUN*	Government of National Unity
ICRC	International Committee of the Red Cross
IOM	International Organization for Migration
MPLA*	People's Movement for the Liberation of Angola
NGO	Nongovernmental Organization
OAU	Organization of African Unity
ONUSAL	United Nations Operation in El Salvador
ONUMOZ	United Nations Operation in Mozambique
PIR*	Rapid Intervention Police
PKO	Peacekeeping Operation
RSS	Reintegration Support Scheme
RUF	Revolutionary United Front (Sierra Leone)
SRSG	Special Representative of the Secretary-General
STAE*	Technical Secretariat for Electoral Administration
SWAPO	South West African People's Organization (Namibia)
TU	Technical Unit for Demobilization
UNAVEM	United Nations Angola Verification Mission
UNDP	United Nations Development Programme
UNHCR	United Nations High Commission on Refugees
Unicef	United Nations Children's Fund
UNIDIR	United Nations Institute for Disarmament Research
Unita*	National Union for the Total Independence of Angola
UNOHAC	United Nations Office for Humanitarian Assistance Coordination
UNOSOM	United Nations Operation in Somalia
UNSCERO	United Nations Special Coordinator for Emergency Relief Operations
UNTAC	United Nations Transitional Authority in Cambodia

UNTAG	United Nations Transitional Assistance Group
USAID	United States Agency for International Development
USCR	United States Committee for Refugees
WFP	World Food Programme
WHO	World Health Organization

POLITICAL PARTIES AND COALITIONS IN MOZAMBIQUE DURING THE PEACE PROCESS

AP	Patriotic Alliance
CDR	Democratic Reflection Center
FAP	Patriotic Action Front
Frelimo	Mozambique Liberation Front
Fumo	Mozambique United Front
Monamo	Mozambican Nationalist Movement
Pacode	Democratic Congress Party
Pademo	Mozambique Democratic Party
Palmo	Mozambique Liberal Democratic Party
Panade	National Democratic Party
Panamo	Mozambique National Party
PCD	Democratic Convergence Party
PCN	National Convention Party
Pimo	Mozambique Independent Party
PPLM	Mozambique Liberal Progress Party
PPPM	Mozambique People's Progress Party
PRD	Democratic Renewal Party
PSD	Social Democratic Party
PT	Workers' Party
Renamo	Mozambican National Resistance
SOL	Social Liberal and Democratic Party
UD	Democratic Union
Unamo	National Mozambican Union

CHRONOLOGY, 1992–94

1992

October 4	Signing of the General Peace Agreement in Rome
October 13	Security Council Resolution 782 welcomes the agreement, approves the dispatch of military observers, and confirms the appointment of Aldo Ajello as SRSG
October 15	SRSG and first military observers arrive in Mozambique Cease-fire begins with minor violations in the following days
November 4	First meeting of CSC
December 16	Security Council Resolution 797 establishes ONUMOZ

1993

March 4	First Italian peacekeeping troops arrive
March 6	Renamo boycotts peace commissions
April 14	Security Council Resolution 818
April 15	Italian contingent replaces Zimbabwean troops on Beira corridor
May 14	Mozambique government and United Nations sign status-of-forces agreement
May 20	Renamo trust fund authorized by United Nations
June	Full deployment of ONUMOZ contingents Number of refugees returned reaches 250,000
June 3	Renamo resumes participation on peace commissions
July 9	Security Council Resolution 850 approves ONUMOZ chairmanship of CCFADM and sets October 1994 date for elections
August 21	Dhlakama's first visit to Maputo for meetings with Chissano

September 3	Dhlakama leaves Maputo
September 13	Security Council Resolution 863
October 18	Boutros-Ghali meets Chissano and Dhlakama in Maputo
October 22	CSC approves new timetable for the peace process
October 29	Security Council Resolution 879
November 5	Security Council Resolution 882 extends ONUMOZ mandate to May 5, 1994
November 30	CSC finalizes agreements on electoral law and on the assembly of troops
December	Assembly of troops commences at fifteen assembly areas Number of refugees returned reaches 600,000
December 20	More assembly areas opened, bringing total to thirty-five

1994

January 12	Demobilization of paramilitary forces, militia, and irregulars begins
February 15	CNE commences preparations for elections
February 21	Last assembly areas opened, bringing total to forty-nine
February 23	Security Council Resolution 898 approves deployment of 1,144 Civpol monitors
March 10	First demobilization of FAM troops
March 18	First demobilization of Renamo troops
April 6	Joint commanders of FADM sworn in
April 28	Assembly total reaches nearly 50,000, of whom 13,000 have been demobilized
May 5	Security Council Resolution 916 extends ONUMOZ mandate to November 15
June	Number of refugees returned reaches 1 million Registration of voters begins 1,000 Civpol are deployed throughout the country
July	Rioting intensifies in the assembly areas as demobilization is delayed (55 percent of assembled FAM troops and 29 percent of assembled Renamo troops have been demobilized)
July 11	Assembly of troops declared virtually complete

July 20	South Africa's new president, Nelson Mandela, visits Mozambique
July 25	Number of FADM troops recruited stands at 4,500
August 15	Agreed final deadline for demobilization passes with 16,813 troops still in the assembly areas
August 30	CCF begins verification of arms depots and caches
September 2	Registration of voters ends
September 22	Electoral campaign begins
October	Number of demobilized soldiers exceeds 90,000 Number of FADM recruits reaches 11,000
October 24	Electoral campaign ends
October 26	Dhlakama says Renamo will boycott elections
October 27	Voting begins across the country
October 28	Dhlakama calls off boycott
October 29	Voting extends to third day
November 7	Preliminary results indicate a Frelimo victory
November 15	Security Council Resolution 957 extends ONUMOZ mandate by one month Withdrawal of ONUMOZ military component begins
November 19	Election results announced: Chissano wins 53 percent of presidential vote to Dhlakama's 34 percent; in the National Assembly, Frelimo wins 129 seats to Renamo's 112
November 21	Security Council Resolution 960 calls on parties to accept the election results
December 6	Last meeting of the CSC
December 9	Chissano inaugurated as president ONUMOZ mandate expires

MOZAMBIQUE

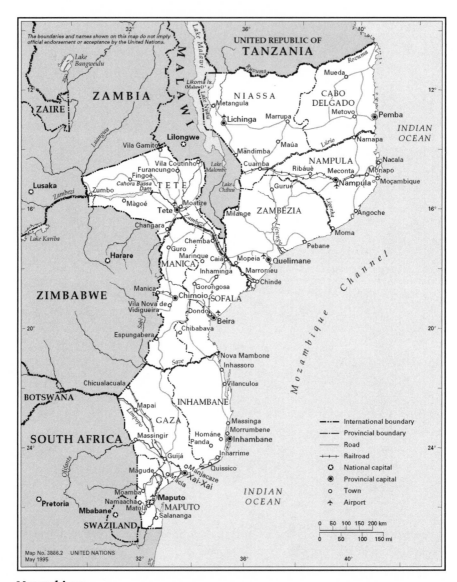

Mozambique

From *The United Nations and Mozambique, 1992–1995* (New York: United Nations, 1995), map 3886.2 (May 1995). Reprinted with permission of the United Nations Publications Board.

1.

MOZAMBIQUE AND THE CHALLENGES OF PEACEKEEPING IN AFRICA

As things stand in the late 1990s, more than a few African states are certain to require some combination of peacemaking, peace-keeping, and peacebuilding to help them face the future. This is why it is useful to analyze such operations already undertaken in the continent and to assess their achievements and weaknesses. The experience of Mozambique, where between 1992 and 1994 the United Nations scored one of its rare peacekeeping successes, is an unusually rich source of lessons for an international community that finds itself increasingly challenged to deal with complex emergencies and conflicts in Africa.

Demands for new and different kinds of conflict resolution have already been generated by the recent phenomena of state collapse (as in Liberia and Somalia), genocide (as in Burundi and Rwanda), rebellions fueled by instability in neighboring states (as in Uganda and Sierra Leone), or implacable confrontation between forces that control vast areas of national territory (as in Angola and Sudan). Further complex political and humanitarian crises are certain to arise in the years ahead. Different combinations of civil disorder and famine could again create demands for the kind of peace enforcement already controversially pioneered in Somalia.

The more extreme forms of national collapse have encouraged the notion that the international community ought to intervene to limit wide-spread loss of life by whatever means are available, disregarding conventional notions of sovereignty.[1] UN agencies involved in huge relief

3

operations mounted for Ethiopia in 1984–85 and Southern Sudan in 1989–93 sought ways of operating with a degree of independence from host governments that were engaged in conflict with rebels. The pattern of achieving access on the basis of need rather than through detailed consultation with official authorities was set by Operation Lifeline Sudan and was later followed by the operation to protect relief supplies in Somalia—a pattern also adopted in the former Yugoslavia. In these cases, humanitarian crises that were caused or exacerbated by war succeeded in generating sufficient concern and urgency for the international community to take decisive action with military support.

Increasingly, the world's attention has to be focused on preventing such crises getting out of hand. Events in Liberia, Rwanda, Burundi, and Zaire (renamed Congo in spring 1997) have required the international community, UN agencies, and nongovernmental organizations to relieve suffering in conditions of political meltdown; in such circumstances, the delivery of emergency relief can all too easily become part of the political bargaining. To prevent a proliferation of similar conflicts, more attention has to be given to mediation and to achieving more efficient delivery of humanitarian aid, as well as to the prospects of achieving a transition from conflict to peace.[2] Interventionist peacekeeping may still be needed, but the evidence shows that it will rarely be successful outside the context of saving lives or supporting viable peace agreements.

Africa is not guaranteed a peaceful future, but experience has shown that fractured states can be put back together, given adequate levels of local and foreign support for the process. To the extent that most wars eventually come to an end—whether through victory, a negotiated solution, or sheer exhaustion—Africa has already seen the satisfactory winding down of a number of long-running conflicts, especially in the two regions most afflicted by the Cold War syndrome, namely Southern Africa and the Horn, where superpower rivalry ensured active military support for governments and rebel movements alike. Since 1990 and the end of the Cold War, successful mediation has produced promising long-term solutions for Namibia, South Africa, Ethiopia, Eritrea, and Mozambique, all of which suffered conflicts deemed "ripe for resolution" as long ago as 1984.[3] The emergence of these states from war or the threat of war provides an important measure of hope for Africa. Although new points of tension are emerging, a significant number of the continent's major conflicts have been put to rest.

The United Nations Operation in Mozambique (ONUMOZ) provides an important example of how a peace process can be conducted under international supervision. It need not be taken as a perfect model. Just as the African context does not present a uniform set of problems, peace-keeping is by its nature an inexact science, bedeviled by hidden depths of uncertainty and volatility. Any peacekeeping operation (PKO), once launched, is subject to high levels of risk, as well as to shifts of perception and of performance by both sponsors and warring parties. The UN operation in Mozambique somehow managed to avoid the pitfalls that have beset many other peacekeeping operations. It deserves to be examined, in the interests of peacekeeping elsewhere, to establish how responsive and relevant the operation was to the situation on the ground, to assess the political authority that the United Nations was able to exert throughout the process, to consider the role of the international community as a whole, and to assess the legacy the undertaking left behind in Mozambique.

There are clear parallels between the kind of conflict that laid waste to much of Mozambique in the 1980s and the cruel hit-and-run insurrections, sometimes backed by outside forces, that are continuing to create instability in other parts of Africa. Africa regularly poses challenges for the international community comparable with those that emerged over many years in Mozambique. The current challenges include stemming the flow of weapons fueled by, or fueling, conflict; responding to complex humanitarian emergencies resulting from prolonged conflict; achieving viable mediation channels; responding to the results of such mediation through formulas and processes for the separation of forces, demobilization, disarmament, resettling refugees, and safeguarding human rights; and converting armed conflicts into peaceful political contests.

There is also a case for examining ONUMOZ in the light of the difficulties experienced by the United Nations in Angola since 1991. Although the parallels with Angola should not be overstated, the sometimes close synergy between developments in the two countries—dating from their shared history as the largest Portuguese colonies in Africa, their adoption of Marxist policies after 1975, and their common experience of South African destabilization policies of the 1970s and 1980s—continued into the 1990s as parallel international efforts were made to bring an end to their respective internal wars. As events turned out, the disastrous failure of the second Angola Verification Mission (UNAVEM II) in the last months of 1992 became a major factor in persuading the Security Council of the need for a substantial mission in Mozambique. The subsequent success of ONUMOZ contrasted sharply with the failure in Angola and, naturally enough, some of the new lessons were applied in the formulation of UNAVEM III in 1995. Such lessons necessarily had to be adjusted to the reality that the Angolan conflict was sustained by very different dynamics from those that had earlier prevailed in Mozambique. Between 1992 and 1994, the Angolan parties demonstrated a relentless capacity and will to keep on fighting, each believing that it could defeat the other or, put differently, that it could not face the consequences of losing. In Mozambique, the United Nations's role was made considerably simpler by the genuine desire on both sides to halt the fighting—one of the factors that can make all the difference between success and failure in peacekeeping.

UN Peacekeeping in Africa and Beyond

The UN Security Council has in general been sparing in its approval of peacekeeping operations in Africa, and has preferred to offer its moral support for regional or subregional peacekeeping initiatives. The first direct involvement in the Congo between 1960 and 1964 was a substantial operation, but it was continuously hampered by disagreements in the Security Council, by the changing realities on the ground, and by the evolution of the mandate from one of halting foreign intervention to one of ending a civil war. The Congo experience was as traumatic for the United Nations as was the Vietnam War for the United States. The United Nations did not return to peacekeeping in Africa until the end of the 1980s, and then to verify and monitor agreements reached—without UN participation—by other parties. Following the signing of accords between Angola, Cuba, and South Africa in New York on December 22, 1988, the United Nations was drawn into the scaling down of the same Cold War tensions that had been largely responsible for its own inability to engage in peacemaking or peacekeeping in Africa. The United Nations began monitoring the Cuban troop pullout from Angola under the first Angola Verification Mission (UNAVEM I, 1989–91) and then undertook a much more substantial operation in Namibia, where its Transitional Assistance Group (UNTAG, 1989–90) helped to steer the country to independence from South Africa on March 21, 1990.

UNTAG was a "classic" operation in that it was underpinned by the consent of the principal parties (the South African government and the SWAPO independence movement). It was also an important model for UN "peacebuilding," bringing together the military function of overseeing the withdrawal of hostile forces with the political function of monitoring elections.[4] Although UNTAG initially faced difficulties in securing funding, troop contributions, and adequate staff, the successful outcome in the form of free and fair elections in November 1989, leading directly to Namibia's complete independence, was of tremendous significance to the United Nations, boosting confidence at a time when the organization was beginning to be called upon to mount comparably complex operations in other parts of the world, notably those in Nicaragua (1989–91), El Salvador (1991–94), and Cambodia (1991–93).

The growth in demand for post–Cold War peacekeeping operations from mid-1991 onward significantly strained the United Nations's political consultative process and the administrative capacities of the new Department of Peacekeeping Operations (DPKO) in New York. In Africa, the operations approved at this time included the stillborn Mission for the Referendum in Western Sahara (MINURSO)—launched in 1991 but subsequently stalled by Moroccan foot-dragging—and a second Angola Verification Mission (1991–92), which included substantial monitoring responsibilities (cease-fire, formation of a new army, and elections) but was constrained by a short time frame, a tight budget, and the lack of reconciliation between the warring parties. As Fen Osler Hampson has commented, "UN action could not have been much more efficient unless UNAVEM II had been given a substantially wider mandate to implement the peace process and put more personnel on the ground."[5] Demobilization was ineffective, and the planned new army was not formed ahead of the September 1992 elections. Then the election results were unacceptable to the Unita leader, Jonas Savimbi, and the country rapidly slid back to an outright war more ferocious than anything that had gone before. As the Angola debacle unfolded, the United Nations was also beset by accusations of ineffectiveness in the face of the simultaneous tragedies in the former Yugoslavia and Somalia. The first UN operation in Somalia (UNOSOM I), authorized in April 1992, was collapsing amid dangerous conditions from a lack of agreement over its mandate, inadequate funding, and an international unwillingness to make troop contributions, prompting the outgoing U.S. president, George Bush, to order the U.S.-led Operation Restore Hope in December.

Despite these setbacks, the United Nations was developing its experience of classic peacekeeping and peacebuilding, notably through its substantial operation in Cambodia, which was assembled over the months following the signing in 1991 of that country's Paris peace accords. The

Transitional Authority in Cambodia (UNTAC, 1992–93) had an ambitious and costly mandate to change the political structure of the country with the help of 15,000 military and 7,000 civilian personnel. Although implementation was marred by the refusal of one of the four signatories, the Khmer Rouge, to demobilize its forces, UNTAC remained on course to organize and monitor an acceptable electoral process in 1993.

It was against the background of these African and international developments that Mozambique's General Peace Agreement in Rome was signed on October 4, 1992. Decisions about the level of support for Mozambique were largely determined in the light of the collapse of the Angola operation. The coincidence of timing between the failure of one process in Southern Africa and the start of another helped to concentrate minds on the establishment of ONUMOZ as a "classic" and multifunctional operation, capitalizing on the detailed drafting of the Rome peace agreement and the full consent of the parties. The political outlook was promising although the humanitarian challenge, compounded by a severe Southern African drought, was a cause of concern.

The Possibilities and Limits of Peacekeeping

Different models of peacekeeping have been tried, but endlessly variable political and humanitarian conditions exact demands that are unique to each operation. Peacekeeping is, by its nature, an ad hoc function. Moreover, as many analysts have noted, it is only fully successful when all the parties wish to stop fighting.[6] For the United Nations, peacekeeping operations are best suited to following up, rather than preceding or enforcing, efforts at conflict resolution. The common features of successful operations, as suggested by William Durch, are local consent; international impartiality; support from the major powers, and from the United States in particular; and the willingness of the local parties to alter their priorities from "winning everything to salvaging something" in a peace process.[7]

Beyond these general hypotheses, important lessons can be drawn from each operation. In considering the achievements and weaknesses of ONUMOZ, some useful comparisons can be made with UNTAC in Cambodia, which suffered near-failure but enjoyed eventual success and was clearly an important test case for classic missions of a complex nature. The lessons drawn from UNTAC by Michael Doyle and Nishkala Suntharalingam stress the vital importance of not losing time in the immediate aftermath of a peace agreement and the need for mandates to be "politically well designed."[8] In their view, the designing of mandates should focus on the institutionalization of whatever degree of reconciliation the parties have agreed to in their peace negotiations, the incorporation of bargaining advantages for the UN authority, and as much independent implementation for the United Nations as the parties will accept.

The Australian foreign minister most closely involved in preparing the ground for UNTAC, Gareth Evans, later outlined the basic requirements of such missions as clear and achievable goals, adequate resources, close coordination between peacemaking and peacekeeping, impartiality, local support, external support, and a signposted exit.[9] He also expressed the conviction that the UN Secretariat needs to establish or strengthen its planning units for the specific components of each mission, that deployment should occur as soon as possible after the parties reach agreement, that the United Nations must provide the best possible personnel, and that communications between the force and the UN Secretariat must be strengthened. A significant comment comes from the secretary-general's special representative in Cambodia during the UNTAC mandate, Yasushi Akashi, who urged proper training for military and police contingents "for inculcating sensitivity and respect for local customs and cultures."[10]

An ever present challenge to peacekeeping and humanitarian operations comes from shortages of qualified personnel and managers, shortfalls in funding, and the weaknesses of management and information at the UN Secretariat.[11] Over the period of planning for and deployment of ONUMOZ, these challenges were made particularly intense by the competing demands of Cambodia and the former Yugoslavia. The cost of UN peacekeeping jumped from $500 million in 1991 to $2 billion in 1992, rising again to $3.2 billion in 1993 and $3.9 billion in 1994. By 1994, the United Nations was running seventeen PKOs worldwide, involving 70,000 soldiers. After reaching this peak, demands for UN peacekeeping began to tail off. By 1996, the largest PKO in the world was the third Angola Verification Mission (UNAVEM III), deploying 6,500 soldiers, 500 military observers, and 300 civilian police monitors.

Achievements and Weaknesses of ONUMOZ

The hypotheses and proposals spelled out above are particularly relevant to an operation on the scale of ONUMOZ. Mozambique's two parties wished to stop fighting and adjusted their objectives from seeking victory to accepting compromise, the international community displayed impartiality, and both the United States and the European Union lent strong support. The United Nations's mandate, if not well designed, was at least based on a patiently negotiated formula acceptable to both parties. The mandate sought to institutionalize the process agreed between them and it gave the United Nations considerable authority and leverage over the peace process. The inherent weaknesses and institutional shortcomings of the United Nations—sluggishness, delayed deployment, inadequate funding, a shortage of professional staff, and poor preparation, planning, and training—became apparent at different stages but did not prove fatal to the process.

Although the full conclusions of this study are given in the last chapters, it is appropriate to anticipate some of the overriding themes. First, the obvious achievement of ONUMOZ was that it helped to steer a large, war-torn country firmly in the direction of peace. Thus the principal purpose of the UN mandate was achieved. At the end of the two-year mandate in December 1994, the United Nations and the international community as a whole could claim that they had not only succeeded in keeping Mozambique's sworn enemies, Frelimo and Renamo, from returning to war, but also organized elections that had established a democratic political structure for this war-shattered nation over the longer term. Mozambique was not ignored at a time of great need and the international community acted with a rare degree of unanimity. As earlier in Namibia, the United Nations became the agent of transition and was endowed with a degree of authority and leverage to help to guard against any resumption of conflict.

Second, the circumstances were generally propitious. Events in Southern Africa, and in Mozambique in particular, were dominated by the changes taking place within South Africa—changes that were to lead to the democratic elections there in April 1994. In sharp contrast to the catastrophe in Angola, where the belligerent parties were ready to return to war at a moment's notice, Mozambique was in a state of exhaustion. The Mozambican generals and politicians on the whole remained committed to the peace agreement they had negotiated and signed in Rome. Once the soldiers on the two sides of the conflict were successfully and voluntarily demobilized, the risk of a return to war was effectively eliminated. Moreover, millions of displaced Mozambicans showed their faith in the process by returning spontaneously to their homes as soon as they felt it safe to do so. Ultimately, about 5 million of a population of 16 million took advantage of the return to peace to reclaim land and property.

Third and most remarkable, a determined and enthusiastic electorate overwhelmingly endorsed the peace. Ordinary citizens clearly did not want to miss their first chance to choose parties and individuals to represent them. Despite a last-minute threat of disruption by Renamo's leader, Afonso Dhlakama, the well-organized elections of October 27–29, 1994, confirmed that the people of Mozambique were ready to make a new start.

In terms of the final outcome, therefore, the United Nations was seen to have performed satisfactorily in Mozambique, completing a complex mandate from the Security Council with challenging military, humanitarian, and political components. But peacekeeping is thankless work, even when as apparently successful as this mission turned out to be. As had been the case in so many of its other operations, the United Nations was criticized for its performance. From soon after ONUMOZ was launched in late 1992 until it ended two years later, complaints were voiced that the operation was too slow and bureaucratic, that there was poor cooperation with the different agencies active in Mozambique, that the secretariat in New York sent unprofessional personnel, and that ONUMOZ failed to attend to some of the most urgent priorities while trying to take on several unnecessary or even unachievable functions. The examination of ONUMOZ that follows shows that mistakes were indeed made and that peacekeeping operations have built-in encumbrances and contradictions. The image of the United Nations as a slow-moving and heavy-footed beast was all too often highlighted.

A determination to avoid failure was generated by events in Angola and contributed to an overambitious mandate, but it also stimulated effective political management of the most visible aspects of the peace process. A combination of cooperation by the international community and political dexterity helped to bring Mozambique to a point where ONUMOZ could disengage without shame or rancor. Forceful leadership of ONUMOZ was provided by the UN secretary-general's special representative, the Italian politician and diplomat Aldo Ajello, who after a difficult start was able to use effective persuasion and improvisation to keep the peace process on track. Ajello's energy and commitment ensured the support of a powerful supervisory and monitoring commission that included the ambassadors of countries with influence in Mozambique. Ajello was able to keep ONUMOZ running in tandem with the joint efforts of the donors. Together they extracted just enough cooperation from the Mozambican parties to keep the peace process moving forward to its end.

Politically, the efforts of the donor community and ONUMOZ combined to deliver well-monitored elections in 1994 and put a convincing seal on the Rome peace agreement. It was ultimately fortunate for the United Nations that the elections diverted attention from some of the operation's more obvious weaknesses, such as the poor results recorded in the clearance of landmines and the collection of weapons, the small size of Mozambique's new armed forces, and, above all, the lack of full reconciliation between Frelimo and Renamo. In the event, none of these setbacks was to prove disastrous to the peace process although each raised questions about the longer-term stability of Mozambique.

One of the most persistently difficult questions to answer relates to the actual need for an operation of the ambitious size, scope, and expense of ONUMOZ, which cost at least $700 million, to resolve the political, military, and humanitarian problems of a poor country with a notional gross domestic product of only $1.5 billion. The operation, as first visualized in 1992 and subsequently sustained, certainly represented an important insurance policy for the international community at time of great disappointment over the disaster in Angola, continuing uncertainty within South Africa, and a severe regional drought threatening neighbors that depended on Mozambique's transportation infrastructure. The nature and composition of ONUMOZ was ultimately determined by the Security Council in New York, in its eleven resolutions relating to Mozambique between October 13, 1992, and November 21, 1994. Once established and funded, the operation took on a life of its own. Much of the political decision making occurred in Maputo rather than in New York or Western capitals, which were more often informed rather than consulted about the changing needs on the ground. This allowed for political flexibility, but ONUMOZ was rarely subjected to close examination by its paymasters.

By the time it was withdrawn, ONUMOZ had come to be seen by many as a sledgehammer employed to crack a relatively small nut, and its disengagement was broadly accepted and welcomed by both its paymasters and its beneficiaries. By the end of 1995, the tangible sense of relief in Mozambique that ONUMOZ had departed was accompanied by some concern about its longer-term impact on the Mozambican polity and society. Mozambicans of all persuasions had often been offended by the overbearing influence and behavior of UN personnel. Moreover, the donor community appeared to be more comfortable with the notion of exerting political influence through normal diplomatic channels than with the role it had played as party to the overt political power wielded by ONUMOZ. The vacuum left by its withdrawal was filled by a consortium of donors, including the United Nations's own agencies.

It will become clear in the course of this study that the entity known as ONUMOZ was in a number of its activities more of an abstraction than a reality. Although the management of the entire peace process was nominally entrusted by the UN Security Council to ONUMOZ, much of the work was in fact conducted by units operating outside the UN system and funded directly by bilateral donors. The phenomenon of donors working in parallel with ONUMOZ became particularly evident during the demobilization phase and the preparation for elections. Despite great difficulties of coordination in some areas, most donors managed to keep in step with the overall aims and objectives of ONUMOZ, if not with its frustrating bureaucracy. Perhaps ironically, it was usually the UN agencies with long experience of Mozambique that proved the most reluctant to cooperate with the new, inexperienced, and entirely temporary ONUMOZ staff, who came to be viewed almost as invaders.

The varied perceptions of ONUMOZ revealed in this study help to illustrate both its achievements and its weaknesses. Criticism of the operation from the Mozambican parties and the local press was continuous, but this actually helped to keep the operation alert, if not always responsive, to the expectations of Mozambican citizens. Once ONUMOZ was launched, concern about its performance was also repeatedly expressed within the international community in Maputo. It was to Ajello's credit that he encouraged and used debate and criticism as essential tools in his mission.

To the extent that the ONUMOZ period in Mozambique provides insights into the theory and practice of peacekeeping and into the political, humanitarian, and economic challenges facing Africa, the conclusions and lessons are presented in the concluding chapters.

2.

THE SPIRIT OF ROME

The Peace Accords and the Belated Invitation to the United Nations

The process of negotiating an end to Mozambique's devastating war was a skilled balancing act conducted by Italian mediators who managed to combine a good understanding of the complexities of Mozambique with extraordinary patience. Once the talks began in July 1990, the mediators built on the barest minimum of common ground between the government and Renamo, despite apparently irreconcilable differences. At first, the success of the talks depended on discretion, lack of publicity, and not raising international expectations. There was considerable skepticism, both in Mozambique and among the international community as a whole, about the prospects of success. It took more than a year to forge the basic agreement on principles and a further six months to start to deal with the substantive issues. The momentum for constructing a comprehensive peace agreement developed only after May 1992, and even then there were doubts about the outcome and timing. Although peace was already breaking out around the country by the time that the General Peace Agreement (GPA) was eventually signed in October 1992, the international community was scarcely ready for the challenge of a major peacekeeping operation in Mozambique.[1]

A State of Exhaustion

By the beginning of 1992, the Mozambican nation was at the extremes of distress. The war that had been fought for fifteen years overshadowed all

15

movement and economic activity throughout this vast, impoverished country. The onset of the 1991–92 drought was exacerbating dependence on foreign aid and assistance. There seemed to be no prospect of accelerating the painfully slow process of negotiating an end to the conflict that had begun in Rome in 1990 under the auspices of the Italian government and the Sant'Egidio community, a Roman Catholic group of intellectuals and volunteers dedicated to helping immigrants and solving problems in their home countries. The situation on the ground was as dangerous as ever. The government still controlled all the major cities and provincial capitals but was unable to ensure the safety of the internal transportation network. Although a partial cease-fire had been observed since December 1990 along the main transportation corridors leading into Zimbabwe and Malawi, Renamo was still capable of acting destructively throughout large areas of the country. The rebel movement was losing the South African logistic backing that had sustained it throughout the 1980s. But although it lacked the military capacity to threaten the cities, Renamo could still maintain its psychological advantage by the threat of disruption and surprise attack. Without a cease-fire, both the state of war and the humanitarian crisis could bring only further misery.

Renamo's heartland was the central provinces of Sofala and Manica. Its skill at exploiting the government's military weakness had, since the late 1980s, given it the means to operate throughout the country, seizing government weaponry, destroying the economic infrastructure, and disrupting the transportation of goods and food relief. Although Renamo's claims to control more than 80 percent of the country were highly exaggerated, it more or less permanently controlled about 25 percent of Mozambique in zones scattered throughout the country, and was certainly disruptive in about 80 percent of the country.[2] The government's portrayal of Renamo as an African equivalent of the Khmer Rouge could not hide the fact that the movement had established a basic form of administration in many areas and was winning over the support or acquiescence of traditional chiefs and significant sections of the rural population. It had committed atrocities in provinces where its presence was weaker, particularly in the south, but the government's military methods were often as destructive and had a self-defeating tendency to alienate those who had not fled to escape the fighting.[3] By 1992, a strategic stalemate prevailed. Tactically the government was in no position to reverse the gradual gains that Renamo was making in the north-central region, particularly in Tete, Zambezia, and Nampula provinces. Millions of people there had already been displaced, many of them into refugee camps in the cities and neighboring Malawi. Any resumption of struggles over territory would have laid further waste to regions that are Mozambique's agricultural heartland. Renamo was, however, showing signs of being weakened by drought and by its lack of direct access to food relief.

In the wake of the 1991–92 drought, most regions of the country were being pushed to the limits of survival. The areas that Renamo controlled were especially badly hit, although the movement's persistent denial of access to outsiders had prevented international, bilateral, or nongovernmental organizations (NGOs) from assessing needs or providing humanitarian relief. Such agencies could provide emergency relief only for the needy people who were within reach, whether displaced within the country or living as refugees in neighboring countries. By 1992, armed escorts had to be provided for convoys delivering food to more than half the districts in the country.[4] Such was the scale of Mozambique's humanitarian problems that the nation was host to no fewer than 26 UN agencies, 6 multilateral non-UN agencies, 44 bilateral donors, official agencies from 35 countries, and 143 external NGOs from 23 countries.[5] There was already an impressive degree of coordination among donors. A key body was the Aid for Democracy Group, a gathering of ambassadors who closely followed the negotiations in Rome and concerned themselves with the issues of democratization, decentralization, and public-sector reform.

Progress in Rome

The negotiations in Rome did not at first bring the international community fully into the frame or even involve close consultation with the United Nations. The first agreements dealt with largely abstract political questions relating to the final elements of a peace process, not the essentials of a peacekeeping operation. Protocol I of the GPA, signed on October 18, 1991, established only the basic principles upon which the rest of the peace agreement could be constructed. Formulated with the help of the mediators (the Sant'Egidio community and the Italian government), this agreement accepted that Renamo should become a political party, that the government should effectively limit its political monopoly, and that there should be a supervisory peace commission in which the United Nations and third-party governments would be invited to participate. Although this laid a notional basis for UN involvement, the peace process still lacked sufficiently concrete definition to justify detailed planning—even after Protocols II and III, on the formation of political parties and the electoral law, respectively, were signed on November 13, 1991, and March 12, 1992.[6]

The parties and their mediators made a broad assumption that the international community would have to play an implementing role, but the international community was not even represented at the talks.[7] It was an essential part of the Sant'Egidio formula that the two sides should move forward at their own pace without being subjected to undue pressure. The formal involvement of Portugal and the United States, both of which had taken a close interest from the outset of the talks in 1990, was eventually proposed sometime between March and June 1992, as the talks at last became more purposeful. If an effective cease-fire were to be agreed upon, there would be a need for international observers. Renamo strongly favored giving the United Nations the leading role, but the government, fearing loss of sovereignty, would have preferred a largely African operation led by the Organization of African Unity. At the same time, it was becoming apparent that humanitarian issues, in which the United Nations was already extensively involved, could no longer be kept out of the discussion.

Within Mozambique itself, the growing hardships were increasing pressure on both Frelimo and Renamo to reach an understanding as soon as possible. The country's churches took the lead in campaigning for faster progress in Rome. Militarily, the two sides had fought themselves to a standstill. The government army was threatening mutiny over unpaid wages; Renamo areas of the country were facing shortages of food. There was also a risk of a wider social breakdown, particularly in view of the millions of automatic weapons in the hands of civilians in Mozambique.[8] Neighboring countries—themselves facing the prospect of food shortages and heavily dependent on Mozambique as a vital supply route—were fearful that they would be overwhelmed by any further exodus of refugees from Mozambique.

When Afonso Dhlakama met U.S. Assistant Secretary of State Herman Cohen in Malawi in April 1992, the Renamo leader welcomed the proposal that the United States should participate as an observer at the Rome negotiations. Meanwhile, progress in Rome began to be monitored by UN headquarters in New York, and particularly by Under-Secretary-General James Jonah, who held informal consultations with member states of the Security Council. But there were still few indications that a large UN operation was necessary or desirable, and full consideration of the issue was hampered by uncertainty about the chances of success in Rome.

Toward the end of May, invitations to observe the Rome talks were issued to Portugal and to three permanent members of the Security Council—the United States, the United Kingdom, and France. The United Nations was invited only after all four countries had themselves agreed to participate. They emphasized their role as observers rather than mediators, although as far as the Mozambican government was concerned there was "no very precise boundary between mediating, observing and influencing."[9] President Chissano sent a letter to the secretary-general on June 1, 1992, inviting the United Nations to join the observers in Rome. The UN Secretariat responded by dispatching Colonel Romeo Ferreira of the Brazilian armed forces, who had served with the ONUSAL operation in El Salvador.

In Rome, Ferreira's presence helped to keep New York informed of progress. By early July, he was reporting on a potential breakthrough in the discussions of military issues and the structure of the peace commissions. The Italian delegation at the Rome talks was proposing a joint political and military commission, comprising the parties, representatives of the mediators, the United Nations, and a number of countries. The Italians were also proposing a range of subcommissions, some with and some without UN involvement, prompting UN officials in New York to suggest the need for a more hierarchical structure. No more than 700 military personnel were being proposed (100 observers to verify the cease-fire and 100 observers and 500 troops to verify military aspects of demobilization). Daily reports from Ferreira helped keep UN Under-Secretary-General Marrack Goulding closely informed about the developments in Rome. The messages being sent back from New York to Rome at this time hinted that the United Nations should not be expected to accept automatically whatever role might be envisaged for it by the negotiators.

After Chissano and Dhlakama had met face-to-face in Rome in early August, Goulding and Jonah sent their first full briefing to the secretary-general, pointing out that the United Nations was soon likely to be asked to monitor the entire peace process in Mozambique. The briefing raised questions about whether the United Nations should chair the peace commission and subcommissions, about the kind of mandate involved, about the need to integrate all aspects of the peace process, and about financing—with the cost at this stage estimated at little more than $80 million, the annual budget of UNAVEM II in Angola. Although the United

Nations had arrived late in the Rome process, its role as guarantor of the peace was becoming central. This role was now apparently accepted by the parties, the mediators, and the observer nations alike. The joint declaration signed in Rome on August 7 by the two leaders formally accepted the role of the international community and the United Nations in monitoring and guaranteeing the cease-fire and the electoral process envisaged in the peace agreement.

In the second week of August, the United Nations upgraded its presence in Rome by sending Tayeb Merchoug, an Algerian and a high-ranking political affairs officer in Jonah's office. Aware that the United Nations was being required to implement a process that it had played little part in mediating, Merchoug found himself uncomfortably restricted in his capacity as observer rather than mediator, especially when questions were raised about the amount of authority the United Nations should exert. Renamo was pressing for the United Nations to mount a Cambodia-style operation to exercise extensive political and administrative powers for the duration of its mandate. Merchoug succeeded in resisting this pressure, but he stressed that the United Nations would be in favor of exercising an impartial role through chairmanship of the peace commissions.[10]

Following discussions between Jonah and the Mozambican permanent representative at the United Nations, Pedro Comissario Afonso, the secretariat on August 18 sent a short "non-paper" (an informal aide-mémoire, not for attribution) to the government in Maputo. The non-paper pointed out the need for an agreement defining the status of a UN operation and suggested the presence of a special representative of the secretary-general to supervise the military and electoral aspects of an operation. Mention was also made of the possible need for a police division and for the United Nations to take on a humanitarian coordination function. Also raised was the possibility that the secretary-general might not be able to obtain Security Council authority for an operation until after the signing of the full peace agreement, which, it was now suggested, could take place on October 1.

Indicating its general acceptance of the UN role as proposed by New York, the Mozambican government invited planning teams to visit the country as soon as possible to assess the scale of the likely involvement. A technical mission, composed of experts on military and electoral affairs, arrived in September, very late in the day in view of the fact that the negotiations in Rome were drawing to a close. The team consulted and traveled widely, speaking to the government in Maputo and, on

September 20, to Dhlakama in Maringue. The report on the military aspects, issued on September 29, was the first to underline the need to guarantee security on the transportation corridors, because the Zimbabwean and Malawian troops patrolling the corridors were to be withdrawn as part of the peace agreement. The link between the peace process and the distribution of humanitarian aid was stressed and programs to rehabilitate infrastructure and to carry out demining were recommended. The report also urged that a status-of-mission agreement be signed with the Mozambique government before an operation commenced.

With only a matter of days to go before the date set for signing the GPA and all its remaining protocols, the UN Secretariat found itself being confronted with a Mozambican operation that could not be done cheaply. In the circumstances, UN officials felt that there was little option other than to let the deal be struck first. The operation could be planned afterward and imperfections in the peace agreement itself corrected as the implications for the international community became clearer.

The United Nations was already overstretched in similar situations around the world and was concerned about overcommitting itself. But the secretariat could not avoid the conclusion that a Mozambique mission would have to be larger than the mission deployed in Angola. If it were to succeed, things should not be left to chance. This meant that the role of the United Nations should be central in guiding the peace process. Influenced by the difficulties being experienced in Angola, the discussions in New York at this time centered on the importance of ensuring full demobilization of the parties as well as UN chairmanship of the key supervisory commission. The issue of the chairmanship was clarified only in the closing stages of the Rome talks. In terms of the kind of mandate being considered, the closest parallel in the United Nations's experience was ONUSAL in El Salvador.

The reports from the technical team returning from Mozambique showed that a large, complex, and expensive mission was unavoidable. On September 24, the secretary-general's office had begun to prepare a presentation to the Security Council. The DPKO stressed its view that the peace commissions be chaired by the United Nations and that assembly areas for the two armies be identified. It pointed out that a deployment of troops along the three principal transportation corridors would greatly add to the size, complexity, and cost of the operation and would take several months to arrange. The secretary-general's letter of September 29 to the president of the Security Council urged that the question of troop deployment be resolved before the signing of the GPA.[11] There was no time for this to be done before the signing, so the first delays in mounting the operation became inevitable.

Merchoug's presence in Rome, and that of James Jonah during the final days before the signing of the GPA in early October, helped to bring the negotiations to conclusion, even though the United Nations remained ill prepared to shoulder the responsibility of another substantial operation. In the last few days of September, Merchoug advised New York that it was best to let the signing go ahead, whatever reservations the secretariat might have. Arriving in Rome on October 1, Jonah learned that both parties were becoming concerned about the readiness of the United Nations to have a presence in Mozambique, particularly because the peace agreement proposed that a cease-fire would come into effect within a matter of days after the signing. Jonah gave assurances that the United Nations would provide at least a symbolic presence on the ground at an early date. Dhlakama continued to hesitate, arriving in Rome too late for a planned signing on October 1, and then raising a number of objections to details in the final protocols. (Dhlakama agreed to travel to Rome only after the Tiny Rowland, chief executive of the British multinational corporation Lonrho, sent his private jet to collect the Renamo leader.) Eventually, assurances of financial support from both Rowland and the Italian government persuaded Dhlakama to sign on October 4.[12]

In a statement welcoming the signing, Secretary-General Boutros Boutros-Ghali said that the GPA envisaged a central and large role for the United Nations. Pointing out that "the United Nations role will require greater effort and more resources than was the case in Angola," he promised that the matter would be brought before the Security Council as early as possible so that the United Nations would be in a position to carry out "the extremely important responsibilities assigned to it by this agreement."[13]

As Cameron Hume notes in his detailed account of the Rome negotiations, the mediators had done a splendid job of securing legitimacy for the GPA, but the agreement itself was flawed. The parties never seriously discussed the practical elements of the protocols on military questions, guarantees, and the cease-fire, partly because of the sheer difficulty of reaching common ground on these sensitive issues and partly because of inadequate information on the deployment of the parties' own forces. Neither side had a clear idea of how to establish or operate the numerous commissions, committees, and subcommittees that the parties themselves had insisted upon building into the agreement. Hume, himself a member of the U.S. observer team, noted that the parties "had stipulated a time-table that they could not possibly keep to, even in the first weeks after a cease-fire."[14] Moreover, last-minute negotiations over the administration of territory produced a poorly phrased compromise that allowed for different interpretations and would raise considerable difficulties later. The United Nations was assuming responsibility for implementing an agreement that would require effective renegotiation on a number of fronts.

The General Peace Agreement

In that it appeared to provide a comprehensive framework that accommodated the principal concerns of the two parties, the GPA was relatively sophisticated. It had received the full assent of the leadership of both parties, and it set up agreed procedures and precise timetables. It was therefore an essential text to guide the peace process. But its sheer complexity meant that it imposed heavy demands on those required to implement it. It did not realistically allow the United Nations to take up its functions in an organized or coherent manner and, for many of the stipulations, logistics had not been taken into account. Both sides, more concerned with managing developments in the short term, looked to the international community to provide the organizational framework of the peace process. Renamo, in particular, had a very personalized and rudimentary system of command and control and had considered neither the logistics of assembly and its other commitments nor how to find trained and literate people to staff the large number of commissions proposed in the agreement.

The GPA contained seven different protocols, of which the most complex were those covering political and military matters. The first three protocols settled only the questions of legitimacy. Protocol I on Basic Principles established the commitment of both sides to dialogue and co-operation as indispensable to peace. The government undertook not to promulgate any legislation contrary to the agreements reached. Renamo committed itself to respect the laws and institutions of the state. Protocol II on Political Parties provided guarantees for multiparty democracy and, specifically, established the principles governing the formation of political parties. Protocol III on the Principles of the Electoral Law dealt with the electoral process, including freedom of the press and access to the media, freedom of movement and domicile in the country, the return of refugees and displaced Mozambicans and their reintegration into society, the electoral procedures, a pluralistic system, guarantees, and the role of international observers.

The remaining four protocols, all of which were signed on October 4, 1992, contained substantial challenges for the international community and the parties alike. Protocol IV on Military Questions provided for the formation of a single joint army; established its numerical strength at thirty thousand; and established a calendar for the withdrawal of foreign troops from Mozambique, the dismantling of private and irregular armed groups, the functioning of the secret service, the restructuring of the police and their delinking from party structures, and the reintegration of demobilized soldiers. Protocol V on Guarantees established the calendar of the electoral process, provided for the creation of a supervision and monitoring commission, and established mechanisms for the implementation of agreements. Protocol VI on the Cease-Fire provided for the end of the armed conflict and established a 180-day calendar for the cease-fire, separation and concentration of forces, and full demobilization of both sides' armed forces. Its failure to identify the assembly areas had already created the potential for prolonged further negotiation. Protocol VI also failed to give a realistic framework for the disarmament of the two sides' forces. The last protocol, Protocol VII, on a Donors' Conference, called for a conference to guarantee the provision of funding for both the electoral process and humanitarian assistance programs. It established that part of the funds donated should be allocated to the political parties.[15]

The GPA envisaged that the United Nations would assume chairmanship of three commissions: the Supervision and Control Commission, the Cease-Fire Commission, and the Reintegration Commission (for demobilized soldiers). Other commissions to be established under the terms of the GPA, albeit envisaged as having no UN participation, were a Commission for the Joint Armed Forces for the Defense of Mozambique, a National Information Commission, a National Police Affairs Commission, a National Elections Commission, and a National Territorial Administration Commission.

The timetables in the GPA foresaw completion of the entire peace process in a mere twelve months, but the United Nations was far from ready to set up the kind of machinery that would be needed to implement such a calendar. It could take only the most tentative of first steps. The UN Secretariat needed more time to assess the full needs of the process, and in the days after the signing of the GPA, it could do little more than attend to the most immediate task, deploying observers to verify the cease-fire that was due to begin on October 15. Only thereafter could the rest of the process start to unfold.

3.

THE LAUNCH OF ONUMOZ

Inauspicious Beginnings, Troublesome Bureaucracy

For several months after the signing of the General Peace Agreement, UN action in Mozambique was little more than symbolic. The maintenance of peace depended on the two parties' combat exhaustion and the Mozambican people's obvious enthusiasm for a new era without war. The buildup of the UN presence was far too slow to maintain the pace of the process expected in the GPA, and the parties themselves started to reassess their prospects in the light of the kind of UN operation being considered and planned in New York and Western capitals.

The thinking of the UN Security Council and the secretariat about Mozambique was guided by the simultaneous collapse of Angola's peace process in October. Angola, whose colonial history and recent experience closely resembled that of Mozambique, was returning rapidly to outright civil war—a war far more devastating than the conflict that had gone before. The fundamental lesson for those planning a Mozambican operation was that elections should take place only after the satisfactory demobilization of troops and formation of a new army. It was accepted that the elections themselves would have to be more thoroughly prepared and observed than those in Angola, in order to minimize the risk of dispute over the results.

The Security Council in December 1992 approved a UN Operation in Mozambique (ONUMOZ) that was both substantial and multifunctional, but until the second half of February 1993 the only effective evidence of UN engagement was a small advance force of military observers. The parties were able to capitalize on the delay by exploiting inconsistencies in the GPA and by establishing new conditions for both the peace process and UN involvement. Renamo declared that it would not start to demobilize until UN troops arrived in large numbers. Some in the government felt that the UN mandate was an infringement of national sovereignty. In the circumstances, the United Nations and the special representative of the secretary-general had little choice other than to improvise and build up the elements of the peace process incrementally. Operationally, ONUMOZ was hampered by bureaucracy; politically, it had to reformulate the agreements reached in Rome. Only persistent efforts against challenging odds kept the peace process alive through its first unpromising year.

Venture into the Unknown

On October 4, Aldo Ajello was summoned at short notice from Geneva to New York to be told of his assignment as interim special representative of the secretary-general (SRSG). One of the most senior Italians in the UN system, with the rank of assistant secretary-general, Ajello was serving as director of the bureau of external relations of the United Nations Development Programme (UNDP). In an earlier career as a politician between 1979 and 1983, Ajello had been a member of the Italian Parliament and had taken a close interest in foreign affairs, playing a leading role in the substantial growth of the Italian international aid budget in the early 1980s. Since joining UNDP in 1984, he had served as a director in the European office until 1988 and then, until 1991, as director for special activities, where he became familiar with UNDP's substantial programs in Central America, including the coordination of humanitarian assistance.

In New York, Ajello was briefed by Dimitry Titov of the Department of Peacekeeping Operations and officials of the Department of Political Affairs. He familiarized himself with the GPA and made a preliminary assessment of the needs of the operation. The secretary-general reported to the Security Council on October 9 that the United Nations could not establish more than a token presence by October 15, the date set for the start of the cease-fire, but that the interim SRSG would travel to Maputo to help the parties set up the joint machinery to be chaired by the United Nations, to finalize the modalities, and to ensure access for relief workers. On October 13, Security Council Resolution 782 approved Ajello's appointment and the dispatch of twenty-five military observers.[1] On October 15, Ajello arrived in Maputo with the military observers, who were drawn mainly from peacekeeping duty in Cyprus and were led by Colonel Sinha of India.

Although the signing of the GPA in Rome had been greeted joyfully by Mozambicans, nothing had yet been done in Maputo to prepare operations or to establish the mechanisms of the peace process. On October 16, Ajello met with Chissano, who was ready to move forward, and on October 19 in Maringue, Sofala province, with Dhlakama, who was far from ready. Dhlakama was still weighing his options following the final Rome negotiations and indicated that he was not prepared to leave his headquarters in the bush for the capital until the government provided suitable housing for himself and his colleagues in Maputo. The status and security of the Renamo leadership in the new situation were uppermost in his mind.

In Maputo, Ajello held wide-ranging talks with representatives of the international community and of Sant'Egidio, as well as with the small group of military observers. He was briefed about the preliminary plans for demobilization that had already been made by a group of donors led by Switzerland. He accepted the argument put to him that demobilization should be managed by two components, a small number of military observers and a larger civilian technical unit to work on the logistics of accommodation, provisioning, registration, and reintegration. Ajello also held detailed discussions with the representatives of Portugal, the United States, and the United Kingdom, and began to draw up plans for deploying the UN battalions needed to replace foreign troops along the transportation corridors. Although few of the embassies saw the need for a major deployment of troops, the collapsing peace process in Angola was creating new international pressure for a large mission, something that Ajello himself had little difficulty in supporting. Anticipating the debate of these issues at the United Nations, Ajello quickly familiarized himself with the requirements of the GPA and the views of the international community in Maputo.

Despite the obvious joy and celebration after the signing the GPA, the cease-fire was not assured. On October 20, the day after Ajello's meeting with Dhlakama, Renamo forces were reported to have captured four towns in Zambezia and Nampula provinces in flagrant breach of the cease-fire and possibly in defiance of the movement's own leadership. Although the government quickly regained control of Angoche, Maganja da Costa, and Memba, the fourth town, Lugela, was not retaken until November. The violations drew a quick condemnation from the Security

Council, a signal of international concern that Ajello sought to build upon by calling for a high-level meeting of the two sides in Maputo. A gamble that gave a foretaste of Ajello's political style, it worked, allowing for a clear indication on Mozambican soil of the two parties' acceptance of a peace that had been negotiated thousands of miles away in Rome. To Mozambicans, the meeting was proof that things were changing and that dialogue was now the order of the day. Follow-up meetings were held in Maputo between the two sides' chief negotiators in Rome, Armando Guebuza and Raul Domingos, and by November 3 Ajello had won agreements to establish the four key commissions and to provide housing for Dhlakama in the capital. On November 4, the Supervision and Control Commission, the first basic building block for a UN operation, met for the first time. Immediately afterwards, Ajello flew to New York, and subsequently Washington, to lobby for approval of the substantial multifunctional UN force that he had begun to sense might be achievable.

Avoiding Another Angola

The timing for mounting yet another major peacekeeping operation was as difficult as it was propitious. In the same weeks that the Security Council and the U.S. government were considering the prospect of a U.S.-led mission to Somalia, the international community was witnessing the catastrophic aftermath of the Angolan elections and could ill afford a further conflagration in Southern Africa. The Angola precedent fed directly into the planning for Mozambique. The international community had watched helplessly in the weeks following Angola's elections of September 29–30, when Jonas Savimbi and his Unita party refused to accept their electoral defeat and denounced the international community's endorsement of the results; all attempts at reconciliation failed to stop the return to war. Unita's ability to regroup its forces made the compelling case that the priority in Mozambique should be to ensure a complete demobilization of the two armies and the formation of new joint army before elections were held. It also implied the need for a stronger and more forceful international presence in Mozambique than had been mandated in Angola.

The problems encountered by the Angola mission, UNAVEM II, had their origins in some of the ambiguities of the Bicesse Accords, which had been mediated by Portugal and signed by the MPLA government and Unita in May 1991, and in the lack of authority given to the third parties in the peace commissions.[2] Most analysts agreed that UNAVEM's weakness was its mandate, which was restricted to monitoring and verifying the steps agreed on by the parties. The United Nations had no powers to intervene to ensure implementation.[3] Also, the operation was small, with only 350 military observers, 125 police observers, and, in the final phase, an electoral division of 100, bolstered briefly by 400 monitors for the elections.

The Angolan peace process came unstuck on several fronts. "High levels of mistrust characterized relations between Unita and the MPLA during both the negotiation and implementation phases of the Bicesse Accords," notes Fen Hampson.[4] Demobilization of the two armies was not carried out in good faith and their integration into a single national force was not achieved. UNAVEM suffered financial and logistic constraints, was often ill informed about the situation in different parts of the country, and, toward the end, was even undermined by the imminence of a Mozambican operation, as plans were made for UNAVEM equipment and material to be shipped to Mozambique.[5] During October, as Angola's cease-fire moved toward complete collapse, the international community was powerless to intervene. Full-scale war broke out in Luanda on October 31, rapidly spreading to the rest of the country, where the two opposing armies' primary objective was to gain control of the principal cities, provinces, and economic production zones, particularly those rich in oil and diamonds. A succinct summary of the new conflict was given by a Unita official: "The problem is that you have two forces fighting for power and each one believes that if it lays down its arms, the other will subjugate it." In January 1993, the SRSG in Angola, Margaret Anstee, remarked, "One could say, with lessons of hindsight, that the UN should never have accepted the mandate."[6]

Planning for ONUMOZ

Aware of the mistakes that had been made in Angola, but encouraged by the still promising atmosphere within Mozambique, the UN Secretariat and the Security Council proceeded to construct the operational plan, using the comprehensive formula of the GPA as a guide. In New York, Ajello met the UN ambassadors of France, Italy, Portugal, Sweden, the United Kingdom, and Zimbabwe. They discussed the military, political, and economic aspects of the operation, and Ajello received positive support for his assessment of the need for armed troops. On November 20 in Washington, Ajello's meetings at the State Department and the Pentagon produced approval for a large UN mission, something Ajello later described as a "miracle." He attributed the U.S. position to two things: his achievement in Mozambique in keeping Renamo in play after the risk of a breakdown in the cease-fire; and the timing in Washington, where the incoming administration of President Bill Clinton, rather than the outgoing administration of President George Bush, would have to worry about meeting the United States's share of the cost.[7] Initially reluctant to support even three battalions, the United States eventually gave its go-ahead for five, accepting the argument that there should be protection not only for the transit of goods across Mozambique on the three main corridors (Nacala, Beira, and Limpopo) between the coast and its landlocked neighbors, Malawi and Zimbabwe, but also on the Tete corridor that links those two countries and on the main domestic highway between Maputo and Beira (Route No. 1). The United States also accepted that Italy should be the leading contributor of troops and that Italian forces would be positioned on the key Beira corridor.

Despite concerns about cost and the shortage of human resources in the UN system (in the midst of the massive operation in Cambodia), the Mozambique operation was becoming more substantial. Inputs into the planning were made by the Departments for Political Affairs, Peacekeeping, and Humanitarian Affairs; the UNDP's Africa Bureau; and other major UN agencies. The DPKO was determined to create a credible system of verification for the assembly of troops and was concerned that troops should be disarmed and completely demobilized before returning to civilian life. The department was also aware of the desirability of a civilian police-monitoring element, although the GPA did not request it. Ajello favored a police component, but his immediate concerns were about the time needed to provide observers for demobilization, the need for demining and rehabilitating roads, and the potential problems posed by the withdrawal of Zimbabwean troops from the Beira corridor. (It was already becoming apparent that Dhlakama was unwilling to start demobilization until UN contingents arrived to replace the Zimbabweans.) By the time the finishing touches were being put to the report of the secretary-general to the Security Council at the end of November, the proposed operation was palpably growing in size and scope. The report tried to address the practical challenges but in doing so added elements that the parties had not foreseen. The perceived need to give credible underpinning to the authority of the United Nations, and to deal simultaneously with the related issues of delivery of humanitarian aid and the Southern African drought, was generating an operation that would require more time and, possibly, new negotiations to set in motion.

On November 23, Ajello travelled to Rome, arriving in the midst of a debate about what kind of intervention Italy should undertake in Somalia and accusations that the government was contemplating a "neocolonial" mission in its former colony there. Ajello was able to persuade the Italian government that an operation in Mozambique led by Italian troops with full UN endorsement was an entirely acceptable option and an appropriate follow-up to the Rome peace negotiations. Italy, however, was unwilling to send the troops ahead of a Security Council resolution, which was still being prepared, and the Rome government's ability to act was also hampered by the ongoing political crisis in Italy. Even after the Security Council's ruling in December, Italy had problems arranging transport for its contingent. Fortunately, Dhlakama's impatience for the arrival of UN contingents was softened by a meeting with Zimbabwe's president, Robert Mugabe, who persuaded the Renamo leader to continue to accept the presence of the Zimbabwean forces until UN troops arrived, however long that might take.

Ajello's absence from Maputo meant that little was happening on the ground. The cease-fire appeared to be holding well and the two sides fulfilled their promise to name their preferred locations for the forty-nine assembly areas for the armies. Following a visit to Maputo by representatives of the United Nations's newly established Department of Humanitarian Affairs, there were discussions in Maputo about the establishment of a United Nations Office for Humanitarian Assistance Coordination (UNOHAC—see chapter 5). A program for the reintegration of returnees, displaced persons, and demobilized soldiers was prepared for presentation to donors in Rome in December. The Cease-Fire Commission (CCF) met on November 25, issuing a rebuke to the government for resorting to force to eject Renamo from Lugela, but the Supervision and Control Commission (CSC) could not meet without the United Nations in the chair, and Ajello was still away. Five of the CSC ambassadors went to Chissano and asked him to suggest to Boutros-Ghali that the UNDP resident representative, Erick de Mul, be asked to act as chairman. This allowed the CSC to meet for a second time on December 2, when it discussed the parameters for verifying the cease-fire and agreed to invite Germany to join the commission. But the arrangement led to early strains in the relationship between Ajello and de Mul; these strains were later to be aggravated by UNOHAC's takeover of the humanitarian coordination functions that long been carried out under the aegis of UNDP.

As the cease-fire continued to hold, Mozambicans were beginning to wake from their long nightmare. Freedom of movement was now possible at least throughout government-controlled zones, although landmines made travel hazardous on both roads and bush paths. Rural Renamo-controlled zones remained inaccessible, and in many of them people were prevented from leaving or entering. Renamo leaders routinely prevented the entry of government officials, NGOs, and journalists, while exacting taxes from people coming to do business. The government, for its part, insisted that there could be only one administration for the country and was particularly angered by a bilateral arrangement reached between Renamo and the International Committee of the Red Cross (ICRC) for demining roads in Renamo areas. The government prevented a British contractor, Defence Systems Ltd., from starting work, arguing that the GPA did not allow Renamo to have independent links with international agencies. Tensions remained high in Zambezia and Nampula provinces, where Renamo was continuing to block all access and where independent armed groups, such as the progovernment Naparama army, which campaigned for its own demobilization, were staging blockades on main roads.

The ONUMOZ concept was hammered out in New York during November and early December. Ajello took the risk of proposing the inclusion of a civilian police component, a suggestion that was strongly rebuffed by the government, although it was eventually to become an acceptable and vital element of ONUMOZ (see chapters 4 and 7). Officials in the secretariat presented a variety of opinions on the optimum size of the electoral verification operation and on the precise requirements for the management of troops being demobilized in the assembly areas, but the mission that was eventually recommended by Goulding was generally in line with the multifunctional project favored by Ajello. The Mozambique government lobbied the Security Council to limit the size of the operation but the council was by now generally agreed upon spending a bit more than necessary so as to avoid the costly embarrassment of another UNAVEM II.[8] The secretary-general's report to the Security Council (reprinted here as appendix I) proposed 354 military observers, about 5,500 troops, 130 police, hundreds of civilian officials, and up to 1,200 international observers during the elections. The operation was costed at $332 million over a twelve-month period, of which $158 million was budgeted to cover military aspects and the remaining $174 million to provide civilian staff and services. It was suggested that the delays that had already crept into the twelve-month schedule meant that this first-year budget could probably be reduced to $260 million.

Security Council Approval

In Resolution 797 of December 16 (reprinted here as appendix II), the Security Council approved the establishment of ONUMOZ as a multi-functional mission with four interlinked components: political, military, electoral, and humanitarian. The political function was to facilitate implementation of the GPA and to chair the CSC. The military function was to monitor and verify the cease-fire, the concentration of forces, and demobilization, as well as to provide security for vital infrastructures and all UN and other international activities. The electoral function was to provide technical assistance and monitor the entire electoral process. The humanitarian function was broadly defined as coordinating and monitoring all humanitarian assistance operations.[9] The U.S. ambassador to the United Nations, Edward Perkins, put on record his government's view that the introduction of peacekeeping forces should be phased and that the secretary-general should make regular reports on progress at least every three months. He confirmed U.S. financial support for aspects of the process, including elections, repatriation of refugees, and reintegration of demobilized soldiers. Perkins also endorsed Ajello's "energetic and highly effective efforts."

The Security Council's decision provided a clear signal for donors to proceed with their pledges. A World Bank consultative group, meeting in Paris in December, raised $760 million in credits, grants, and food aid. A second conference in Rome considered humanitarian issues relating to the peace process and produced initial pledges of $320 million, of which $107 million was promised by Italy alone. Italy also gave assurances that it would help raise the money for the political parties. It was revealed only later that Italy agreed to give $15 million to Renamo for the express purpose of turning itself into a political party. When, in the crisis that overwhelmed the Italian political establishment in the first months of 1993, the money did not materialize, Renamo publicized the deal.

In Maputo, members of the Mozambique government began openly to express concern at the size and functions of the mission proposed by the Security Council and the lack of consultation over the size of the Italian contingent being prepared for deployment along the Beira corridor. One member of the government was quoted as saying, "We are not a protectorate of the Security Council; we are a member of the United Nations. The UN is here as observers, not as a peacekeeping force."[10] A Frelimo representative, Narciso Matos, speaking in parliament in December, warned that the United Nations could become "a state within a state."

Ajello returned to Mozambique after the donors' conferences in mid-December. His promise to Dhlakama that he would organize the early arrival of a battalion of Italian troops to guard the Beira corridor provided the context for the first of many tests of will between ONUMOZ and the Maputo government. Ajello informed the government on December 23 that an advance party of thirteen Italian officers was already flying to Beira. The government responded by refusing landing permission, and the plane had to return to Italy. These developments prompted Dhlakama to write to Boutros-Ghali on January 7 that Renamo would not move troops to assembly points until 65 percent of the UN troops were in Mozambique. He also demanded the presence of some UN troops in Renamo areas.[11] The secretary-general later said that this demand was seriously affecting progress.

Renamo was simultaneously engaged in a war of words with the government over the administration of the areas that it controlled. The Renamo foreign secretary, Jose de Castro, emphasized his party's claim that the GPA divided the country into two independently governed zones.[12] The dispute delayed the deployment of tripartite teams sent to oversee the beginning of demining operations, and many vital roads seemed likely to remain closed for some time. Dhlakama, meanwhile, kept up his political offensive, accusing the government of recruiting former soldiers and security agents into its police force, as had been done by the Angolan government in response to demobilization there.

Dhlakama's failure to arrive in Maputo by the end of the year, as Ajello and Chissano had publicly said he would, was widely interpreted as a sign of his determination to exact further concessions from the government. "Both Renamo and Frelimo seem surprised at just how much they conceded during the Rome negotiations, and are trying to recoup some of those concessions now," wrote a correspondent in Maputo.[13] Renamo's secretary-general, Vicente Ululu, blamed the government for trying to "sabotage the peace process" by not providing houses as agreed in Rome. But while remaining at odds with the government, Renamo was equally concerned to score points with the international community by giving repeated assurances that it was not contemplating a return to war. Ululu stressed that, whatever cause it had appeared to espouse during the war, Renamo was now entirely in favor of plural democracy, justice, free enterprise, and private health and education.[14]

ONUMOZ Struggles to Be Born

By February, the physical enactment of the peace process, as spelled out in the GPA, had not begun, but the United Nations was managing to play for time. Already, the consensus among senior diplomats in Maputo was that elections could not now be held in 1993 and that the ONUMOZ mandate would have to be extended by nine months or even a year. While Renamo was stepping up its campaign both for greater evidence of a UN presence and for the financial support it had demanded to help it transform itself into a political party, the government in Maputo was showing its determination not to be rushed into anything and became increasingly resentful of UN moves that appeared to threaten its sovereignty.

Members of the CSC at this time noted that the cease-fire was holding because Mozambicans themselves had universally decided to stop fighting and were now more interested in reoccupying their homes and cultivating their fields than with supporting either party to the conflict. They also credited Renamo as having proved itself more disciplined than they had expected, although the party still was ill equipped to implement the timetable of the peace agreement. "They cannot man the commissions and they want to consolidate their hold on the areas they control," said the British ambassador, Richard Edis.[15]

The creation of ONUMOZ was further delayed by infighting in New York. UN headquarters was still reluctant to send a large number of troops, and the Field Operations Division was clearly overwhelmed with the unprecedented number of its peacekeeping operations around the world. Procedures such as internal reviews and screening of personnel proved extraordinarily complex and slow. Ajello's appointment as full SRSG and the ONUMOZ budget were confirmed only after long bureaucratic battles. Uncertainties about the future of James Jonah cast a shadow over ONUMOZ because it was likely that, if he were to be appointed as SRSG, he would want to make several of his own key appointments. Only after Jonah was reappointed for a further term as under-secretary-general in UN headquarters in February 1993 did Ajello's position became more secure, allowing him to appoint more staff. He later commented that "when you start having rumors about people replacing you, you lose authority and things become difficult."[16] Ajello was effectively confirmed in the post by April, although there was no public announcement to this effect.

Finance was a problem, at least until the UN General Assembly approved its first ONUMOZ budget in March. A small advance of $9.5 million had been made available pending approval of the budget. The purchase of equipment, leasing of office space and aircraft, and recruitment and deployment of key personnel were all delayed. In a private interview, one official blamed what he termed "suicidal" rules and procedures for the slow start. ONUMOZ was not authorized to purchase capital equipment and so was forced to rely on expensive short-term contracts, much to the benefit of South African car rental and other services companies. In an interview in March, Ajello criticized the tedious budgetary process in New York, saying, "It's nonsense that they left us with $9.5 million. . . . That means we couldn't place any orders, we couldn't order any vehicles, any equipment. . . . I cannot use military observers without vehicles, without radio, without anything. It's pure nonsense, our budgetary process."[17]

In New York, the General Assembly's advisory committee on budgetary questions demanded detailed justification of the amounts to be paid to staff, the costs of mine clearance and air operations, and the sources of financing of humanitarian programs. Eventually, on March 15, the General Assembly approved an initial budget of $140 million. ONUMOZ could at last order the capital equipment it needed, including vehicles and communications equipment, which still took some months to arrive. "What nearly killed ONUMOZ in the early months was the lack of staff and the tortuous budgetary process," said a senior aide to Ajello. "The system proved remarkably inept in terms of structures and procedures."[18]

An outstanding problem between the Mozambique government and the United Nations was the absence of a status-of-forces agreement that would allow the UN forces the freedom of movement they required and exemptions from taxes and duties. It was a situation complicated by the donors' pressure on Mozambique to raise revenue from all available sources. After meeting Chissano, Ajello accepted the argument that the government was too poor to offer free accommodation to the United Nations, and it was agreed that office and housing rents would be paid. However, senior members of the government continued to resist the idea that the UN troops should have complete freedom of movement and to assert that the United Nations was meant only to observe, not to act as a peacekeeping force. One was quoted as accusing the United Nations of wanting to act as an "occupation force." In response, UN officials accused the government of wanting to milk as much tax money as possible before signing the status agreement.[19]

The secretariat had sent a first draft of the agreement to the government in November, but it had not pushed for a signing before the Security Council resolution in December. By February the United Nations was still asking the government to sign the agreement by the end of March. The government then insisted on close consultation with different ministries and did not respond until mid-April. The agreement was eventually signed in May and granted diplomatic immunity to ONUMOZ personnel, unlimited freedom of movement, and exemption from taxes and duties.

Renamo Provides Political Delays

Prevarication by both the government and Renamo early in 1993 bought the United Nations badly needed time to establish the operation's various components. The search for military contingents and civilian professionals was prolonged. By the end of February 1993, the UN presence consisted of 184 unarmed military observers and the beginnings of a civilian administration at the Rovuma Hotel in central Maputo, which was to become the nerve center of ONUMOZ. Although operating with a skeleton staff, Ajello set up an active process of consultation and negotiation with the international community, especially the international representatives on the CSC and the top levels of the government and Renamo. To maintain close contact with Dhlakama, Ajello used the services of Eric Lubin, a French diplomat seconded to ONUMOZ, who flew regularly back and forth between Maputo and Renamo's bush headquarters at Maringue.

The issue of suitable housing in Maputo for the Renamo leadership, which had been merely an irritant before, became the main cause of delay to the political process. Dhlakama's agreement to each step of the process, still crucial at this early phase, could be secured only on flying visits to Maringue by Ajello, Lubin, or international delegations. Although Dhlakama's close lieutenants, Raul Domingos and Vicente Ululu, took up residence in Maputo and received financial support from the Italian government, the ten houses and apartments first allocated by the government were still deemed insufficient and another fifteen, including a large and secure mansion for Dhlakama himself, were demanded. The wrangles over the housing issue were an effective smokescreen for Renamo's unpreparedness to engage fully in the work of the CSC or any of the other commissions. In March, Ajello noted that "the work of the commissions has been hampered by the policy of the empty chair."[20]

Dhlakama's personal dominance of Renamo's central structures had inhibited independent thought and action among his commanders and political adjutants, many of whom were illiterate or inexperienced in debate or committee procedures. At this early stage, Dhlakama was in any case principally interested in testing his movement's political strength. On February 28, Renamo staged its first public rally in government-held territory, in Beira, the country's second city. The event attracted a large and peaceful crowd and allowed Renamo to sign up many new members.

The lack of progress in implementing the GPA was beginning to throw up problems as government and Renamo soldiers continued to wait for news of their possible demobilization. Government soldiers occasionally looted food from warehouses or staged protests complaining of late wage payments and demanding increases in pay. Soldiers already demobilized before the peace process, including former members of the presidential guard, created disturbances around Maputo, claiming unpaid pensions and other benefits. Small groups of armed men also began to threaten civilians on roads in a number of provinces, including Maputo, Sofala, Zambezia, and Nampula.

Interviewed in March 1993, Ajello described most of the disturbances on both sides as "marginal," although he expressed concern about the poor morale of government soldiers. "One of the major problems we face when we start the demobilization of troops will be to provide these soldiers with the back wages." He attributed the delay in demobilization to the distrust between the two sides and to Renamo's insistence on the prior arrival of the UN troops. He hoped to start opening the assembly areas by April. Confirming that "everybody agrees that there is no way we can have elections in October," Ajello expressed his frustrations at the "completely unrealistic and unprofessional" timetable of the GPA.[21]

Although the peace process received a boost with the arrival in Beira on March 4 of the first planeload of 185 Italian soldiers, it simultaneously received its worst setback to date when Renamo refused to attend CSC meetings or to cooperate with the CCF's investigations into serious violations being alleged by the government—including claims that Renamo had infiltrated a battalion of troops from Malawi and was training Zimbabwean dissidents in Gorongosa district. Raul Domingos refused to attend a CSC meeting called by Ajello for March 6 and three days later left Maputo for Maringue. He accused the government of refusing to provide food for Renamo delegates who, he claimed, were now going hungry and could not be expected to attend meetings on an empty stomach. After a briefing from Domingos, Dhlakama gave a press conference in Maringue on March 10 at which he demanded that the government also feed his party officials.

Renamo's demands for money received a new response from Italy, which offered the party $65,000 for its March expenses, as well as cars, computers, and fax machines, and from Ajello, who announced on March 12 that a UN trust fund was to be established to provide Renamo with the resources needed for its people to stay in Maputo. Ajello said that Renamo needed the "minimum resources to compete" if it were not to go back to the bush and fight. He added that Dhlakama wanted personal, military, and financial security and was not prepared to start demobilization until he had all the guarantees he needed.[22] The feeling in the international community was that a meeting between Chissano and Dhlakama could help resolve some of the distrust, but tentative arrangements for such a meeting came to nothing.

ONUMOZ officials publicly and privately expressed their serious concerns about the impasse, but Ajello turned the Renamo boycott to his advantage, seeing that it would give more time to fulfill Renamo's conditions about the deployment of the military contingents and to fund its financial requirements. "There is no crisis. Time has not been wasted," Ajello said on April 5, adding that Renamo had underestimated the number and quality of the people it needed to staff the commissions and that forty-five of its members had been selected to attend a monthlong training seminar in Maringue.[23] Even after this training, however, Renamo delayed its return to Maputo until it received assurances on the promised housing and funds. Ajello was still trying to establish the trust fund machinery. In a tour of Europe in April and May, Dhlakama won pledges of funding from some governments, but only on condition that Renamo lived up to its promises.

Inaccessible Renamo Territory

Renamo areas still remained inaccessible to both UN and government officials in April. Some NGOs and journalists had been allowed limited access, but Renamo was insisting on the right to distribute food and relief materials. The GPA tried to resolve the problem by giving Renamo authority to administer its areas while also requiring it to obey existing state laws; however, the issue remained a bone of contention. In some districts, each side tried to enforce control over territory claimed by the other. Renamo was not ready to name its representatives on the territorial commission, which the GPA said would decide the relationship between the government and Renamo-administered areas. A Renamo press statement in May 1993 again insisted that the peace accords recognized two administrations in the country and that all "economic agents" had to ask Renamo for permission before entering Renamo-held zones.[24] In Sofala province, Renamo banned timber companies and hunters from entering, and in Zambezia it prevented the transportation of stone and wood for construction. International agencies and NGOs continued to report constraints on access. Only after mid-1993 did Renamo's reluctance to open up its areas to NGOs begin to ease. The ICRC, which did have access, did much to open the way for others; one of its own initiatives was to return child soldiers from Renamo areas to their homes.

Contingents Arrive

The full contingent of 1,043 Italian troops was in place along the Beira corridor in April. The withdrawal of Zimbabwean troops by April 15 was marked by a ceremony at Chimoio attended by Presidents Chissano and Mugabe. The Italians were self-sufficient, with more than 500 road vehicles, 17 helicopters, and 3 aircraft. Botswana's infantry battalion of 743 men arrived in April to guard the Tete corridor, and in May battalions arrived from Bangladesh, Zambia, and Uruguay to guard the Nacala and Limpopo corridors and the main Maputo-Beira highway, respectively. Portugal sent a communications unit, Argentina a medical unit, and India a logistics unit. By June, UN troops totaled nearly 5,300 and military observers 247. The Malawian troops protecting the Nacala corridor, the last non-UN foreign troops in the country, departed on June 9. By July, the UN military presence reached 6,222 armed troops and 294 unarmed military observers.

Although the Italian contingent was fully self-sufficient, those from Third World countries were ill prepared for the difficult conditions, and the planning for their deployment was minimal. When the Uruguayan contingent set up camp, it was provided with neither food nor water for the first two days, and half the battalion found itself deployed to a point forty kilometers from the highway it was to patrol. Few briefings were

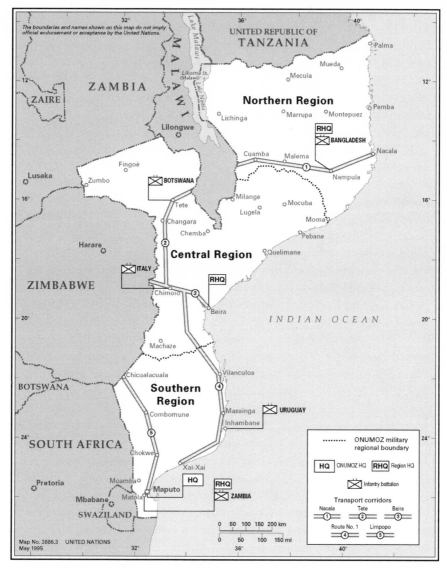

Initial ONUMOZ Military Deployment along Transport Corridors, May 1993

From *The United Nations and Mozambique, 1992–1995* (New York: United Nations, 1995), map 3886.3 (May 1995). Reprinted with permission of the United Nations Publications Board.

given about local history, culture, or the health risks, especially from AIDS. Isolated and restricted in their mandate, few of the UN troops resisted engaging in sexual contact with Mozambican women and young girls; this was to become a matter of considerable concern to NGO social and health workers. Most of the contingents were also criticized for failing to make a positive contribution to rehabilitating the country's shattered infrastructure, although Bangladeshi engineers proved an exception by repairing roads in Nampula province.

In the months after the replacement of the Zimbabweans by the Italians on the Beira corridor, the number of armed attacks on the road rose noticeably. The first Force Commander, Major General Lelio Goncalves Rodrigues da Silva, insisted on a strict interpretation of the mandate, at first refusing to allow troops to intervene to prevent acts of banditry. Because of this passivity, the military presence attracted little criticism, although supporters of the government sometimes voiced their dislike of the presence of Portuguese military personnel, who were seen as an unpleasant reminder of the country's painful colonial history.

Although the cease-fire continued to hold, the delay in proceeding to demobilization raised the possibility that the troops might be needed for more than patrolling duties. Ajello was in favor of deployment if the need arose outside the corridors, and especially in Zambezia province, the scene of much of the fiercest fighting in the 1980s and a potential theater for renewed conflict. It was evident that any disputes about the control of Zambezia and its north-south roads could severely disrupt the peace process. During 1993, after banditry by former soldiers was reported on the road between the provincial capital, Quelimane, and Nicoadala, Ajello strongly recommended deployment to the secretary-general, who on August 30 said he was studying the proposal. Eventually in early 1994, after the appointment of Major General Mohammad Abdus Salam of Bangladesh as the new force commander, two Brazilian companies were deployed to Mocuba in Zambezia, where they were confronted by some potentially dangerous situations, particularly after the start of demobilization.

Starts and Stops

The deal that brought Renamo back to Maputo involved the establishment of the trust fund and provision of accommodation for Renamo officials. Ajello played a major part in the negotiations, persuading the government of the need to accord status by providing good-quality accommodation in the capital and convincing the international community of the need to channel funds for the conversion of Renamo into a political rather than military entity. Italy was the principal contributor, although in view of its own mounting political crisis at home, it had difficulty in releasing the money. The United Nations would have preferred not to take responsibility, as to do so created a precedent of involvement in the establishment of political parties and was hard to justify to the Mozambican government. (Nevertheless, once such a precedent is created, it can enter into the canon of potential action, and the secretary-general's "Agenda for Democracy"—published in the form of a report to the UN General Assembly in August 1995—cites the Renamo case, commenting that the trust fund "played a particularly positive role" in transforming Renamo into a political party.)[25] However, under pressure from Ajello, the secretariat reluctantly accepted that the establishment of the fund was an obligation—deriving from the GPA and from the subsequent understandings reached between Italy and Renamo. In an announcement made in New York on May 20, 1992, the United Nations described the fund as a "Trust Fund for the Implementation of the Peace Process in Mozambique," noting that its purpose was to ensure the implementation of Protocol III, Article 7 (b) of the GPA and that it was "earmarked to cover costs associated with requirements for, among others, transport, office space, and communications facilities." The fund was to be managed by the SRSG. The statement added that various member states had made commitments, including Italy, which had already made an initial contribution of $5.8 million.[26]

Ever the pragmatist, Ajello saw that money could play an important part in softening up Renamo's reluctance to keep participating in the process. In an interview at the time he said, "I don't believe Dhlakama is an angel. But I look at his real interests. He will try to get what he can, money, a political deal, a good life. But his final interest is to play this game and not another one."[27] Ajello managed to overcome the skepticism of most donors, who doubted that contributions to the trust fund would be money well spent. "The relatively small amount of money needed for the trust fund was the insurance that everything else would work," Ajello said later.[28]

A group of Renamo officials returned to Maputo at the beginning of June, enabling the CSC and the CCF to hold their first meetings in three months on June 3. Both the government and Renamo presented their lists of delegates to sit on the other principal commissions. But Renamo delegates still had to refer to Dhlakama in Maringue for all important decisions, and UN officials and other diplomats also had to fly to Maringue to sustain the peace process, prompting one UN official to comment that they were playing into Dhlakama's hands: "The international community is supporting his view of himself as king of the bush. He is a hero there and he is in total control. . . . He keeps visitors waiting and offers them a meal or not on whim."[29]

The establishment of the trust fund did not prevent Renamo from making new demands. During a follow-up donors' meeting in Maputo on June 8 and 9, Renamo asked for the provision of offices, communications equipment, food, money for foreign travel, training centers for demobilized soldiers, uniforms, and clothing. Raul Domingos and his colleagues at the meeting set a new price tag of $100 million and demanded assistance for the opening of Renamo embassies wherever the Maputo government was represented around the world. Donors were in general affronted by these requests, although representatives of Sant'Egidio said that Renamo's attitude was understandable, as it saw Frelimo as having an unequal advantage in being able to use the machinery of the state. The donors made no new concessions in the face of these new demands, but expressed concern about the delays in the process. They did, however, firm up their commitments, made in Rome in December 1992, to furnish humanitarian assistance. An additional $70 million was pledged for a wide range of activities, including demobilization, repatriation of refugees, and demining. Working groups were set up, one to deal with the needs of refugees, displaced persons, and demobilized soldiers; one on rehabilitation; and another on the application of pledged funds amounting to $450 million, including contributions to a number of other trust funds that had been set up after the Rome meeting.

Dhlakama himself steadfastly refused to go to Maputo or to meet Chissano. He and his colleagues cited new conditions on demobilization, including the right to name governors in a number of provinces, as well as representatives in the mass media and the ministry of the interior. Ajello identified the main problems as the continuing mistrust between the two sides, and criticized the inability of Renamo delegates on the commissions to make decisions without referring to Maringue. When the U.S. assistant secretary of state for Africa, George Moose, visited Maringue during June, Dhlakama promised to meet Chissano in Maputo in July but later changed his mind. This prompted the United States to issue its first public criticism of Renamo and to exert pressure through Kenya and South Africa, both of which sent envoys to meet the Renamo leader. This pressure led to arrangements for a face-to-face meeting between Chissano and Dhlakama, which finally took place in August.

At a special meeting of the Security Council on Mozambique on July 9, the U.S. ambassador, Madeleine Albright, said that her government continued to support ONUMOZ and had a "well-founded confidence in its prospects for success," but was concerned by the delays in starting demobilization and preparations for training the new army and for elections. She added that the new proposed date for elections, in September or October 1994, was realistic but that her government would find it difficult to support any postponement past October 1994. She expressed her appreciation of Ajello's "skillful and energetic efforts" and her pleasure that he had now been confirmed in his post.

Although the international community became increasingly frustrated by Renamo's delaying tactics, broken promises, and escalating demands, it was also quick to criticize some of the government's actions. Ajello was quoted as saying that "quiet diplomacy did not work." Reports of a government violation of the cease-fire in July, in the form of action to expel Renamo from three villages in Tete province, provoked a strong reaction from Ajello. At a press conference on July 23, he admitted that the situation had deteriorated, and in early August he accused both sides of "playing stupid games."[30]

Territorial administration remained the principal sticking point. In early July, Dhlakama presented the Italian ambassador, Manfredo di Camerana, with a demand for Renamo-nominated governors, a demand that di Camerana passed to the government. Renamo's national council restated its insistence upon a "division of territorial administration" at a meeting on August 1, whereupon Dhlakama declared that he intended to negotiate with Chissano the naming of Renamo-approved governors for five provinces, saying, "We control our zones. These must be integrated in the state administration." In response, Alcidio Guenha of Frelimo's political commission said that his party would not agree to the demand for governors and claimed that "Renamo is afraid of elections, so they want to divide administration of the country now and threaten not to demobilize their troops until we give them governors." Interviewed by the independent newsletter Mediafax, di Camerana regretted that "no-one makes an effort to understand Renamo." He urged the United Nations to be more pragmatic.[31]

The hiatus in the process meant that several issues that obstensibly had been settled in Rome were reopened. Ideas were floated by a variety of foreign missions in Maputo about the formation of a transitional government or a formula for postelection power sharing. After a visit to UN headquarters in July, Ajello commented, "Some people in New York think the Western winner-takes-all model of democracy is too geometrical for Africa, and some kind of pre-election compromise on power is viable." This was to become a serious issue in the run-up to the elections the following year (see chapter 7). Another area of discussion concerned money and access to resources. Some diplomats in Maputo suggested that because Renamo was clearly determined to gain access to relief aid, its leaders could also be bought off by being given access to farms, businesses, and loans. There were reports in September 1993 that Renamo was making contacts with South African firms with a view to awarding timber and mining concessions in the areas it controlled.[32]

The Cease-Fire and the CCF

Despite the continuing political logjam, the cease-fire held. Traffic returned to the roads and gradually supply routes for food aid and medicines were opened up to rural villages. Good rains in the 1992–93 season meant that the harvests were exceptionally good and that the country's long-term reliance on food aid might now begin to tail off. But by June 1993, eight months after the cease-fire began, there was considerable concern about the potential for discontent in the military camps of both sides. The government side was the least disciplined, and there were repeated strikes and demonstrations by soldiers and ex-soldiers demanding their unpaid wages.

Following the long interruption caused by Renamo's absence from Maputo between March and June 1993, at least the work of the CCF was able to resume to consider about forty complaints of violations. After investigation by military observers, Renamo's occupation since November 1992 of Salamanga, south of Maputo, caused the CCF to criticize Renamo's presence there and to condemn subsequent actions in the area, where Renamo detained ten people for three weeks in June and July 1993. The CCF also condemned the government's occupation of villages in Tete province in June and was backed up by a strongly worded statement from the international members of the CSC, who took exception to the fact that the government acted after making a formal complaint about

Renamo activities in the same area. Ajello described the government's retaliation as a serious violation and added: "I am very concerned by the attitude of some high-ranking government authorities who think they have the right to counterattack when Renamo occupies an area illegally. That's a dangerous philosophy. It would make the UN useless here and could lead to renewed conflict."[33] Accusations and counteraccusations continued to fly between the two sides. The government claimed that Renamo was receiving training from South Africans in Kenya and receiving military supplies while stockpiling new weapons in caches around the country. Renamo claimed that the government was moving thousands of soldiers into the police force.

Assembly of Troops Stalled

ONUMOZ was hampered both politically and logistically from moving toward the assembly of troops that was to precede demobilization of the two armies. Progress was agonizingly slow in the identification of suitable assembly areas that both parties and ONUMOZ could agree to. There were difficulties with most of the forty-nine assembly areas planned for in the GPA (twenty-nine for the government and twenty for Renamo). A first group of twelve assembly points had been inspected and initially approved by the end of January 1993, prompting Ajello to express the hope during February that assembly could begin within a month. But as the inspections continued, it was becoming increasingly apparent that the parties' first choice of areas had been based on strategic rather than practical considerations. Each party wanted to counter the advantage of the other in any particular district and regarded the proposals of the other as an attempt either to consolidate its hold in a disputed zone or simply to acquire more territory. Few of the nominated areas had access to water and other basic facilities appropriate for temporary habitation by large numbers of soldiers.

Complaints by either side were made in the first instance to the CCF, which in turn referred the most serious disputes to the CSC. By late April 1993, ONUMOZ observers had inspected nineteen assembly areas but had approved only thirteen (nine government and four Renamo). Three of the original sites had been rejected as totally inaccessible, and the observers recommended that two others be moved. Many of the sites proposed by Renamo were particularly unsuitable because of the suspected or confirmed presence of landmines on the roads leading to them. Following the suspension of all the commissions in early March, a hiatus lasted until meetings of the CCF resumed in June.

When the reconnaissance teams rejected an area, finding a substitute was a time-consuming process involving complex political and logistic considerations. ONUMOZ repeatedly had to explain the minimum conditions for the assembly areas, including their accessibility, the need for water supplies, and the existence of basic infrastructure. For its own part, ONUMOZ was hampered by cumbersome procurement procedures for the essential inputs for troop assembly. Many items had to be obtained through UN headquarters in New York, which eventually opted for accommodation equipment that was to be transported by air from a supplier in Canada, at extraordinarily high cost. By June, ONUMOZ was at last ready to declare open the first six assembly areas, which were chosen in the interests of political balance to give one for each party in each of the three operational regions (north, center, and south). Food and medicines were made available, in the hopes of exerting political pressure on the parties to start demobilizing, despite the risk that the supplies would deteriorate before the assembly process actually started.

Ajello authorized an innovative division of labor between civilian and military arms of ONUMOZ to handle the logistics of assembly and demobilization. Following up the preparatory work already undertaken by the Swiss Development Cooperation (a government aid agency) in 1991, funds had already been reserved by a number of donors for a substantial reduction of the oversized and underpaid government army. A Swiss-led coordinating group prepared a logistical framework that ONUMOZ readily adopted.[34] A civilian Technical Unit for Demobilization (TU) was created to handle logistics as essential support for the ONUMOZ military observer group. Responsible directly to Ajello, the TU worked out the procedures for establishing the assembly areas and planned the provision of basic facilities and health care, providing support for food distribution, organizing transportation, and undertaking the paperwork for registration and demobilization.

Despite the delays in starting the assembly process, ONUMOZ gained valuable experience in demobilization during 1993 with a preliminary exercise for nearly fourteen thousand government soldiers who had received their demobilization notices in the months preceding the peace agreement. The need for this first demobilization was underlined by demonstrations and strikes by government soldiers demanding both back pay and demobilization money in the first months of 1993. Starting in

May, the TU registered the soldiers while the government released agreed payments, and the UNDP and the Dutch government helped to organize transportation home. The total number of formerly demobilized soldiers assisted in this way eventually reached 13,776, somewhat less than the 16,000 originally estimated by the government. News of the payments provoked further incidents, however, and there were protests by ex-soldiers in different parts of the country, by security guards working at government-owned factories, and by serving soldiers tired of being paid inadequately and increasingly irregularly. A parachute brigade demonstrated in Nacala during May, demanding payment of danger money for every jump the soldiers had ever made.

The New Army and Electoral Preparations

The Commission for the Joint Armed Forces for the Defense of Mozambique (CCFADM) was initially composed of the government, Renamo, France, Portugal, and the United Kingdom. The troika of European members, which had all agreed to play a part in training the army, met in Lisbon in March 1993 to define their contributions. The resulting "Lisbon proposal" provided the framework for their initiatives and was used as a means of coordination with both parties. Each member of the troika then sent advisory teams to Mozambique. Portugal undertook to train three battalions of special forces and one company of marines and to provide training for officers and sergeants. The Portuguese team also later worked with both parties to draft the fundamental documentation of the new army (to be known as the Armed Forces for the Defense of Mozambique—the FADM). Britain agreed to train 540 instructors at a special camp in Zimbabwe. France was committed to training a company of deminers. The chairmanship of CCFADM remained vacant until the two parties agreed to offer it to the United Nations, and the Security Council agreed to this in July.[35] After the CCFADM held its first plenary meeting on July 22, 1993, it established a pattern of meetings on a plenary, tripartite, and bilateral basis.

The first steps toward elections were made in March 1993 with the publication by the government of its draft electoral law, drawn up with the help of experts from the European Union. The original timetable included a special session of parliament in May 1993 to consider the electoral law and accompanying laws on access to radio and on the role of the international observers. The appointment of an election commission had been scheduled for June. The electoral timetable fell apart after Renamo's boycott of the peace process between March and June and because of dissent from the smaller parties. What was expected to be a routine conference to discuss the law on April 27—albeit without the presence of Renamo—turned into a concerted attempt by the minority parties to increase their bargaining power. Twelve of the small parties walked out of the conference immediately after President Chissano made the opening speech and issued a statement accusing the government of not respecting the opposition and not being serious about democracy. Imitating Renamo's tactics, they demanded office space for their own political work. They also called for a power-sharing transitional government, in which they could play a part, to rule until the elections could be held. However, the parties did not keep common cause for long, as shown by a number of splits in party leaderships over the following weeks.

After various false starts, a renewed attempt to discuss the draft election law began again on July 29 at an open-ended conference attended by Frelimo, Renamo, and the smaller parties. Renamo opened the proceedings with objections to large sections of the draft. The conference dragged on until it collapsed on September 18, having proceeded no further than Article 16, which dealt with the composition of the electoral commission. The government wanted majority representation on a body consisting of twenty-one members. Eight of the twelve smaller parties decided to abandon the conference and urged the government to try to reach agreement with Renamo. The justice minister, Ali Dauto, said that a new draft would be published in October and the government would now hold bilateral negotiations with Renamo. The state administration minister, Aguiar Mazula, added that the government would "find other mechanisms for consultation, not only with political parties but also with civil society."[36]

Conclusions

The calendar set down by the GPA came to be described by Ajello as "perfect nonsense." This was as true for the parties as it was for the United Nations. The GPA had laid the foundation stone, but the construction of a lasting peace in Mozambique required still more negotiation and planning. Renamo was not ready to engage in the work of the peace commissions and, once it had taken steps to train its people, was reluctant to start demobilizing. The government had doubts about the role that the United Nations would play and resented what it saw as infringements of sovereignty. The United Nations itself underestimated the logistic difficulties of assembling its operation. The delays in deploying ONUMOZ military contingents and in mounting other elements of its mandate tended to limit the SRSG's authority and ability to hold the two parties to their agreements.

By the middle of 1993, the international community had accepted that the peace process would take at least until October 1994 to complete but was determined that there should be no further slippage beyond that. The political challenge was to convince Dhlakama to come out of the bush and to engage in serious talk. The main logistic challenges lay ahead in preparing for demobilization and elections. Fortunately for ONUMOZ, the latter programs were receiving the close attention of the international community as a whole and the necessary funding and management were already available. Ajello increasingly saw that a successful completion of the peace process would depend on the efforts of the bilateral donors and the UN agencies on the ground and he used the group of international ambassadors in the main peace commission, the CSC, as his principal source of authority and support.

Renamo's delaying tactics created a political logjam that could be broken only by a renewal of direct talks between Chissano and Dhlakama and a reexamination and rescheduling of key elements of the GPA. Time had to be allowed for the issues to be examined by the two leaderships, in the hopes that a new demobilization timetable and the electoral program could be agreed before the end of the year. Fortunately, peace continued to hold, refugees were returning in the hundreds of thousands from neighboring countries, and humanitarian relief was successfully reaching the neediest people.

4.

ASSEMBLING THE PARTIES
AND THEIR ARMIES
Overcoming Doubts and Hesitations

A breakthrough in the stalled peace process came with Afonso Dhlakama's long-awaited arrival in Maputo at the end of August 1993 and his first meetings on Mozambican soil with President Joaquim Chissano. Some issues that had not been adequately addressed by the GPA, especially matters of territory and the police, were resolved. There was still little movement toward demobilization, and Renamo was clearly the more reluctant. Renamo maintained no-go areas around its military bases and used the implied threat of a possible return to war as a bargaining chip to extract as much as its leaders thought they could gain out of the peace process.

ONUMOZ and the international community expended considerable effort in persuading Renamo, and in particular Dhlakama, to abandon the military option and to prepare for elections. A visit to Maputo by UN Secretary-General Boutros Boutros-Ghali in October 1993 was particularly helpful.

The Dhlakama-Chissano Agreements

The Renamo leader's arrival in Maputo on August 21, 1993, was in itself a significant breakthrough. Greeted by Renamo supporters in the capital, Dhlakama was driven freely and noisily around the city under the protection of his own armed bodyguards. The agenda that Renamo prepared for its leader's long-delayed talks with Chissano not only covered the subjects of territory, the police, and the media but also included a proposal for the establishment of a new national high authority or supreme commission, which Renamo hoped would put its leader on an equal footing with the president and the prime minister.

Between August 23 and September 3, there were face-to-face meetings between Chissano and Dhlakama, as well as plenary sessions of delegations of both parties and a meeting between provincial governors and Renamo's own provincial delegates. The results were useful, if not dramatic. On territorial questions, it was agreed that Renamo would nominate advisers to the provincial governors to advise on all matters, including social and economic issues, with regard to zones under Renamo control. All decisions relating to Renamo-controlled zones would be made after the advisers had given their opinion. Situations that could not be resolved with the provincial governors or the central government would be referred to the administration commission. The main concession made by the government was its agreement that once the advisers were in place, Renamo would have the right to nominate officials in areas it controlled. The two sides also agreed to ask the United Nations to send civilian police observers to monitor all the police in the country and to give technical assistance to the proposed police commission.[1] This agreement prompted the Security Council to authorize a survey team to report on the size and functions of a police contingent.[2]

The presence of international civilian police monitors in UN peacekeeping operations has tended to be an afterthought, and in this ONUMOZ was no exception, although Ajello had long held out for such a presence in the face of resistance from the Maputo government. Human rights organizations had been urging the United Nations to develop a more coherent and consistent approach and saw Mozambique as a test case. Amnesty International went on record to say there was need for "vigorous attention to human rights concerns when designing and implementing peace settlements," and urged a "specialized international civilian human rights monitoring component" as an essential part of all PKOs. In Angola, the United Nations's inability to speak out or respond effectively in the face of violations of the peace accords "contributed to the contempt for and the eventual total breakdown of the peace process," and the weaknesses of the UNAVEM II mandate were "echoed somewhat" in ONUMOZ, Amnesty International claimed.[3] In Mozambique, the Dhlakama-Chissano agreements did at last lay the groundwork for a civilian police contingent, although its deployment possibly came too late to be entirely effective (see chapters 7 and 8).

False Start

Dhlakama left Maputo immediately after the talks. Another delay then ensued, while both Dhlakama and Chissano traveled abroad to explain their positions. The Sant'Egidio community at this time criticized the United Nations for trying "to solve problems by direct intervention" rather than by pursuing the "spirit of Rome" and "seeking what unites." "Mozambican politics are full of nuances," wrote one Sant'Egidio representative. "They cannot be understood simply through the relationship with the international community." The future success of the Rome accords lay, he said, in keeping three elements in balance: the transformation of Renamo into a political party; self-limitation by the Mozambique government; and the need for the United Nations to play a political role in almost all key sectors.[4]

On September 20, Ajello presented the government and Renamo with a new calendar, calling for demobilization to start in October. This was immediately rejected by Renamo, whose delegates to the CSC once again abandoned Maputo for Maringue. Renamo made no attempt to appoint its advisers to the provincial governors and refused to move toward demobilization unless the UN police monitors arrived and the government began dismantling its irregular forces and private security operations. By retreating into its habitual isolation, Renamo seemed to be indicating that it had not yet given up its military option.

"Dhlakama was inventing new excuses every day," said Ajello later, "and so I used a carrot-and-stick approach."[5] While holding out the promise of direct payments to Dhlakama from the Renamo trust fund, he also threatened that the United Nations could not continue to bear the cost of maintaining its presence, which was now estimated at $1 million a day. He warned Dhlakama that, unless he began demobilization, the United Nations would not stay to oversee the elections. Renamo would thus be at the mercy of elections organized by the government.

Boutros-Ghali Visits

Before the planned visit by the UN secretary-general to Maputo between October 17 and 20, 1993, Ajello prepared the ground carefully, setting three basic targets: to obtain a new starting date for demobilization, to resolve the dispute over the election law, and to secure a firm commitment to elections by October 1994. He negotiated a revised timetable that set the opening of the first assembly areas for November and December, with March 1994 as the target for the demobilization of half the troops and May 1994 for completion of the process. On elections, the timetable set November 1993 for approval of the electoral law and appointment of the electoral commission, April through June 1994 for registration of voters, and September and October 1994 for the election campaign. For the creation of the new army, December 1993 was set as the beginning of Portuguese training, which would continue until August 1994, so that the new army could become operational in September.

The visit secured tangible progress. After meeting with Chissano and Dhlakama on October 18 and, subsequently, with diplomats in the capital, Boutros-Ghali announced that the two leaders had promised to sign the revised timetable, that Renamo had agreed to start demobilization at the same time as the government dismantled its irregular forces and before the UN police observers arrived, and that progress had been made in negotiations over the composition of the commissions to deal with elections, security matters, police, and territory. In Maputo, the secretary-general also met South African leaders, including Foreign Minister Roelof "Pik" Botha, who took the opportunity to stage a ceremony marking the transformation of South Africa's trade mission in Maputo into an embassy and emphasized the need to stem the flow of illegal arms from Mozambique.

Boutros-Ghali told journalists that his role was that of "a catalyst rather than an alchemist" and stressed that the United Nations could not impose peace. "The new danger is, if there's no political will from the opposing parties, the UN will pull out." He warned that Africa was becoming increasingly marginal to the international interests of powerful countries and that one more disaster would turn them against the whole continent. He said that most of around $1.2 billion in promised grants and loans was on hold until donors saw an advance in the process.[6]

The explicit threat of a withdrawal of international support and money produced results. The difficulties being experienced by the United Nations elsewhere in Africa were convincing proof that international support for ONUMOZ was not limitless. Ajello underlined these problems in a statement made after the secretary-general's departure, stressing "the huge responsibility President Chissano and Mr. Dhlakama have at this present moment—not only for Mozambique, but at a continental level and for peacekeeping operations throughout the world. . . . At this time, when the international community is tending to withdraw support from peacekeeping operations, it is obvious that a success story in one country would have a global impact."[7] The Security Council also stepped up the pressure by putting ONUMOZ on a short leash. On October 29, two days before the existing mandate was due to expire, it was extended by only six days to await the secretary-general's report. Thereupon, with some members of the Security Council wanting the mandate renewed for only three months at a time, the council agreed to extend it for six months, subject to a review in ninety days.

Money for Dhlakama

Behind the scenes, the offer of new money for the Renamo trust fund was helping to engage Dhlakama more seriously than before. After Boutros-Ghali left the country, Dhlakama stayed an extra week in Maputo and indicated his intention to take up residence there, raising the Renamo flag on the house he had been allocated, a beachfront mansion formerly occupied by the representative of the European Union. The secretary-general's report to the Security Council on November 1 now put the blame more openly on Renamo, noting that the movement had for a long time been reluctant to begin the assembly and demobilization of troops and had linked conditions to the process. But the report also stressed the need for the international community to give money to Renamo: "Certain expenditures associated with the transformation of Renamo into a political party . . . cannot be easily met through a United Nations–administered fund [and] governments should give some money directly to the party."[8]

The United Nations's own fund had by this time brought in $6 million, with a further $4 million expected. Substantial disbursements from the fund had been made to Lonrho in consideration of the accommodation being provided for the eighty Renamo officials at the company's Hotel Cardoso since July. Dhlakama had been under the impression that Lonrho would provide not only accommodation but also cash to Renamo, but this did not happen. Dhlakama was further irritated that pledges from European governments had not yet materialized. Moreover, the use of UN trust funds was subject to tight bureaucratic restrictions. Before it could authorize any payments, ONUMOZ had to monitor Renamo's spending and required evidence that the fund was being used for allowable and receipted expenditures. To ease the paperwork problem, Renamo frequently asked ONUMOZ for assistance in making purchases, but this left nothing that could be used at the discretion of the leadership.

Ajello decided to arrange direct cash payments to Dhlakama in return for his full cooperation with the peace process. Italy, Portugal, and South Africa were the main contributors. Starting in September 1993, Dhlakama was paid $300,000 per month. (The payments continued for thirteen months until October 1994 and eventually totaled $3.9 million.) Before each payment, Ajello had to certify that Renamo was not obstructing the process. The expenditures were audited.

"Dhlakama gave his word and kept his word," Ajello said later.[9] However, having expended considerable effort to keep Renamo in play, Ajello was soon to be faced with a greater reluctance on the side of the government. While Dhlakama kept his strong personal hold over his movement, Chissano was subject to a wide range of pressures from his political and military chiefs, as well from his restive troops. Impoverished and undisciplined, the government's forces rioted for wages in Tete and Sofala provinces during October, reinforcing the government's fear of being forced into a more rapid demobilization than that required of Renamo, which was able to enforce tighter discipline among its troops.

The Security Council on November 5 renewed the ONUMOZ mandate for a further six months, but set tough conditions, insisting that the assembly of troops should begin and that the electoral law be approved before the end of November.[10] The secretary-general wrote to both Chissano and Dhlakama saying that it was vital to work together "to maintain the momentum that has been created."[11] Chissano and Dhlakama met on November 24 and reached an understanding on both the electoral law and the electoral structures. To meet the deadline set by the Security Council, the CSC sat late into the night of November 30 to finalize both the electoral and assembly agreements, whereupon ONUMOZ could declare that all thirty-six assembly areas approved by the CCF were ready to receive troops, and that the parties had agreed to start assembly in twenty of the areas (twelve government and eight Renamo). At a consultative group meeting in Paris on December 8, donors emphasized the importance of keeping the revised peace process on track but also backed a new scheme for supporting the reintegration of demobilized troops. A significant proportion of the commitments was specifically targeted to demobilization, resettlement, and elections. Credits and grants totaling $1.04 billion were announced.

Preparations for Assembly

By August 1993, twenty-nine assembly areas had been approved (twenty-two government and seven Renamo) and twelve (eight government and four Renamo) were ready to receive troops, but with no troops arriving, the UN teams in the prepared sites were getting bored. Renamo was in no hurry to start assembly. The government, for pressing economic reasons, was impatient to shed the burden of its vast and ill-disciplined army, and indicated that it was prepared to start the demobilization in those provinces in which all the sites had been agreed upon by the parties. ONUMOZ, however, could not start the process without being sure that both sides would comply in parallel.

The logistic problems of surveying, approving, and preparing Renamo sites persisted, although bureaucratic confusion on the UN side sometimes made matters worse. An offer by a Swedish humanitarian agency, SwedRelief, to speed the survey and preparation of Renamo sites by clearing mines from access roads to the assembly areas was declined by UNOHAC. Delays in the European Union's funding of water systems, a job being undertaken by Unicef (the UN Children's Fund), also slowed progress. Eventually by November 1993, thirty-six assembly areas were approved (twenty-six government and ten Renamo). Most of the sites originally proposed by the government had been accepted; most of those proposed by Renamo were changed in the interests of accessibility and manageability. Approval of the other thirteen remained obstructed, mainly as a result of political disputes over the control of territory.

As assembly finally became a possibility, the TU became the principal manager of the logistics of demobilization. Although the TU worked with the military observer group led by Colonel Ghobashi, the unit's independence from ONUMOZ finance and procurement gave it a degree of flexibility that the operation's military division clearly lacked. The TU's brief expanded to include providing the assembly areas with accommodation, water, and health facilities, coordinating the supply of food, organizing transport, undertaking registration, and providing information to the assembled troops and preparing for reintegration. The TU's registration and data-management program had to allow for control and verification of the process; to register all the troops who were arriving at the assembly areas and other units that were to be registered in the "non-assembled" areas (certain groups—such as administrative sections, the navy, the air force, and provincial military command units—could not be sent to assembly areas in the bush and were deemed to be "assembled" at their place of work); and to issue lists of registered soldiers from which each party would select troops to be integrated into the new army. The information was to be circulated to the parties and to the various organizations involved in supply and implementation.

With its budget supplemented by contributions and personnel from a number of donors, the TU's headquarters was run by ten international staff members. Its three regional offices were staffed with coordinators provided by SwedRelief and about seventy UN volunteers. Other personnel were provided by the World Health Organization, Unicef, and ONUMOZ. The World Food Programme was on standby to distribute food to the assembly areas, and the International Organization for Migration was engaged to transport demobilized soldiers back home. When problems arose at the interface between military, logistical, and humanitarian work, Ajello came increasingly to rely on the TU chief, Ton Pardoel, who reported directly to Ajello.

The TU faced the statistical challenge of working out how many troops would be arriving for assembly, how many would be demobilized, and how many would join the new army. The government, in particular, did not have a reliable count of how many troops it had in different parts of the country, and there was a long history of corruption, with commanders claiming pay for units that did not exist. Although both sides turned in lists of men and weaponry at the end of July 1993, these were incomplete and unreliable. As delays grew, provision also had to be made for the assembly areas without a clear idea of how long the soldiers would be staying.

Assembling the Troops

As soon as assembly began during December, disputes arose over the interpretation of the numbers accommodated in the camps. The government questioned the ONUMOZ system of publishing numbers as soon as soldiers had registered, surrendered their weapons, and received their identity cards, and accused ONUMOZ of deliberately understating the low numbers of government troops.[12] In the first three weeks of December, nearly 5,894 government troops were registered out of 6,844 arrivals; for Renamo 1,357 were registered out of 2,518 arrivals.

Using the revised timetable as leverage, the international members of the CSC now showed that they were determined to flex their muscles. In a statement on December 12, they noted with concern that five of the first twenty assembly areas were still not agreed upon and that Renamo had used only three of its assembly areas, had sent very few troops to them, and had turned in insignificant quantities of weapons. The CSC also urged the government to begin to demobilize its irregular forces and warned that further delays could have a negative impact on Security Council deliberations.

Arguments between the two parties over territorial control were still delaying decisions over the locations of Renamo assembly areas at Salamanga, Dunda, Savane, and Nhangau. After careful preparatory negotiations, Ajello on December 14 put forward to a CSC meeting a formula to separate out the military, logistic, and political factors governing decisions over locations. He suggested that troops that had occupied new territory after October 4, 1992, had to withdraw, but without giving the right to the other party to occupy the space vacated. He also proposed that purely logistic justifications for troop movements might be accepted by the CCF, without having implications for decisions on territorial control. Both the government and Renamo accepted this interpretation, although bilateral consultations were still needed to resolve the specific cases of Salamanga and Dunda, where the government maintained that Renamo's claims to territory were not based on its positions at the time of the cease-fire. A U.S. embassy official at the meeting, Christopher Dell, clarified the point that a Renamo withdrawal from a site did not prejudice Renamo's right to request to use it as an assembly area.[13]

The government insisted on equilibrium and complained that Renamo had begun to assemble only in the north of the country, not in the center and south. Renamo, in response, said it was also concerned with simultaneity and demanded the disbanding of the government's paramilitary forces. The CSC took upon itself the task of monitoring the activities of private security organizations, which Renamo alleged to be using militias and paramilitary troops.[14]

A second group of fifteen assembly areas was formally opened on December 20, bringing the total to thirty-five (twenty-one government and fourteen Renamo). A further twelve were ready (eight government and four Renamo) and were declared open on February 1, 1994, but the two remaining Renamo sites at Salamanga and Dunda took some weeks longer to be approved. Assembly proceeded well during January, and by January 27 the total numbers of assembled troops were 11,567 for the government and 7,199 for Renamo. As proportions of the two sides' declared totals, these figures amounted to 19 percent of the government's forces and 38 percent of Renamo's. In other words, Renamo was assembling twice as fast as the government.

It soon became clear that neither side was assembling its most important forces. In particular, the government's nine main brigades (the "Red Berets") and its special forces (the "Nyangas") remained in their barracks. Moreover, the weapons being turned in were the oldest and least effective. Officers in the government's army—the Armed Forces of Mozambique, known as FAM—were reportedly reluctant to order their troops to the assembly areas until the government's intentions about back pay and the selection of troops for the new army were clarified. Unrest among government troops demanding back pay produced riots in several military bases around the country during January. Instability was chronic along the Nacala corridor.

The government, which had long been under pressure from the World Bank and other donors to reduce its military spending, expressed strong resentment about UN officials' questioning of its inability to pay its troops. When Ajello said in January that he would like to know what happened to the defense budget, the government's chief delegate to the CSC, Armando Guebuza, responded: "We proposed ages ago to raise army salaries, and we wanted to extend demobilization pay, but our creditors said no—now they accuse us of not paying enough. The UN says we should offer better conditions to soldiers, so they don't disrupt the peace process—but the World Bank says we must cut the budget, tighten credit, and limit defense spending."[15] The size of the defense budget remained a point of tension between the government and the United Nations, and a source of considerable confusion for all concerned throughout the process of recruitment into the new army.

In operational terms, ONUMOZ was overstretched in the huge central region of the country, where both parties had almost half of their assembly areas. Problems were looming in Renamo assembly areas, some of which were becoming severely overcrowded. Dhlakama protested to ONUMOZ and Ajello about the lack of food at assembly areas in Sofala province, while water was being transported by helicopter for ONUMOZ personnel. Ajello asked the World Food Programme to increase the rations, but this did not prevent the soldiers in the camps from becoming restless and anxious about their fate. Many were inclined to desert but were held back by the possibility of receiving their demobilization pay. A few attempted to register twice in the hopes of a double payoff.

The TU had initially hoped to have a "two-door" entry and exit process, whereby there would be a steady flow of troops through each assembly area, without the requirement for a long stay. But as it became clear that both the government and Renamo were reluctant to start demobilizing troops until they were assembled in large numbers, ONU-MOZ had to plan on the basis that the troops would stay for at least eight weeks, to allow time for registration, the compilation of lists, the selection of troops for the new joint army, and the organization of the demobilization packages, including pay.

Soldiers on both sides were proving reluctant to enter the new army, disproving the parties' assumptions about the numbers of troops they could contribute. The government, thinking it would have more volunteers than the 15,000 it had agreed to contribute, intended to select from among volunteers. Renamo, meanwhile, was convinced that most of its 20,000 fighters would volunteer in order to enjoy better conditions and to receive salaries for the first time in their lives. In fact, neither party had started assembly with an accurate idea of its troop numbers or the wishes of the soldiers. As soon as the process started, it emerged that fewer than 10 percent of soldiers wanted to volunteer (fewer than 7 percent of the government's soldiers and fewer than 13 percent of Renamo's troops). When the volunteer rate fell further, the two parties indicated that they would resort to conscription. Ajello anticipated the problems that this could cause but chose to let the parties find out for themselves.

Donors Alter the Reintegration Package

Severe disagreements among donors about reintegration support for the demobilized soldiers arose toward the end of 1993 and were eventually resolved in early 1994. The director of UNOHAC, Bernt Bernander, had worked hard with the Reintegration Commission to develop a three-year reintegration scheme that included vocational training, an employment-creation fund, and a kits and credit scheme. The most important donors opposed Bernander's ideas and pushed for a faster program to remove the immediate threat posed by a disaffected military waiting to be demobilized. They favored an unprecedented formula, namely, giving the soldiers an additional eighteen months' salary, on top of the six months' pay they were already guaranteed. After Ajello announced the decision somewhat prematurely in January, a donors' meeting in Maputo formally approved a $20 million package, calling it the Reintegration Support Scheme (RSS).

The main contributions to the RSS were made by Denmark, Germany, Italy, the Netherlands, Norway, Portugal, Spain, Sweden, and Switzerland. Although payment of the eighteen months' additional support seemed to go against the principles and procedures of bilateral and multilateral agencies alike, it was a formula that the donors agreed to be both justifiable and viable to ensure peaceful demobilization. The move forced UNOHAC to switch money from other programs and increased the burden on the TU, which at short notice had to collect new information on the intentions of the assembled soldiers so that arrangements could be made for them to receive their RSS payments.

The new package could hardly fail to persuade a soldier to choose demobilization rather than continued service. It now included (1) six months' salary (half on demobilization day); (2) transportation with the soldier's family to any part of Mozambique, where food for three months and a kit of tools and vegetable seeds would be provided and the other half of the six months' salary would be paid; (3) an additional eighteen months' salary, based on the ex-soldier's former rank and payable in two-monthly installments; (4) an information and referral system; (5) occupational training; and (6) a provincial fund to support ex-soldiers' activities in their communities. The RSS provided a tangible incentive for demobilization that eventually overwhelmed the attempts of the parties to keep back troops. The prospect of two years' salary did more to bring the soldiers into the assembly areas than did any instructions from their commanders. Once assembled, the soldiers also soon began to clamor, sometimes violently, for demobilization rather than recruitment into the new army.

Conclusions

Between August 1993 and January 1994 the considerable distrust between the government and Renamo did not diminish, but the prospects for a practical fulfillment of the ONUMOZ mandate did improve. The first visit of the Renamo leader to Maputo helped to relaunch the stalled peace process and to resolve disputes about territory and the police. A new timetable could then be formulated for the most essential elements of the peace process: assembly and demobilization of soldiers, formation of the new army, and elections. But the greatest challenge was the reluctance of Dhlakama to abandon Renamo's military options in favor of entering the political and electoral contest that could bring the peace process to conclusion. For Dhlakama it was largely a question of resources.

He had expected Western governments to provide more substantial sums to fund Renamo's transformation into a political party than they were willing or able to deliver. Once the SRSG had persuaded governments to provide additional finance to Renamo, Dhlakama proved ready to comply with the new assembly and electoral timetable.

ONUMOZ gained leverage over Renamo, but it could not establish a complementary relationship with the Maputo government, many of whose members tended to resent what they saw as the international community using both Renamo and the entire peace process to limit Frelimo's authority and power. Consequently, although the assembly of troops began well and good progress was made toward establishing an electoral process, the government began to show signs of a less confident and more defensive attitude toward the work of ONUMOZ.

The peace process was, nevertheless, producing good results throughout Mozambique. Refugees and displaced people were continuing to return to their homes and freedom of movement was increasing. Food was more widely available. The start of troop assembly was also a sign that the previous restrictions on movement into and out of areas controlled by Renamo were now beginning to disappear.

5.

LANDMINES IN THE PEACE PROCESS

Problems in Coordinating Humanitarian Assistance

Mozambique's peace agreement signaled to the international community that, for the first time, it might now be possible to provide food and other emergency assistance to Mozambicans in all parts of the country. The years of war-induced hardship, the displacement of at least 5 million people, and the threat posed by the 1991–92 drought created a moral imperative. Once the fighting had ended, the survival of Mozambicans had to be guaranteed and the basis laid for a peaceful and productive future. A long-awaited chance had arrived to help Mozambicans break the cycle of violence that had destroyed their infrastructure, had forced many to flee, and had made any economic activity, even subsistence farming, a high-risk venture. An immediate effort was needed to save lives, and UN agencies and other donors were quick to mobilize programs and projects that had not been possible under conditions of war.

The attitude of the Mozambican parties and their soldiers provided important encouragement. Within days of the signing of the GPA, government troops were seen sharing their emergency food rations with Renamo fighters. Where there had been extortion, violence, and inhumanity, there was a beginning of cooperation and compassion. Once the parties had called off the fighting, ordinary Mozambicans showed themselves determined to return to their homes and to rebuild their lives, without waiting for help from outside.

At first, the return to normality proceeded only gradually, hampered by Renamo's ingrained reluctance to allow access into its areas and by the landmines that were widely scattered along roads and footpaths throughout the entire country. Despite long delays in undertaking the nationwide demining program, most of the humanitarian challenges were tackled in a pragmatic manner, with ad hoc coordination and inputs from a wide range of agencies and governments. Emergency assistance generally arrived where it was most needed.

Good coordination among donors in this field did not depend upon ONUMOZ, despite the initial intention that it should play a major and strategic role. From the outset, the delays affecting the establishment of ONUMOZ undermined its ability to act as a coordinator of humanitarian aid. Later, its humanitarian arm, UNOHAC, came to be accused of inefficiency and needless bureaucracy. Its efforts to reinforce the neutrality of ONUMOZ and to provide a flow of reliable information to the donor community as a whole were appreciated but did not redeem its poor reputation. UNOHAC failed both to coordinate and to deliver on the key items in its mandate, and the achievements of ONUMOZ in the humanitarian field were largely attributable to the collective efforts of donors and other UN agencies. Nevertheless, by the end of the peace process, there was serious concern that the emphasis on achieving quick results had undermined Mozambique's own capacity to manage its longer-term development needs.

The Humanitarian Imperative and UNOHAC

Mozambique's war created a vicious circle of dependence upon international aid and humanitarian assistance; indeed, by the early 1990s the country was sometimes cynically referred to as the "Donors' Republic of Mozambique." The more Renamo disrupted the economy, and the larger the numbers of displaced people and refugees escaping the conflict, the more assistance was needed. Food relief itself became a strategic target that Renamo sought either to seize or to destroy. Only after Renamo had given assurances in mid-1992 that it would allow free access to humanitarian relief did the picture began to change. By the time the GPA was signed, the international community was getting ready to support a nationwide humanitarian effort.

As in Somalia, Liberia, and Angola, the danger existed that the availability and distribution of relief aid would fuel or revive conflict. Commenting on the lessons to be drawn from international intervention in Somalia, Chester Crocker remarked that "it is hard to escape the conclusion that humanitarian intervention requires a linkage to political strategies of peacemaking and conflict resolution."[1] Although in Mozambique the risk of a dangerous entanglement of humanitarian relief and war was much reduced after the signing of the GPA, the potential contradictions between the political and humanitarian requirements of the peace process were an ever present source of concern and debate. In New York, institutional pressure to give the United Nations Department of Humanitarian Affairs (DHA) an active role in Mozambique led to ONUMOZ's becoming the first UN peacekeeping operation to establish a large humanitarian component within its own structure. As recommended by the secretary-general, and endorsed by the Security Council in December 1992, UNOHAC replaced the existing office of the United Nations Special Coordinator for Emergency Relief Operations (UNSCERO) in Maputo and was put under the authority of the SRSG.[2] UNOHAC's specific "humanitarian diplomacy" mandates included providing access for humanitarian aid to Renamo areas, facilitating contact between government and Renamo, developing mine-clearance programs, and promoting the social and economic integration of demobilized soldiers.

Although they were entirely rational in concept, the decisions in New York raised problems in Maputo, where the aims and management of UNOHAC were subjected to scrutiny by a long-established community of international, bilateral, and nongovernmental humanitarian agencies. A high degree of coordination already existed, both formally and informally, and these organizations found it hard to accept the need for an additional agency. Thus, UNOHAC came into being without the consent or cooperation of the dozens of humanitarian organizations already on the ground. The leading UN agencies were already engaged in turf battles. Both the World Food Programme and Unicef had reservations about working with UNOHAC's predecessor, UNSCERO. Some UN agencies, used to working as counterparts to government agencies, were also reluctant to meet the peace agreement's requirement that they should deal with Renamo as an equal partner to the government. Each agency had its different links to government, either through the ministries of finance or cooperation or through specific emergency management bodies such as the National Executive Committee for the Emergency (CENE) and the Department for the Prevention and Combat of Natural Disasters (DPCCN), or its coordinating body (CCPPCCN).

The perception of "a somewhat fluid and amorphous situation," as Ajello put it later, contributed to the decision to transfer the UNSCERO office's functions to UNOHAC, which was seen as becoming a high-level operation under the overall guidance of the SRSG.[3] The local UNDP office was not in favor, but was caught short-handed, the resident representative having been replaced in the week before the GPA was signed. Peter Simkin, the outgoing head of both UNDP and UNSCERO, had developed irreplaceable experience in opening up contacts with Renamo and negotiating humanitarian access, but he was not around to argue the case for UNDP to remain in charge of coordination. Interagency rivalries in New York also confused matters. As a new entity, DHA was still evolving its own coordination strategies and was operating without a clear relationship with DPKO.

Political imperatives prevailed and UNOHAC was mandated as a support unit, to provide ONUMOZ with a full picture and to help solve problems with and between the government and Renamo. But the mandate overlapped with so many ongoing donor-coordination activities that UNOHAC from the outset found it hard to define its own sphere of operations or to fend off competition from the rest of the donor community. The first UNOHAC director, Bernt Bernander, commented in mid-1993 that he had never seen coordination on the scale that was being attempted in Mozambique, and he expressed the hope that each agency could, as he put it, "develop a stake in the process." At the same time, he observed that although Unicef, the World Health Organization (WHO), and the International Organization for Migration (IOM) were represented in UNOHAC, two major agencies, the World Food Programme (WFP) and the United Nations High Commission on Refugees (UNHCR), were still not represented.

UNOHAC reported to DHA and was not always able or willing to respond to the demands of ONUMOZ or the SRSG in ways that were initially envisaged. UNOHAC's financial and bureaucratic constraints limited its effectiveness, especially in its program to clear landmines. Even after a special UN trust fund for humanitarian assistance was established for relief assistance, reintegration, demobilization, and demining, DHA had only limited authority over the allocation of the donors' funds. UNOHAC did not help its case by clearly emphasizing a long-term developmental philosophy rather than concentrating on the immediate and short-term needs of the peace process. The Consolidated Humanitarian Assistance Program (CHAP), first outlined in Rome in December 1992 and subsequently refined by UNOHAC, came to be seen by donors as an entirely worthy but wholly inappropriate statement of intent, focusing as it did on the need for humanitarian assistance to conform to a macroeconomic framework.[4] This approach was attributed to the particular concerns and outlook of Bernander, who was much respected for his professionalism, sincerity, and commitment but who was clearly a "development man" rather than a "peacekeeping man" and came under particularly heavy criticism from the United States Agency for International Development (USAID). UNOHAC's marginalization was increased by the low priority of the peace commission to which it was most directly linked, the Reintegration Commission, which could not play a major part until demobilization of combatants actually began. By the time this happened, the strategy of reintegrating the demobilized into civilian society over a number of years was abruptly abandoned in favor of entirely different proposals for a system of cash payments (see chapter 4).

"The question of coordination is a problem everywhere in the UN system," Ajello said later.[5] The creation of two new UN coordinating structures in Maputo, ONUMOZ and UNOHAC, meant that the existing UN agencies in the country lost staff to a new agency under the authority of managers dispatched from New York, who had a direct line to the secretary-general but had almost no knowledge of Mozambique before they arrived. Essentially, the case for enforcing humanitarian coordination was not as strong in Mozambique as it was in situations where war continued to rage. By contrast, DHA's counterpart operation in Angola, established in 1993 after the resumption of hostilities there, ensured a coherent distribution of responsibilities and created a sense of collaboration rather than competition among UN agencies.[6]

Donors and NGOs

UNOHAC aside, coordination among donors was generally efficient. In particular, the Nordic countries (which, with Canada, the Netherlands, and Switzerland, had come to be known as the "like-minded group"), the European Union, and the United States had a strong commitment to work together and were able to bring effective pressure on ONUMOZ, the government, and Renamo to keep the process moving forward. Money was available when necessary, and donors emphasized the need to complement existing activities and the ability to deliver. The two largest UN agencies in Mozambique, WFP and UNHCR, stayed aloof from formal coordination with ONUMOZ, but each helped to create the essential conditions for a normalization of life in Mozambique by delivering food and assisting in the largest return of refugees ever witnessed in Africa. As a provider of transportation, the principal newcomer on the scene was IOM, an intergovernmental body that provides support for displaced populations. Its facilities were vital for the return and reintegration of displaced persons, refugees, and demobilized soldiers and for the later deployment of Mozambican monitors to observe the elections.

The substantial NGO community, which had long played a significant, and sometimes overbearing, role in Mozambique's management of its emergencies, grew even larger and even more important.[7] The number of active international NGOs rose from about 150 to nearly 250 between 1992 and 1994. Donors relied on NGOs to perform essential work, and some donors deliberately used the NGOs as an alternative to working with the Maputo government. Not all NGOs performed well, and their presence in such numbers tended to undermine rather than bolster the capacity of Mozambicans to deal with their own humanitarian and developmental challenges. A coordinating body, Link, tried to represent the NGO case in the peace process on behalf of both the international and Mozambican organizations, but NGOs were often treated with suspicion by both the government and Renamo. The government, which resented the sheer quantity of resources available to the NGO community, continued to refuse all requests for duty exemptions on their imports, including medicine, seeds, tools, vehicles, and computers, and thus effectively taxed these donations to the country, succeeding with the NGOs where it had failed to tax ONUMOZ itself. A Link official described the customs procedures as the single greatest impediment to implementing humanitarian assistance in Mozambique.

NGOs were nearly always the first outsiders to go into Renamo areas, where they undertook a wide range of responsibilities, from delivering food to restoring water sources, opening health centers, and reopening schools. Renamo obstructed NGO access to most of its zones throughout the first year of the peace process, relenting only after a meeting between Dhlakama and a group of leading NGOs in November 1993. Although Dhlakama told the NGOs that their work was being manipulated by the government "for its own strategic interests," his promise to give them support at the local level led to a significant easing of Renamo's restrictions in the second year.

Access for the Convoys

The disruption of war and the onset of drought meant that, by 1992, Mozambique's own crops could satisfy only between 60 and 70 percent of the nation's food needs, putting an estimated 4 million people at risk. The international community responded to this emergency by pledging sufficient food aid in May 1992 to carry Mozambique through most of 1993, as long as Renamo permitted access to its own areas, where food was most scarce. WFP and Unicef became the first agencies to fly into Maringue and to talk directly to Renamo and Dhlakama. Their influence helped in the formulation of the Rome agreement of July 16, 1992, by which Renamo agreed to permit the delivery of aid throughout the country and to suspend attacks on relief convoys passing through government areas.[8] But Renamo was nervous about allowing vehicles into its own zones and asked to be supplied by air, which the agencies at first refused because of the high cost and the lack of suitable landing strips.

Eventually, in September, Renamo agreed to permit convoys escorted by the ICRC into a few Renamo areas that were accessible by two land routes, one from Beira and one from the Zimbabwe border. Negotiations on further access proved difficult. UNSCERO proposed opening another eight supply routes from within the country but Renamo rejected these, demanding deliveries from Malawi and South Africa over roads that UNSCERO deemed to be either impassable or mined. The agencies were naturally wary that food could be used to prolong the war and refused to deliver supplies on the basis of Renamo's own exaggerated population estimates. They were trying to avoid a situation whereby Renamo could stockpile food to prevent the captive population from leaving the zones it controlled.

By the time the GPA was signed, serious famine was threatening both government and Renamo areas, particularly in Manica and Sofala provinces. The ICRC reported that in Chibava district, in southern Sofala, between ten and twenty people were dying each day in the Renamo-held locality of Magunde, and that the daily toll was as high as forty in government-held localities.[9] People in the two provinces were either crowding into the Beira corridor to be within reach of relief food or fleeing into Zimbabwe. Only after the cease-fire took effect on October 15 did the flow of refugees subside and the great return begin.

The peace agreement was the signal that a more coordinated supply and delivery of food aid within the country could at last proceed. WFP committed nearly half a million tons of food at a total cost of $192 million, opening suboffices in eight provincial capitals and registering numerous NGOs as partners for transporting and distributing its food. In November 1992, WFP created a special logistics unit to move food and other aid to all parts of the country, including government and Renamo areas, using airlifts where no other access was possible. To help the central unit plan for supply routes using convoys, airlifts, or coastal shipping, logistics officers assessed local needs and gathered information on landmines and other obstacles. In the first months, armed groups staged a few attacks and seized supplies, but as the operation reached more communities, the number of such incidents began to decrease. In the first months of 1993, WFP was delivering 19,000 tons of food a month and providing airlifts to five different localities.

Thanks to the good rains of 1992–93, the food situation improved, but the continuing influx of returnees meant that substantial supplies of emergency food had to be available throughout the country. Deliveries reached 30,000 tons a month at the end of 1993. After the roads to Caia and Maringue in Sofala province were opened in September 1993, WFP suspended its airlifts, using the money it saved on rebuilding bridges, repairing roads, and extending the reach of its overland supplies. Road access also improved in Zambezia and Nampula provinces. Nearly all Renamo areas became accessible to emergency relief in the second year of the peace process. By the end of 1994, at least forty different agencies and NGOs had been established in former Renamo areas in 78 of Mozambique's 128 districts. Over the two years of the ONUMOZ mandate, an estimated 116,000 tons, approximately one-third of all the food delivered, were delivered to Renamo areas.[10]

The effectiveness of relief operations has been measured by the sharp reduction in the numbers of people needing food aid, from 3.8 million in 1992 to 1.5 million, of whom half were returnees, by 1995. Nationwide food distribution started to wind down in the second half of 1994 to be replaced by targeted distribution aimed at vulnerable groups. Although as relief supplies began to tail off there were several cases of civilians demanding food by demonstrating or staging road blocks, such protests were usually prompted by the actions of assembled or demobilized soldiers.

WFP was a key player in the peace process. It was in a position to supply food relatively quickly and efficiently as needs changed, and found ways to reach isolated communities, to assist returning refugees, and, later, to provide food to the assembly areas during the demobilization process. In coordination with the TU, WFP supplied food to both assembled and unassembled troops on both sides and provided three months of rations to the demobilized soldiers and their dependents at a total cost of around $5.8 million, including 17,000 tons of food and funds to pay for internal transportation. The agency also provided food for voter registration brigades that were deployed around the country from June 1994.

Reliable figures for food production are not available. Even so, the revival of farm output clearly contributed substantially to the official 19 percent increase in the country's overall economic output in 1993. The improving food situation also encouraged the spontaneous return of Mozambicans to their home districts. The continuation of the peace enabled people to plant 10 percent more land in the 1993–94 season, but the rains were late, short, and irregular. Although the harvests were good in the north, they were less so in the center, and were generally poor in the south. At the end of the peace process in late 1994, with large numbers of people continuing to return to their homes, there were renewed concerns for food security, prompting a variety of aid agencies to step up their distribution of seeds and agricultural tools. Even at the end of the process, the food security situation throughout the country had to be monitored until a self-sustaining agricultural production and marketing system could be reestablished. All food aid operations risk creating a persistent dependence on free food and a weakening of the market for local crops. To counteract this, donors tried to contribute to the development of a domestic food market. By early 1995, WFP was confident that food production would "increase exponentially" and declared that "if government and donors can also build a food security net to deal with any future disasters, Mozambique may regain the self-sufficiency it once had in food production, even producing for export."[11] As it turned out, however, a greater obstacle to the recovery of agriculture in Mozambique has been the lack of clarity over rights to land and the long delay in establishing a coherent land law.

The Problem of Landmines

Initially, action to solve Mozambique's acute landmine problem seemed to be gathering momentum, with the drafting in late 1992 of a mine-clearance plan for more than two thousand kilometers of priority roads (both for access to assembly points and to assist the repatriation of refugees) and early agreement on the need for a detailed landmine survey and the establishment of a training school for Mozambican deminers. Twenty-eight priority roads had been identified by the ICRC as soon as the GPA was signed, and the CSC had given its approval for their clearance on December 31, 1992. But this early momentum was lost after

UNDP in New York was given responsibility for implementing the road-clearance program and the survey, with an allocation of $14 million, half from the ONUMOZ budget and half from the DHA trust fund.

Management of the demining program was placed under UNOHAC, which reported to DHA rather than to the SRSG. UNOHAC delayed a number of important decisions and insisted that all work should be approved by the demining subcommittee of the CCF, which Renamo boycotted throughout the early months of 1993. The persistent failure of the peace commissions to meet and the wariness of both parties about opening up roads that linked Renamo with government areas resulted in prolonged delays in approving the projects at this level, although the money was available and the implementing agencies such as Norwegian People's Aid and Halo Trust were ready to start work.

The rivalry between DHA and UNDP in New York over program jurisdiction (a classic case of UN bureaucratic entanglement) played a major part in the confusion and failure to act in clearing landmines. UNDP in New York was unwilling to approve projects and programs proposed by UNOHAC, arguing over the wording of contracts, tendering procedures, and quality control. Eventually, by the end of March 1994, the mine survey was well under way but by no means completed. Negotiations were still stalled over a major $4.8 million contract for the clearance of priority roads, mainly in Sofala and Manica provinces. The contract was highly controversial because it had been won by a joint venture consisting of Lonrho, Royal Ordnance, and the South African armaments company Mechem, the latter two of which were specialists in the manufacture of landmines.

As result of this long chain of delays, only $1.5 million of the original $14 million budget had been committed by May 1994, by which time, following complaints from Sweden and other contributors to the DHA trust fund, the secretary-general's office intervened. UNDP was ordered to sign the road-clearance contract with the joint venture but the remainder of the demining budget was taken away from UNDP in New York and given to UNOHAC in Maputo, which had begun to act more decisively—having awarded the mine survey contract to Halo Trust without consulting UNDP. One of the priorities for Felix Downes-Thomas after he arrived in Maputo as the new UNOHAC director in March 1994 was to clear the demining logjam and to prevent exasperated donors (particularly the Netherlands and Sweden) from withdrawing their funds. The first demining budget of $14 million was increased to $18.5 million—$11 million from the ONUMOZ budget and $7.5 million from the contributions of donors to the trust fund.

Independently and out of frustration with the United Nations's faltering efforts, several donors and agencies had gone ahead with their own programs. To facilitate food distribution, WFP and its NGO partners became involved in landmine clearance at an early stage. In October 1992, WFP had contracted the British firm, Defence Systems Ltd., to survey two thousand kilometers of roads in the central provinces, and in early 1993 it supplied twenty trained mine detectors to clear mines in Sofala province. In February 1993, the European Union hired Lonrho and Gurkha security guards to provide four teams to clear mines on two hundred kilometers of roads around the Renamo-held town of Inhaminga. Norwegian People's Aid trained deminers and cleared roads in Maputo, Tete, Sofala, and Zambezia provinces. In late 1993, USAID appointed a U.S. contractor, Ronco, to clear mines from priority roads in Manica, Sofala, and Zambezia. Funded by the British government, Halo Trust also undertook extensive demining in Zambezia province, starting in May 1994. A U.S. embassy cable in May 1994 described the situation succinctly: "The progress of the mine clearance efforts to date has been inversely proportional to the degree of dependence on the UN for support."

In June 1994, UNOHAC launched its new Accelerated Demining Program (ADP) to train 450 Mozambican deminers for deployment by November, to strengthen the management of field operations, and to develop a mine-survey capability. By December, the program had cleared forty thousand square meters and lifted over eight hundred mines. Despite opposition from some donors, the ADP continued after the departure of ONUMOZ under the management of UNDP in Maputo. In the closing months of ONUMOZ, the U.S. embassy strongly criticized UNOHAC's proposals for the creation of a new Mozambican government department for the coordination and implementation of mine clearance and called for the United Nations to delegate responsibility for supervision and demining to the existing operations, transferring its unused funds to the agencies already active in the field. During 1995 a National Demining Commission was established, but most of the work of management and field operations was indeed undertaken by outside agencies.

The first Halo Trust national mine survey completed in mid-1994 identified 981 mined areas in Mozambique. The most heavily mined provinces were found to be Inhambane, Manica, Maputo, Sofala, Tete, and Zambezia. Of the 115 districts in the country, 41 had at least ten identified mine sites and a further 37 had at least five. By the time ONUMOZ departed, the different agencies involved in landmine removal had cleared 3,262 kilometers of roads and 1.5 million square meters of territory and had disabled 1,827 antipersonnel mines, 17 antitank mines, and 10,957 items of unexploded ordnance.[12] Subsequent operations in 1995 undertaken by the ADP, Norwegian People's Aid, Halo Trust, and Minetech Zimbabwe improved substantially on this performance: 5,793 kilometers of roads and 17.9 million square meters of territory cleared, and 8,379 antipersonnel mines, 1,332 fragmentation mines, 109 antitank mines, and 11,165 items of unexploded ordnance destroyed by October 1995.[13] By late 1995, the total number of identified mined areas had risen to more than two thousand, as the ADP developed the original Halo Trust mine survey.

Both Halo Trust and Handicap International hazarded the guess that at least fifteen hundred people died from mine accidents during the peace process, although there was no way to confirm these estimates.[14] Accidents involving deaths and the destruction of vehicles on the roads were more often reported than were accidents suffered by individuals in the open countryside. Survivors often sustained very severe injuries, requiring the amputation of limbs. Handicap International recorded that 936 amputees attended its orthopedic centers between 1992 and 1994, and that a further 385 attended in the first six months of 1995, as the return of peace and mobility exposed increasing numbers of people to the landmine hazard.

Landmine accidents are likely to continue in Mozambique for many years. The mines lie along and beside roads and footpaths, in open farming country, around wells, schools, clinics, and other buildings. Most accidents have occurred away from main roads and at least half the victims of accidents have died before receiving any form of medical care. In Maputo province, eighty-one accidents were recorded between June 1994 and October 1995. In Inhambane province, thirty-seven accidents claimed fifty-three victims between March 1994 and March 1995. In Zambezia province, fifty-one accidents were recorded in the first seven months of 1995.[15]

Refugees and the Displaced

At the signing of the peace agreement, it was estimated that, in addition to nearly 2 million refugees in neighboring countries, more than 3 million people were displaced within the country. UNHCR figures for

Mozambican refugees in 1992 showed that more than 1 million were in Malawi, while the remainder were scattered, mainly unregistered, in South Africa, Zimbabwe, Zambia, Tanzania, and Swaziland.[16] Of the 3 million people displaced within Mozambique, about 1 million were living in squatter camps around the cities, and another three hundred thousand were returnees, often living in camps in different parts of the country. The number of displaced people within Renamo areas could never be accurately estimated.[17]

Studies showed that the refugees and returnees were generally able to work out their own survival strategies, although the refugees in particular remained critically dependent on food aid and there was an urgent need to clear and rehabilitate roads and bridges to facilitate the return and to lower the risk of landmine accidents. By June 1993, more than 250,000 refugees had returned from neighboring countries without assistance. Most of these were entering from Malawi, at a rate of more than one thousand a day, mainly into Tete, Sofala, and Zambezia provinces. UNHCR itself was hardly prepared for the scale of the movement, and was only beginning to get itself organized by August 1993, after it had secured a budget of $203 million. Moreover, the slow pace of the peace process in its early months created an imbalance between the assistance available and the areas of greatest need. Most of the refugees were returning to Renamo areas but much of the assistance was going to Frelimo areas because the Renamo authorities were either obstructive or too poorly organized to ask for assistance. The government and donors had still not agreed on a repatriation strategy. The original program proposed a return "in conditions of security and dignity," but this implied a much more elaborate program and ignored the reality that people were already streaming back. The government, meanwhile, demanded that money and resources be made available to help the returnees directly.

The United States Committee for Refugees (USCR) described the return to Mozambique as the largest repatriation of refugees in African history. The committee's report expressed concern about the conditions facing the returnees: "Many refugees will find no towns, no markets, no schools, no health clinics . . . virtually nothing with which to reintegrate. They will have no choice but to rebuild an entire economic and social structure from scratch."[18] An NGO worker was quoted as saying that "there is a tendency to assume when refugees return home, the problem is over. That is when the problem begins. Mozambique is devastated. Reconstruction would be simpler if Mozambique wasn't such a poor country. There is nothing there." The areas of return tended to be, in the words of one UNHCR official, "the most remote, devastated, and traditionally neglected" parts of the country.[19]

UNHCR reached repatriation accords with Malawi, Swaziland, Zambia, and Zimbabwe but took somewhat longer to reach agreement with South Africa, which had not previously recognized the refugee status of migrants and had a long history of forcibly repatriating and detaining Africans from neighboring countries. After South Africa signed its agreement on September 6, 1993, UNHCR began its registration and assessments. The South Africa Defense Force provided transport for returnees until IOM took over in January 1994. The real numbers of Mozambican refugees in South Africa are unlikely ever to be known. Economic migration has continued over several decades, and genuine refugees probably accounted for only part of the total. When UNHCR organized transport for refugees from South Africa, few took the opportunity to return, and some of those who did stayed only long enough to see their families and friends before going back to their more promising existence in exile. However, of the one hundred thousand potential returnees in South Africa estimated by UNHCR, about sixty-seven thousand did return between 1992 and 1995.

The agency undertook organized repatriations from Swaziland, Tanzania, Zambia, and Zimbabwe—although at times there were problems of coordination with operations in the asylum countries.[20] Out of the estimated six hundred thousand refugees who returned during 1993, only twenty thousand received formal assistance from UNHCR, which was still appealing for donors to produce the funds they had pledged. In mid-1994, by which time UNHCR had at last assembled its full complement of staff to undertake its programs and quick-impact projects, the total number who had returned exceeded 1 million and more were accepting the assistance being offered. In September 1995, UNHCR estimated the number of returning refugees since the signing of the GPA at 1.73 million, of whom more than 378,000 had received the agency's transportation assistance.[21] UNHCR may have played a useful role in encouraging refugees seeking to resettle in their home districts, but by the end of 1995 its programs were widely felt to be insufficient to sustain the livelihoods of the returnees after the agency's departure in 1996. Officials expressed the hope that a longer-term program would be launched to rebuild the social, economic, and administrative structures of a society shattered by war.[22] A USCR report written in 1993 noted that "experts predict that the country will labor for a full generation before most Mozambicans can regain the meager standard of living they had in 1980";[23] by late 1995, there was no reason to revise that prediction.

Similar concern was felt about the programs for internally displaced people. An internal IOM evaluation in August 1995 concluded that considerable work needed to be done to improve conditions for the returnees in their places of resettlement. Because IOM was involved in diverse logistic operations throughout the peace process, some members of its staff found themselves overstretched; the limitations on their time and energy particularly affected the programs for the internally displaced. Most internally displaced people had already reached their intended destinations by December 1994. Traveling home, many spontaneous returnees found themselves threatened by landmines, crime, and general insecurity. Sudden surges in population also created tensions in areas where water, food, employment, and social facilities were in short supply. "Mass internal migration has created a wide range of sociodemographic and economic problems," noted the IOM report.[24]

UNOHAC and Demobilization

Differences within the donor community came into sharp focus over UNOHAC's plans for the reintegration of the soldiers after their demobilization. UNOHAC took its brief from the Rome donors' conference of December 1992. With suffering and famine widespread throughout Mozambique, most donors opposed treating the demobilized as a privileged category in the peace process. UNOHAC nevertheless soon came under fire from donors over its socially uncontroversial plans for a three-year program of training, employment, and credit for the demobilized soldiers. Approved by UNOHAC's first director, Bernt Bernander, and accepted by the Reintegration Commission (CORE), the program was based on a long-term reintegration plan with an emphasis on community projects, training, employment creation, and skills development. Its main weakness was that it was unlikely to start up until late 1994, some time after the soldiers were due to return home.

Aware of the political urgency to provide the demobilized soldiers with more attractive and tangible incentives to rejoin civilian life, the donors began to favor programs that could produce results within the short time frame of the peace process itself. The so-called like-minded donor group argued for the shorter-term RSS, to provide a cash subsidy for eighteen months to follow the government's provision of a six-month subsidy. USAID meanwhile proposed a low-budget information and referral service at the provincial level. Bypassing UNOHAC and CORE, donors meeting in Maputo on January 31, 1994, accepted both these programs, which reallocated a number of existing commitments into the RSS. By the end of the process, UNOHAC was prepared to admit that "CORE did not enjoy the support and confidence of the larger system, which greatly undermined its authority and its ability to mobilize action on policies and programs it advocated."[25] CORE was most effective in coordinating meetings between the government and Renamo in tripartite working groups. During the assembly process, it also produced information packs for the assembled soldiers; this literature, although distributed late, did help significantly in explaining the options facing soldiers being demobilized.

Ajello later characterized the disputes over the reintegration support package as the result of tensions in the "culture of development versus peacekeeping."[26] Ajello wanted results within the time frame of the peacekeeping operation; professionals working in the field of humanitarian relief were understandably concerned about doing the job thoroughly. At the end of the process, Downes-Thomas, the director of UNOHAC, was still arguing for the establishment of a clear national authority to manage the reintegration of the demobilized, saying that cash payments alone did not guarantee successful reintegration.[27]

The Challenges of Coordination

In their analysis of war and humanitarianism, Larry Minear and Thomas Weiss state that "coordination at its best can harmonize and energize activities, replace centripetal with centrifugal action, and enhance individual contributions. Coordination at its worst can require costly investments of time and money, frustrate action, centralize functions that are better left decentralized, and politicize humanitarian action."[28] By the end of the peace process, UNOHAC tended to be seen as an example of the latter definition. The forms of coordination that it tried to impose were on the whole deemed to be unnecessary. As an implementing agency it was seen to be inefficient. UNOHAC's problems derived primarily from an inadequate definition of its role at the outset, compounded by political pressure for the newly created DHA to "establish its image." It failed to build upon the existing coordination of humanitarian action within Mozambique. The advantages of integrating UNOHAC within ONUMOZ were later judged to be far smaller than the disadvantages. As a political operation, ONUMOZ had little understanding of humanitarian issues. UNOHAC was caught in the middle, misunderstood by its political bosses and resented by the rest of the humanitarian community.[29]

UNOHAC had an international staff of thirty-five people: twenty-four professionals and eleven seconded from UN or other international agencies. The central office was set up in Maputo to facilitate contact between the government and Renamo, to liaise with the international community, and to gather information. A field presence was established in the ten provincial capitals to promote operational coordination and to ensure neutrality. UNOHAC was also given the task of managing a $32 million DHA trust fund (to which the contributors were Denmark, Italy, the Netherlands, Sweden, and Switzerland) to cover demobilization, mine clearance, reintegration, and general humanitarian assistance, although the donors retained the authority to control these resources. In helping to open up Renamo areas to humanitarian access, in facilitating contact between government and Renamo, and in building up a reliable and accurate database of humanitarian activities in Mozambique, UNOHAC achieved some success. But in mine clearance it bungled badly, and in assisting the reintegration of demobilized soldiers it failed altogether. Rather than building upon the United Nations's long-established coordination mechanisms, UNOHAC caused disruption. "The UNOHAC mandate was wrongly interpreted as setting up a huge bureaucracy at the Rovuma Hotel [ONUMOZ headquarters] to coordinate everything, pushing aside the previous coordination work involving UNDP and UNHCR," declared the USAID director in Mozambique, Roger Carlson.

As the local expression of DHA, UNOHAC had considerable seniority within the UN system but its performance fell short of its promise. It generated unproductive antagonism from other UN agencies and failed to win respect from the donor community upon which it vitally depended. UNDP officials privately blamed the "myopic view of the UN Secretariat" for disrupting the inherited coordination system, and bilateral donors openly denounced UNOHAC as unnecessary, expensive, inefficient, and plagued by bad management. "UNOHAC saw itself as coordinating all development issues in the country, but the donor community saw UNOHAC as losing track of what should be done and its programs as out of sync," said Carlson.[30]

DHA later concluded that UNOHAC might have succeeded if its primary functions had been more clearly defined early on and if it had had greater control over disbursements from the trust fund. Among the donors and humanitarian agencies in Mozambique, there was a feeling that UNOHAC should have been what one called "a small and lean operation" to help donors focus their resources on the requirements of the peace process. Some took the view that, from the outset, the different agencies could have been given the lead in their particular areas of expertise, in which case a more appropriate role for UNOHAC might have been to supplement rather than to replace existing coordination. Many felt that operational management should have been left to those agencies that already had activities on the ground.

Ajello commented later: "Increasingly, criticism was raised against UNOHAC's excessively bureaucratic rules and procedures, its tendency to build overly heavy structures at central and provincial levels, and its inclination to be involved in medium- and long-term programs where it had no mandate." He strongly defended the principle of the coordination of humanitarian assistance as "an essential component of any peace-keeping operation," in particular in meeting the needs of soldiers during demobilization.[31] But this was exactly where UNOHAC did not match up to its mission, and Ajello himself responded quickly to pressure for a practical alternative. Once donors had decided to meet the needs of the demobilizing soldiers with the RSS, Ajello transferred responsibility for managing the scheme to the TU, bypassing UNOHAC almost entirely.

Unilateral action by donors and ad hoc coordination were thus effectively endorsed by ONUMOZ and Ajello. Individually, donors and agencies seized their opportunities for initiatives and actions and remained wary of submitting to ineffective control and coordination. Some donors also took the view that the peace process gave license for international action without government interference, and this resulted in a sharp downgrading of the government's own relief bodies. Although the national disaster relief organization, DPCCN, continued to receive cooperation from WFP, this was a rare exception. "The peace agreement created a field day for agencies to bypass the government," said an NGO manager later. Some powerful donors argued for a continuation of this practice after the departure of ONUMOZ. Writing in mid-1994 in the UNOHAC publication, *Mozambique Report,* USAID director Roger Carlson argued that the relief and reintegration activities handled by ONUMOZ and UNOHAC should not be given to the government when those agencies closed after the election, even though these activities fall within the natural and proper scope of governments. He suggested that programs be handled by a mix of UN and NGO bodies controlled by the donors.

UNOHAC not only disrupted the formal coordination of UN agency activities but also left a tangled inheritance of projects in its wake when the phase-down proved as difficult as the phase-in. Agencies that had felt displaced now found themselves having to take on numerous activities that UNOHAC had launched but not completed. In late 1995, a UNDP official, commenting that "some of UNOHAC's activities had a life beyond life," asked, "Why create an expensive agency for such a short duration, which then handed a sometimes poisoned inheritance back to the permanent agencies?" No fewer than fifty-three UNOHAC projects were passed to UNDP for continuation, including mine clearance and a series of overlapping projects for demobilized soldiers, such as business and skills development, the provincial fund, vocational training, and the provision of food and other forms of support. UNOHAC did hand its valuable database over to the Ministry of Cooperation and Foreign Affairs, but it was not maintained and quickly became useless.

Opening up the Country

Between 1992 and 1994, life in Mozambique improved dramatically, even if the poor state of the roads still made the drive from the north to the south of the country a six-day expedition. The short-term needs of pacification, resettlement, and reintegration were largely being met, and now the more difficult questions about strategies for long-term development came to the fore. In December 1994, UNOHAC provincial offices gave an honest account of the challenges that lay ahead.[32] Conditions were clearly better in the northern and southern provinces than in the central region where the war had raged for longest. The extent of damage to infrastructure throughout the country virtually ensured that the development of internal markets for food was unlikely to proceed quickly.

The northernmost provinces of Cabo Delgado and Niassa had been least affected by the war. Agriculture was reviving, but access was still a problem along rural roads that were known to be mined. In Nampula, former Renamo-held areas were open for access and development, although roads were poor, food aid was still needed, and education and health coverage was reported as being "far from acceptable." In war-torn Zambezia, once contact between district administrations and the local Renamo authorities had been made after March 1994, the reach of humanitarian assistance improved, but mined roads still left some areas inaccessible. The response of the international community was judged to have been generally effective in helping to stabilize rural society in Zambezia but the challenges ahead included restoring a market for agricultural production, promoting enterprise, and improving health and education.

The provinces requiring the most attention after the departure of ONUMOZ were Tete, Sofala, and Manica. In Tete, the former Renamo areas still needed to be integrated into a unified system. "Progress will be slow until political decisions are taken at a central level over how to combine the two previously separate systems," commented the UNOHAC report. Trade and commerce had flourished since the end of the war, but because hundreds of thousands of returnees from Malawi had not yet been able to harvest a crop, substantial relief would be required for many more months to come. In Sofala, although NGOs had gradually gained access to Renamo areas during 1993, not until July and August 1994 did the government appoint Renamo district administrators, whereupon communications and cooperation with people in Renamo strongholds began to improve. UNOHAC reported that what it called "the preconditions" of peace and development had been established but much more action was still required. It recommended continued support for returning refugees, the reintegration of demobilized soldiers, the development of an agricultural policy, and the clearance of many areas where mines and other explosives still impeded the restoration of essential services. In Manica, progress toward reunification was especially slow and was not complete by the end of the peace process. Restrictions on access to Renamo areas by government officers, teachers, and doctors were not entirely lifted, although most NGOs were able to move freely and trade and commerce enjoyed a modest revival. As more people moved into previously inaccessible areas, the risk of landmine incidents grew considerably. UNOHAC urged that priority be given to the clearance of defensive rings of landmines around villages and towns and along feeder roads and access routes to schools, health clinics, and economic centers throughout Manica.

The arid southern provinces faced problems that were more social and economic than political in nature. Inhambane province was littered with landmines but there was no expectation of difficulties in bringing the few Renamo areas into the government administration. The priorities in Inhambane and Gaza alike were rehabilitation of social infrastructure and the revival of economic activity. The southernmost province of

Maputo was confronted by problems rooted in local social realities. "Overpopulation, large numbers of demobilized soldiers, high cost of living, insufficient social services and lack of employment are leading to an expansion of informal and sometimes illegal business, as well as an increase of banditry and crime," UNOHAC reported. "Special attention should be paid to the reintegration programs of the demobilized soldiers in the urban areas," it urged.[33]

Conclusions

Most of the credit for the successes in the humanitarian field, as in so many other areas of the Mozambican peace process, should go to the country's people. Their patient and cooperative spirit ensured the generally peaceful return home of the refugees, the displaced, and the demobilized soldiers. The generosity of the international community, which kept faith with its long-standing support of Mozambique in earlier years, also played a large part. UN agencies, international organizations, and NGOs generally provided high levels of assistance. Commitments to emergency and rehabilitation programs between October 1992 and December 1994 were calculated to total $633 million.[34]

The organizational and interagency problems besetting the humanitarian relief programs never seriously hindered the generally well-coordinated and accurately targeted delivery of many different forms of emergency assistance. The fact that assistance was available and was provided efficiently and flexibly helped ONUMOZ to perform creditably in its more central functions. It was also fortunate that the need to enforce neutrality, which elsewhere has required DHA to distance itself from the political or military aspects of peacekeeping, did not become a major issue. The armies respected the cease-fire, and emergency supplies were not subject to excessive armed disruption or extortion.

The effective performance throughout the country of many agencies contrasts sharply with UNOHAC's inept handling of two important parts of its mandate, demining and reintegration. Nevertheless, for all of UNOHAC's weaknesses in performance, its two directors seemed to understand better than many of their counterparts the importance of providing a basis for sustainable development over the longer term. UNOHAC was a failure because of the lack of distinction between the needs of humanitarian coordination and the need to mount peace-related projects. It is hard to escape the conclusion that the previous coordination under UNSCERO should have been maintained and, when necessary, dovetailed with the peace process through DHA. UNOHAC's projects should have been left to other, more capable agencies to undertake.

The long-term legacy of humanitarian work during the peace process is more difficult to assess. Donor agencies relied heavily on foreign NGOs to deliver resources, prompting some observers to comment that the donor community was deliberately attempting to weaken the government rather than to promote a healthy balance between state and civil society.[35] The fact that there were more international NGOs in Mozambique at the end of the process than at the time of its launch could be a cause of concern. Although the international community delivered humanitarian assistance effectively, especially in Renamo-held areas, it did not follow this through with a strategy for a balanced, Mozambican-managed completion of the process.

6.

DEMOBILIZATION

A Race against Time

Just as the demobilization of Mozambique's opposing armies had been difficult to initiate, it was hard to sustain. The first stage—assembling the troops—proceeded only intermittently, and the second stage—sending the troops home—was late to start. The parties looked suspiciously at each other, were quick to retreat from their commitments, and indulged in posturing, accusation, and counteraccusation. Concerned by the prospect of further delay, ONUMOZ and the CSC eventually became assertive and drove the process forward over the heads of both the government and Renamo, provoking a fresh round of accusations from the government about infringements of sovereignty.

Eventually, it was the soldiers themselves who broke the stalemate. After months of protests, riots, and disturbances in the assembly areas, the government and Renamo lost their military control and finally had to allow the soldiers to choose freely between demobilization and joining the new army. Thanks to a generous redundancy package supplied by the donor community, demobilization was the preferred choice, even among the elite troops that both parties probably intended to keep back as a military contingency.

At times, concern grew that the breakdown of discipline in the assembly areas could threaten law and order across the society. Fears were also aroused by the small number of volunteers for service in the new, joint army; too small a force would be unlikely to be able to provide security in the future. Moreover, the race against time prevented a complete collection of weapons. Although by the end of the process Mozambique was sufficiently demilitarized to enter the final, electoral phase of the ONUMOZ mandate, there was unfinished business in disarmament and in guaranteeing stability in the longer term.

UN Deployment

The assembly and demobilization processes took place in more promising circumstances in early 1994 than would have been possible a year earlier. ONUMOZ was at least fully deployed, even if it did not always function as efficiently as might have been expected. The CSC had become the cockpit of the peace process. Ajello held regular informal consultations with both parties and the international members of the commission to settle points at issue before formal meetings of the CSC. ONUMOZ itself underwent a number of management changes in February 1994. The new deputy SRSG, replacing Bernt Bernander of UNOHAC, was Behrooz Sadry, an Iranian diplomat who had served in the same post in Cambodia. The first ONUMOZ force commander, Major General Lelio Goncalves Rodriguez da Silva of Brazil, was replaced by Major General Mohammad Abdus Salam of Bangladesh. To replace Bernander as director of UNOHAC, DHA sent one of its most senior officials, Felix Downes-Thomas, whose principal task was to unblock the embarrassing logjam over demining.

In its February 1994 resolution on Mozambique, the Security Council asked ONUMOZ to start making plans for a gradual reduction of its military personnel. At the same time, the Security Council approved the deployment of up to 1,144 civilian police monitors.[1] Italy began reducing the size of its contingent in the Beira corridor in early 1994, withdrawing eight hundred, almost all of its troops, during April. In the same month, the secretary-general proposed the withdrawal of a further fifteen hundred soldiers from the contingents.[2] The Beira corridor came to be patrolled largely by Botswanan and Bangladeshi troops redeployed from the Tete and Nacala corridors. By the end of June, ONUMOZ consisted of 4,261 military personnel, 354 military observers, 806 police, and 200 foreign civilian staff, a level that was largely maintained up to the end of the process.

The expense of maintaining the contingents, which contributed little to the day-to-day momentum of the peace process, was hard to justify in practical terms. The battalions were, however, a guarantee of freedom of movement in the transportation corridors and provided back-up security

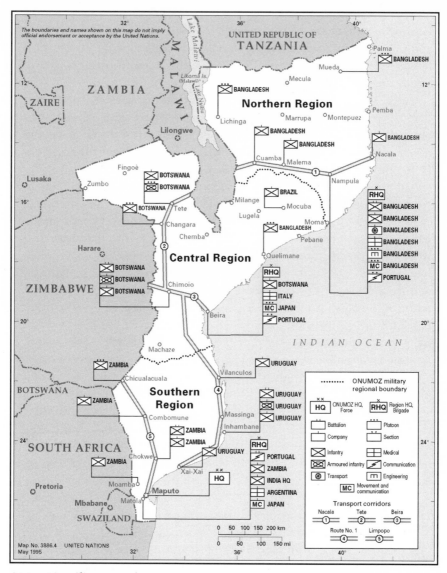

ONUMOZ Military Deployment at Time of Elections, October 1994

From *The United Nations and Mozambique, 1992–1995* (New York: United Nations, 1995), map 3886.4 (May 1995). Reprinted with permission of the United Nations Publications Board.

for the military observers deployed at the assembly areas. The latter role became important during the upsurge of violent incidents between May and July 1994. In essence, the battalions were a symbol of the power of the international community through the difficult and dangerous period of demobilization and the lead-up to elections.

The reputation of the military contingents was damaged by allegations of child abuse. In December 1993, an alliance of Save the Children Fund organizations in Mozambique accused members of the Italian battalion Albatroz of abusing young girls for sexual purposes. A Save the Children Fund official said that prostitution in Beira had increased sharply since the Italian troops had arrived in April 1993 and that UN soldiers in Chimoio were constantly calling on young girls of between twelve and fourteen years of age for sexual services. Ajello set up an investigatory commission, which at a press conference on February 25 announced that the allegations were justified and warned of sanctions against any ONUMOZ personnel found to be, or to have been, involved. No individuals were accused of wrongdoing, but it is worth noting that the entire Albatroz contingent returned to Italy in April (officially, on account of budgetary problems in Italy). It was a humiliation for Italy, which had hoped to establish a good name for its performance in peacekeeping duties. Similar, but unsubstantiated, allegations were made about child abuse by members of other contingents, particularly the Uruguayan battalion, that had been deployed to patrol the main Maputo-Beira highway.

While the deployment of the contingents on the transport corridors eventually became largely unnecessary, the monitoring and verification role of the military observers remained crucial. The observers provided key support for the CCF. Much of the logistical work that might otherwise have been left to the military wing of ONUMOZ was being undertaken by the TU, which proved its value as the key implementing agency for demobilization. Nevertheless, the logistic arrangements were periodically subject to factors beyond the control of ONUMOZ. In late 1993, for instance, UN headquarters in New York suddenly cancelled an ONUMOZ contract with Skylink of Canada, which had been providing cheap and versatile Russian helicopters and crews, awarding it instead to Evergreen of the United States, which provided Bell 212 helicopters with less capacity and a more limited flying range. When ONUMOZ needed to extend its air-transport coverage and capacity for assembly and demobilization in March, Ajello had to seek assistance from South Africa, which at a cost provided larger helicopters more appropriate to the demands in Mozambique.

Maintaining the Balance of Assembly

Before demobilization could begin, there had to be satisfactory assembly of troops from both sides. Some of the assembly areas soon became overcrowded while others remained virtually empty. On both sides, the assembly process was particularly slow in the central provinces that had seen most of the fighting, Manica, Sofala, Tete, and Zambezia. From the outset, the program was dogged by unforeseen problems and by the tendency of each side to find fault with the other's actions. The rate of assembly of the government's FAM troops was initially slow, accelerating between mid-January and mid-February before almost coming to a halt during March. By mid-April only 55 percent (a total of 34,012) of the FAM troops expected had arrived in the assembly areas. Renamo also had cause for suspicion at the government's delay in dismantling its estimated 156,000-strong militia and paramilitary forces, a process that began behind schedule in January. Although Renamo began slowly, in proportional terms it quickly overtook the government's rate of assembly, reaching 58 percent of the expected number of soldiers by the end of January and 81 percent by mid-April, for a total of 15,453 soldiers.

The weapons brought into the assembly areas were generally old and in poor condition, giving rise to well-founded suspicions that the best weapons were being kept back, either on the orders of local commanders or on the initiative of individual soldiers.[3] It was estimated that in the north of the country over 90 percent of the weapons handed in were unserviceable. The reluctance of both parties to allow ONUMOZ inspections of weapons stores revealed a potentially dangerous weakness in both the GPA and the ONUMOZ plan of operations. Clearly, however, the SRSG and his deputy saw the completion of demobilization as more important. They hoped to deal with the arms issue later.

Demobilization could begin only when the two sides had declared their intentions about which combatants were to be discharged and which were to be selected for the new army. Following the agreed-upon procedure, ONUMOZ prepared lists that indicated each soldier's declaration of whether or not he or she wished to volunteer for the new army. Thanks to a sophisticated satellite communications system provided by SwedRelief, the TU had this information available within minutes of each registration exercise. The TU then passed the information to the parties, which had earlier agreed to select their candidates for the army within ten days, so that those not selected could be demobilized. But the parties held on to their lists for weeks that soon stretched into months. The TU's planned methodology of "first in, first out" collapsed, assembly areas rapidly became overcrowded, and indiscipline became endemic. Additional food had to be found for the assembled troops and their families, and the funding of the whole process had to be increased. ONUMOZ resorted to expensive helicopter operations to keep the assembly areas supplied and to be ready to deal with incidents as they arose.

The start of demobilization was half-hearted. A small number of FAM troops were discharged at Massinga assembly area in Inhambane province on March 10; eight days later, a small number of Renamo troops at Neves, also in Inhambane, were discharged. On March 28, the CCF chairman, Colonel Pier Segala, firmly blamed both sides for failing to provide lists of their soldiers to be discharged and for slowing down the rate of assembly. Renamo was also late in providing the first lists of its recruits for the new army. When by mid-April the government had demobilized 12,195 troops, or 20 percent of its estimated total, against only 561 from Renamo, or just 3 percent of its total, the government's reaction was to stop demobilizing its troops altogether.

The potential for crisis over demobilization and the risks of slippage in the timetable were beginning to preoccupy the international community. Attempts to maintain the pressure for forward movement were made during visits in March and April by the OAU secretary-general, Salim Salim; a senior UN official, Ismat Kittani; the U.S. permanent representative to the United Nations, Madeleine Albright; and the United Kingdom's overseas development minister, Baroness Lynda Chalker. Despite these high-level interventions, the standstill in demobilization persisted and was aggravated by a highly charged dispute between ONUMOZ and the government over the total number of FAM troops. Based on the government's declaration of November 1992 that 61,638 soldiers were due for assembly and its subsequent declaration that 14,849 troops were resident in the "non-assembled areas," the number of government troops was assumed to total 76,487. However, on April 21, the government suddenly informed the CCF that its full troop strength at the time of GPA was only 64,118, including both those troops earmarked for assembly and those to be registered as "non-assembled." This revision implied a sudden loss of 12,369 soldiers and immediately led Renamo to suspect that large numbers of troops were being held back.

Questioned by the CCF, the government admitted to poor accounting by the different military and civilian departments and to a tendency by government army field commanders to overstate the number of soldiers under their command in order to get more rations and supplies and to pocket the pay of nonexistent soldiers. These explanations were entirely plausible but had to be treated with caution, given the high level of distrust between the two parties and the possibility of a hidden agenda on the part of the government. The CCF asked for a clear demonstration that the discrepancies were systemic rather than specific to the figures presented for assembly and demobilization, but the government produced no documentation that could clarify the issue or help prove its case.[4] Eventually the government tried to deflect the embarrassment of its overcounting by suggesting that the total included the 13,776 already demobilized during 1992, before the signing of the GPA, and whom the United Nations had already transported home and paid (see chapter 3). The government then produced a new figure of 49,638 troops as the total intended to enter the assembly areas. This was a crude subtraction of 12,000 from the original total and was hardly credible, confirming to ONUMOZ once again that it could not trust figures being presented by either side. There were also glaring inaccuracies in Renamo's troop lists. Not until June, after protracted investigations and negotiations, was the government's total of 49,638 troops for assembly accepted. When 14,828 troops in non-assembled areas were added to the calculation, the total came to 64,466. (The number of FAM troops eventually registered was 67,042—43,409 in the assembly areas and 23,633 in the non-assembled areas.)

The credibility of Renamo's figures was questioned in the light of reports that it was not declaring all its troops in its different bases. Renamo's underreporting was said to be particularly marked in the case of its child soldiers. Ahead of Dhlakama's visit to the United States in June 1994, Renamo admitted that it still had more than 2,000 child soldiers; a Unicef survey had confirmed their presence in tightly guarded bases within Renamo's strongest military zones. A special demobilization program was organized for the benefit of those under fifteen years of age, and the movement's leadership agreed that the child soldiers would be listed as "non-assembled troops." ICRC and Save the Children Fund-USA attempted to reunite many of the discharged youngsters with their families.

In May, ONUMOZ began to register non-assembled troops—those in military bases, headquarters, barracks, hospitals, centers for the disabled, and other installations, of which the government had declared 172 and Renamo 27. The task also involved the collection or deactivation of military equipment. Over the following months, more than thirty thousand personnel were registered at those sites, somewhat higher than the figure of twenty-five thousand anticipated. ONUMOZ encountered resistance only at the more strategic bases, particularly where quantities of heavy equipment, artillery, and tanks were located.

The RSS package, approved by donors in January 1994, did much to encourage the assembled and non-assembled troops alike to opt for demobilization rather than to enlist in the new army, even in defiance of their commanders.[5] During April, those already demobilized in 1993— "the sixteen thousand," as they were known—proved determined to win the same benefits. Their demonstrations elicited agreement from ONUMOZ to meet their demands. Another sustained campaign by disabled soldiers forced the government in June to agree to pension rights for Renamo's war wounded.

As the pressure for demobilization built up, each side used its suspicion that the other was keeping back its best troops and weapons as the excuse for not proceeding. Deadlines came and went. On May 6, the Security Council set a final demobilization deadline of July 15. A CCF meeting in mid-May produced an announcement by the government that it was ready to restart demobilization. A few days later, on May 25, the government again called a halt to demobilization and stopped providing lists to the CCF. On June 13, the CCF, with CSC support, issued a new schedule: for both sides, assembly would end by July 1; demobilization in Renamo areas would be complete by July 29, and in government areas by August 15.

Trouble in the Assembly Areas

Despite growing concern that demobilization might not be concluded in time for the elections to be held as scheduled at the end of October, ONUMOZ, the CSC, and Ajello maintained their pressure and kept the Security Council informed of progress. Meanwhile, the most effective pressure to step up demobilization was coming from the soldiers themselves. Mutinies and protests in assembly points were becoming an everyday occurrence. When both sides tried sending unwilling conscripts into the new army, the incidents and protests multiplied. "The soldiers want to be demobilized as soon as possible," Ajello said on June 17. "They contest the government's lists of who is to be demobilized and who goes into the new army. They don't want to join the new army."[6]

The first incidents had occurred as assembly began at the end of 1993. Government and Renamo soldiers had raided food stores, demanded payments, or held their military commanders hostage. At first such incidents were localized and often promptly resolved. It was not until April that the unrest became more generalized, when the government's repeated suspensions of demobilization prompted soldiers to stage a variety of protests, some of them violent. In May, a group of UN military observers was threatened at a government assembly point at Nhangao, near Beira, by soldiers demanding immediate demobilization. To avoid violence, five hundred troops were immediately processed and demobilized. When a similar incident occurred at Caia (Sofala), Botswanan troops had to be deployed to protect UN property and staff. The worst incidents in May were at Mocuba (Zambezia). On May 21, more than one hundred assembled soldiers rampaged through Mocuba town, injuring civilians, looting houses, and provoking a backlash from the citizens of the town. Other incidents involving government soldiers occurred at Milange (Zambezia), Catandica (Manica), Catembe (Maputo), and Mutarara (Tete).

In Renamo assembly areas, too, there was violence. At Mocubela (Zambezia) in May, soldiers complained that their demobilization pay was insufficient and accused finance ministry officials of stealing their money. They demanded to speak to Renamo's CCF representative, Brigadier Raul Dick, but when he arrived they stripped him and beat him severely. Other incidents occurred in Renamo assembly areas at Mohiua (Zambezia), Namagua (Manica), and Chipanzane (Inhambane), in the latter case causing a temporary withdrawal by the UN staff.

On June 22, the international members of the CSC issued a statement warning that, with the government sending troops into the assembly areas at a rate of only one hundred per day, it would be impossible for the remaining eleven thousand men to be processed through the assembly areas by the deadline of August 15. Accusations and counteraccusations were flying. The head of the government delegation to a CCF meeting of July 4 expressed resentment that the pressure being applied to the government was not being applied equally to Renamo and even accused ONUMOZ of giving "logistical support" to "underground Renamo forces."[7] However, the government did at this point accept a revised deadline of August 15 for the completion of demobilization as set by the CSC and subsequently endorsed by the Security Council in a statement issued on July 19.[8]

By July 5, the government's assembly total was 41,974 (84.6 percent of those now expected), of whom 23,007 had been demobilized and 2,584 had been sent to the new army. This still left a large number, estimated at 16,383, in the assembly areas. By the same date, Renamo's assembled soldiers numbered 17,402 (90.9 percent), of whom 5,099 had been demobilized and 2,268 had joined the new army, leaving 10,035 in the assembly areas. Concern about the implications of the slow pace of demobilization was expressed by the secretary-general, who, in reporting to the Security Council at the beginning of July, warned that if the process were not completed by the agreed dates, and if a large number of soldiers selected for the new army were left in the assembly areas, there would be "a danger that three armies will be in existence in Mozambique during the election period."[9]

The assembly operation, at least, was effectively coming to an end. Some soldiers were still unaccounted for, but Ajello felt able to declare on July 11 that assembly was "virtually complete." Throughout the last weeks of July, small numbers of troops continued to arrive and it was becoming clear that those that did not had opted to stay in the non-assembled areas, where the numbers turned out to be greater than expected (20,281 government troops registered by mid-July compared to the expected figure of 18,912, and 4,731 Renamo troops rather than 4,666).

The Pressure Builds

Assembling the troops without demobilizing them built up the pressure within the assembly areas to the point of explosion. In the first two weeks of July alone, incidents of varying degrees of seriousness occurred in five government areas and in twelve Renamo areas. Colonel Segala put the causes of these incidents into four categories: (1) soldiers were tired of waiting (they had already been waiting up to eight months in some cases); (2) "the overwhelming desire of the soldiers to be demobilized"; (3) their need for additional food and clothing; and (4) their uncertainty about the future. Segala said the incidents had shown that the government and Renamo camp commanders had no control over their troops. He recommended that the parties go to the assembly areas to inform the troops about their future, adding that "it is time that urgent consideration is given to the soldiers' concerns."[10] Ajello increasingly argued in favor of bringing the demobilization to an end as soon as possible.

By July, soldiers in the assembly areas were regularly protesting by blocking roads, holding civilians hostage, and physically resisting being drafted into the new army. Although the mutinies were working in favor of a completion of the peace process, at times the scale of the protests threatened stability by encouraging banditry and tended to engage other armed groups and militias that were not included in the demobilization plan. They also fueled the government's resentment of the United Nations. In July, the government chief of staff, Lieutenant General Antonio Hama Thai, directly accused ONUMOZ personnel of inciting government soldiers not to join the new army. Renamo meanwhile continued to express alarm about the government's Rapid Intervention Police (PIR), which Renamo portrayed as a well-armed military force rather than as a civilian body. (Monitoring of PIR training and equipment by the UN civilian police strongly indicated that Renamo's characterization of the PIR was false.)

Both sides were still holding back their best officers and units from demobilization, as well as out of the new army, but any plans either side may have had to retain these forces as a war contingency were collapsing. Over several days in July, about four hundred Renamo fighters demanding demobilization mutinied in Manica province, stopping traffic on the main north-south road and forcing three hundred people in more than seventy vehicles to drive fifty kilometers to Dombe, where they were held hostage. Colonel Segala intervened and, by ordering the distribution of food rations, succeeded in securing the freedom of the hostages, who had by then been held captive for more than four days.

On July 18, at a government assembly area at Namialo (Nampula), 1,165 troops reacted to the news that only forty-six of their number were to be demobilized. They smashed up their camp and demanded immediate demobilization, threatening to destroy the UN compound. One soldier and two policemen were reported killed when the troops invaded the local police station. They also blocked the roads to Nacala and Nampula. Calm was restored only when it was confirmed on July 21 that all the soldiers would be demobilized. Ugly scenes also occurred at the government assembly area outside Quelimane (Zambezia) when soldiers beat up their camp commander and threatened to kill the UN team if their demands for immediate demobilization were not met. When government police arrived, running battles developed between soldiers and police.

A last attempt by government officers to resist demobilization collapsed towards the end of July following a rebellion by soldiers of the Sixth Tank Brigade at Matola-Gare, an non-assembled location on the outskirts of Maputo. After the brigade commander refused to allow ONUMOZ observers access to the base to disable the brigade's tanks and other armaments, the soldiers mutinied. On July 27, they erected a roadblock on the Machava-Moamba road using armored personnel carriers. They demanded immediate demobilization, money, and food. The following day more soldiers from the base rioted and began looting in Machava, threatening the Argentinean field hospital nearby. The government at first blamed the military observers for encouraging the mutiny, but eventually, after protracted negotiations among the observers, officers, and soldiers, a demobilization date was agreed.

Solutions Are Found

In July, at the height of crises over demobilization and international pressure on the government, the CSC went into high gear, meeting at least once a week. This in turn helped to keep the issue of demobilization under close review by the Security Council, which on July 19 announced that it would consider sending a mission to Mozambique to discuss how best to ensure full and timely implementation of the GPA. The council expressed special concern at the continuing delays in demobilization, without specifically criticizing the government, and stressed that there was "no margin for further delay" in demobilization and the formation of the new army. It demanded that the parties "continue to cooperate with ONUMOZ and with each other" and urged Renamo to allow unimpeded access to areas under its control.[11]

The crisis in both armies was gradually bringing the government and Renamo round to finding a common solution. The CSC meeting of July 20 was a turning point. The head of the government delegation, Armando Guebuza, acknowledged that the situation was "serious and critical" but noted that the two sides now had "a shared objective because both are facing the same problem." His Renamo counterpart, Raul Domingos, echoed this by saying that "both parties were facing equally serious situations in their assembly areas." He pointed out that the GPA had recommended that the new army be a voluntary army and expressed the view that once soldiers had more information about the new army they would want to join.[12]

Ajello underlined the need for a "formal decision in the CSC which could be conveyed to the soldiers in the assembly areas and that could help to quell the current unrest." He asked the parties if they were prepared to make this decision public with a declaration that the soldiers would be given freedom of choice. After long discussion, Guebuza and Domingos agreed to let the soldiers decide for themselves on the basis of information provided directly to the troops by representatives of the CCF, CCFADM, FADM, and ONUMOZ. It was then agreed that four teams would be despatched (two to the central provinces and one each to the north and south) to visit all the assembly areas, to provide soldiers with information, and to ask them to make their choice. Each party was to make public statements to this effect.[13] Unsurprisingly, most soldiers chose demobilization and the reintegration package in preference to an uncertain life in the new army.

By the time of the visit of the Security Council mission, August 8–12, the worst of the political tensions had been resolved. Although violent incidents were continuing, demobilization was by now proceeding more quickly than before and moving toward conclusion. Colonel Segala later reported that 33,000 soldiers were demobilized during August, or more than 42 percent of the final total of 78,000 demobilized over ten months. On the day set for the end of demobilization, August 15, the CCF reported a total of 3,713 soldiers still remaining in the assembly areas, and 13,100 in non-assembly locations. Those in the assembly areas were either soldiers who had failed to report on the day of their demobilization or those who had changed their minds about joining the new army. Those in the non-assembly locations included a possible 5,000 recruits to the new army.

The New Armed Forces

The difficulty of finding willing recruits to serve in the new Armed Forces for the Defense of Mozambique (FADM) had not been contemplated during the peace negotiations in Rome, where plans were laid for an army of 24,000, an air force of 4,000, and a navy of 2,000, to give a total force of 30,000, which was to be drawn equally from each side. Only once the assembly of troops began did it become apparent that few would volunteer to serve. After spending months in the assembly areas, the soldiers became increasingly desperate to be demobilized and suspicious of the conditions they would find in the FADM. According to the first information gathered by the TU, more than 90 percent of FAM soldiers clearly did not want to join. Renamo soldiers were at first unwilling to express an opinion, perhaps out of loyalty to their own commanders or because, in the early stages of assembly, they did not want to miss the opportunity to earn a regular salary for the first time.

The basic foundations of the FADM had been laid in August 1993 when fifty officers from each side were sent to the British army training camp in Nyanga, Zimbabwe. Although 540 instructors went through the training, not all of them wanted to enlist. Those who did had to wait until the proposed infantry battalions began to be trained in April 1994. Portugal, for its part, began training naval gunners at Catembe naval base, south of Maputo, as well as special forces at the Nacala air base, Nampula province.

The government and Renamo presented their first lists of soldiers for the infantry battalions on March 29, 1994. In the following weeks, ONUMOZ provided aircraft and trucks to move two thousand trainees from twenty-seven assembly areas to the three infantry training centers for the first cycle of infantry training. Despite the various training programs, the FADM was at this stage leaderless and in no position to advertise the conditions of service. Belatedly, the chosen joint commanders of the new FADM, Lieutenant General Lagos Lidimo from the government and Lieutenant General Mateus Ngonhamo from Renamo, were sworn in on April 6. The first eighty officers for the high command were appointed in June. Three infantry battalions of the FADM completed their training under British and Mozambican instructors at training camps at Dondo, Boane, and Manhica by early June, but there was a delay in the arrival of uniforms and other military materiel ordered from Portugal. The new army still had no transport or communication equipment and no headquarters staff.

The reluctance of soldiers to volunteer meant that ONUMOZ had to consider how to establish a force of half the intended size, while keeping a further fifteen thousand troops in transit camps for training after the October elections. But developments in the assembly areas were making even this impossible, and eventually the parties agreed that the establishment of a thirty-thousand-strong force should not be a precondition for the holding of elections. Concern about the likely small size of the new army prompted a number of suggestions for consideration by the Commission for the Joint Armed Forces for the Defense of Mozambique (CCFADM), headed by Ajello's deputy, Behrooz Sadry. The risk that the

FADM might be too small to guarantee internal security after the elections was balanced by the advantage that a small army would be less of a financial burden on the national budget, a situation that would help Mozambique score points with the International Monetary Fund. Britain, Portugal, France, Zimbabwe, and Italy had not in any case provided enough resources to train more than fifteen thousand soldiers, and it was clear that accommodation facilities and equipment for the FADM were grossly inadequate. A further point of concern for the CCFADM was the evidence that the new army would be top-heavy with officers hand-picked by the two parties.

Sadry reported to the CSC on July 25 that the total number of personnel in the FADM was only forty-five hundred, including those in the second cycle of training that was then just beginning. He noted that the first three infantry battalions had been deployed to their bases at Chokwe, Cuamba, and Quelimane but estimated that about forty-three hundred trainees were still needed to meet the minimum acceptable requirement of six battalions, and that there would not be enough trainees for a third cycle of training. At the same meeting, Ajello pointed out that rates of desertion from the three existing battalions were high. The battalions had originally numbered 741 soldiers each; now there were only 489 soldiers in Chokwe, 449 in Cuamba, and 629 in Quelimane. He doubted that the existing training programs for an army of fifteen thousand would be completed before elections. Speaking for the government, John Kachamila contended that troops in non-assembled units could still opt to join the FADM and that it might be possible to reach the thirty thousand target. Renamo's delegate, Raul Domingos, was less optimistic, pointing out that a major obstacle to recruitment was the lack of accommodation for soldiers wanting to enlist. He admitted that the situation among non-assembled Renamo units was as tense as it was in the assembly areas and that people merely wanted to leave.[14]

Although the two rival armies had still not been completely disbanded, the formal transfer of authority from the FAM to the FADM went ahead in mid-August and the most senior officers of the FAM and Renamo were ceremonially demobilized in Maputo and Maringue (where Dhlakama declared that he would never wear his uniform again). By this time, the total registered for the FADM was 5,961. Taking the realistic view that even the new target of fifteen thousand troops was beyond reach, Ajello and the international members of the CSC suggested that further recruitment could take place later.

A fifth FADM infantry brigade, trained by Mozambican, British, and Zimbabwean officers at Manhica, Maputo province, was assembled in September. The intake at this time drew heavily from the government's non-assembled forces, of whom nearly 20 percent enlisted, including 633 naval and 1,368 air force personnel. The total strength of the FADM was now close to 11,000 (nearly 8,000 from the government forces and more than 3,000 from Renamo), of whom as many as 4,000 were officers. By November, according to Sadry, the total of FADM personnel was 11,579.

The FADM infantry brigades were trained to a basic level. According to the British representative on the CCFADM, Lieutenant Colonel John Wyatt, they were "integrated and unified" and "reasonably disciplined," but would have to receive further training before being deployed to operational tasks. He strongly emphasized that they were not trained to deal with civil unrest or to maintain crowd control. Nor were they equipped for major deployment or patrols of roads or corridors, since each battalion had only two vehicles. Their morale was dependent upon the regular provision of pay and food. The only camps in a reasonable condition were those at Manhica and Dondo; conditions in the battalion camps at Quelimane, Cuamba, and Chokwe and in the company camps at Chimoio and Lichinga were "very poor."

Wyatt recommended that the FADM high command concentrate on further training, equipment management and control, refurbishment of the infantry barracks, and clear identification of the army's role. "An army is normally required to counter any external threat to the country's borders," Wyatt commented. "In the case of Mozambique, there is no apparent external threat. Internally, the police should be responsible for law and order, only calling on the army when the situation deteriorates beyond its capability. It is therefore in this capacity that the FADM should focus its training—internal security in the event of a complete break-down of law and order."[15]

Incidents and Hidden Troops

Although the political crisis over demobilization had passed by early August, unrest continued in both sides' assembly areas and among non-assembled units. The rioting, blocking of roads, and taking of hostages spread during August to groups such as those already demobilized, disabled troops, militias, and fighters who may have been deliberately held back from assembly. For several days in early August, members of the Naparama militia blocked the main road north from Quelimane, dispersing only after receiving promises of help in returning to civilian life. Incidents in September included a roadblock by about five hundred already demobilized Renamo soldiers at Inhaminga (Sofala). Demanding food, they detained ten cars and one hundred people, and destroyed electoral equipment. At Buzi (Manica), about two hundred people claiming to be Renamo police blocked a road and demanded the same entitlements as demobilized soldiers. A large number of Renamo soldiers also appeared in Mutarara district (Tete), blocking roads, taking hostages, and demanding to be included in the demobilization process.

Renamo groups came out of hiding from bases in Maringue, Dombe, Namanjavira (in Zambezia), and Sinjal (in Tete). In late September, Dhlakama admitted to the presence of such groups and the Renamo foreign secretary, Vicente Ululu, said that Renamo had some fighters who were only "temporarily" demobilized.[16] Once all the forty-nine assembly areas had been dismantled in mid-September, ONUMOZ undertook demobilization without assembly, so as to discharge the considerable numbers of undeclared troops on both sides, particularly in Maringue, where the CCF registered significant numbers of Renamo fighters. The final total of non-assembled troops was registered as 30,758 (23,633 FAM and 7,125 Renamo). Demobilization thus ended conclusively with the return to their homes of nearly 92,000 former combatants and the recruitment of just over 12,000 into the FADM (see table 1). Imbalances in numbers being contributed to the new army by the two sides were compensated for by proportionality. Although the government was contributing twice as many of its soldiers as was Renamo, they numbered only 10 percent of those who had been serving in the FAM. Renamo was contributing 15 percent of its considerably smaller former military force to the FADM.

Although groups of informal forces and ex-soldiers continued to demand pensions and demobilization benefits, ONUMOZ increasingly classed such incidents as criminal rather than military activity and urged the police to take action. The government sent in the PIR to disperse rioters in the different provinces, although this aroused Renamo fears that the elite police might be used against the government's opponents during or after the elections.[17]

Table 1. Final Demobilization Totals.

	Government Troops	Renamo Troops	Total	Percentage of Total
Initial group (1993)				
Registered	13,727	—	13,727	100.00
Demobilized	13,727	—	13,727	100.00
Assembly Areas				
Registered	43,409	17,524	60,933	100.00
Demobilized	39,301	14,142	53,453	87.72
Joined FADM	3,922	3,010	6,932	11.38
Absent	186	361	547	0.90
Non-Assembled Areas				
Registered	23,633	7,125	30,758	100.00
Demobilized	18,260	6,386	24,646	80.13
Joined FADM	4,594	651	5,245	17.05
Absent	779	88	867	2.82
Total				
Registered	80,769	24,649	105,418	100.00
Demobilized	71,288	20,538	91,826	87.11
Joined FADM	8,516	3,661	12,177	11.55
Absent	965	449	1,414	1.34

Source: Ton Pardoel, "Demobilization Programme in Mozambique, Summary Report, October 4, 1995" (privately distributed). (Reprinted with permission of author.)

The Costs of Demobilization

The most easily identifiable elements of the demobilization exercise cost the international community about $85 million. This comprises costs of $52.5 million under the direct management of the TU and the $32 million cost of the RSS.[18] Almost 80 percent of the budget was financed from non-UN sources, including donors and the Mozambique government.[19] The TU effectively coordinated demobilization and reintegration support, managing the distribution of items issued to the ex-combatants with their subsidy payments, basic food rations, transportation vouchers, and tool and seeds kits—which consisted of a bucket, a machete, a hoe, vegetable seeds, an instruction manual, and a *capulana* (two meters of cloth). IOM, for its part, played an important role in providing transportation for the demobilized and hired a private fleet of five hundred vehicles for the purpose.[20]

The RSS was initially costed at about $20 million, although as the final number of demobilized ex-combatants grew by a further twenty thousand, it eventually rose to about $32 million. Administration was handled by UNDP, which coordinated funding, followed up claims and discrepancies, and monitored the payment of subsidies through the banking system. Bank procedures were found to be cumbersome and the communications system was poor. Many districts did not have bank branches, meaning that the demobilized would have to travel long distances to collect their subsidy payments. In some provinces (for example, Tete and Zambezia), the managers of the government-owned People's Development Bank were not even informed about the system until several months after it had been launched.

Donors and agencies continued to discuss the merits of a pacification-oriented as opposed to a development-oriented approach. By the end of the process, most observers agreed that the RSS had succeeded in buying time and providing a breathing space to help the ex-combatants while they identified or generated employment opportunities for themselves, but some agencies felt that the most critical problems confronting the demobilized had "merely been postponed."[21] It was also pointed out that neither the veterans' association (Amodeg) nor the handicapped veterans' association (Adimemo) had received any international support, although they were by definition the organizations most likely to have a long-term interest in the welfare and reintegration of the demobilized into civilian society.

Collecting Weapons

The collection of weapons clearly had a lower priority than other aspects of the peace process, and ONUMOZ units were given neither the responsibility nor the means to oversee comprehensive disarmament until demobilization was drawing to a close. Disarmament was, anyway, strongly resisted by both sides. Although most soldiers brought weapons with them into assembly areas and surrendered them, many soldiers may have hidden their best weapons, and there was plenty of evidence that both parties had established arms caches around the country, possibly for use in the event of a return to war. The CCF chairman, Colonel Segala, reported to the CSC in July 1994 that soldiers had admitted to hiding weapons outside the assembly areas. "The presence of weapons dispersed around the country is a matter of particular concern, and can seriously imperil public security now and especially after the elections once the United Nations has left Mozambique," Segala said.[22]

When troop assembly began in early 1994, both parties objected to the transportation of weapons collected from the assembled soldiers to regional arms deposits, despite the fact that they had agreed to this procedure in the GPA. But as security deteriorated in the assembly areas, the parties eventually agreed that all military equipment in excess of two hundred weapons from each assembly area could be transported by military observers, accompanied by the ONUMOZ contingents. The final plan for ONUMOZ-CCF verification of assembly areas, military installations, and weaponry was eventually drawn up only in July 1994, leaving very little time for comprehensive checking. Arms registered in the assembly and non-assembly areas amounted to 111,531 individual pieces, including 157 tanks and armored personnel carriers and 30 artillery weapons.

Both Renamo and the government obstructed the work of checking for arms caches. Renamo provided misleading or inaccurate information and the government's military leaders proved reluctant to authorize collection. Final verification began only on August 30 and was set to end on October 20. After the closure of the assembly areas, the CCF arranged to visit sites, including arms caches, listed by the two sides as having been in military use. Arms were either to be destroyed or to be taken under UN control for transfer to the new army. Renamo supplied sketchy information about the locations and the nature of its sites, thereby impeding progress by the military observer teams. Nevertheless, the CCF did manage to visit a number of undeclared sites belonging to both sides. In the first five weeks of verification, the CCF found 130 unreported arms caches. Some were large, including truckloads of arms.

Colonel Segala on September 19 reported that the military equipment registered during cantonment and verification was now "posing a military as well as a political problem" as the large quantities "presented a potential for internal and external instability."[23] At a formal meeting of the CCF on November 11, it was agreed that all arms collected by ONUMOZ and under CCF custody would be transferred to the new army. One hundred and eighty thousand weapons were turned over to the new army; twenty-four thousand were destroyed. Ajello later said that ONUMOZ had wanted to destroy a much larger number of weapons but this had not been allowed by the government.[24] A study undertaken by ONUMOZ had also concluded that it was "not economically viable" to arrange for the disposal of weapons locally.[25]

By the end of the process, the CCF had verified 744 locations (603 declared and 141 undeclared). It had examined 498 government sites and 246 Renamo sites, but had run out of time before it had verified all the declared or undeclared Renamo sites. The military equipment it had found in the verified sites amounted to 46,193 weapons, 2.7 million rounds of ammunition, 19,047 mines, and quantities of hand grenades and explosives. In his final report of December 5, Segala confirmed the commission's inability to complete verification of Renamo bases and arms dumps. Renamo had halted verification on September 22, permitting only a limited resumption after October 10. Of Renamo's declared locations of 287, the monitors had visited only 116, or 40 percent of the total. In Manica and Sofala, the CCF had visited only 30 percent of Renamo sites. By contrast, it had visited 99 percent of the government's declared locations around the country. At the conclusion of the peace process, the United Nations offered to provide a small unit to complete the job, but the government declined the offer.

Without doubt, the opportunity to accomplish a comprehensive disarmament in Mozambique was undermined by the extraordinary delays and disruptions that befell the entire demobilization process. However, the failure to achieve better results also stemmed from a reluctance to focus seriously on the problem as a whole. The timetable laid down in the GPA had required the parties to supply the United Nations with "complete inventories of their troop strength, arms, ammunition, mines and other explosives," starting six days before the cease-fire came into effect and continuing at two-week intervals thereafter, and allowing the United Nations to verify this information. The GPA also stipulated that one month after the cease-fire "all collective and individual weapons, including weapons on board aircraft and ships" should be stored in warehouses under UN control.[26] Although the operational plan of ONUMOZ, as spelled out in the secretary-general's report of December 3, 1992, gave the CCF responsibility for the collection and storage of weapons, including those of other armed groups and irregulars, insufficient priority was given to the wider issues of control and collection—other than the recognition in the secretary-general's report that there was an "abundance of arms" in the country and that armed bandits operated outside the control of either side in the conflict.[27] A study conducted by the UN Institute for Disarmament Research noted that the "non-specific nature of much of the GPA" gave both parties room to maneuver in interpreting the plans, and it added that "the UN, therefore, was not able to ensure that the parties adhered to their commitments."[28] The parties simply did not provide the CCF with any of the weapons lists stipulated by the GPA.

The leader of the TU, Ton Pardoel, later noted that the individuals on both sides who best knew the locations of arms caches simply slipped through the net. Many were demobilized without being questioned. Others were not put forward for demobilization until the final weeks of the process. Whatever information the TU itself acquired, it passed to the military observers but no action was taken. Pardoel said that the military observer team waited too long to take action and was then diverted by all the other work it had to do, especially in verifying demobilization in the non-assembled areas. "If ONUMOZ had pushed earlier, more could have been done," Pardoel believed.[29]

ONUMOZ clearly missed the opportunity to reduce the millions of weapons at large in Mozambican society. After ONUMOZ departed, the government agreed on a program for weapons disposal with the South African government while, independently, the Protestant Council of Churches of Mozambique launched a "guns into hoes" program, but the resources for such efforts fell far short of those available during the UN presence. Crime levels in Mozambique continued to be disturbing after ONUMOZ departed. The easy availability of AK-47–type weapons fueled a flourishing cross-border trade into South Africa and other countries, with an impact upon security and stability throughout the region. Although more arms caches were found during 1995 and 1996, suspicions circulated that police and military officials may themselves have been involved in gun-running activities.[30]

Conclusions

With considerable difficulty and uncertainty, the international community worked together to ensure that demobilization went ahead. The United Nations and the international members of the CSC acted forcefully— some would say arrogantly—to hold the parties to commitments they evidently found hard to sustain. Direct pressure on the leadership of the parties was complemented by the frustrations of the assembled soldiers, whose desire to rejoin civilian life was the most effective limitation on the parties' chances of returning to war. Demobilization finally put an end to the military options of both sides, and laid the basic foundations of a new joint army, although this was evidently a shaky institution.

In operational terms, demobilization was as thorough and effective as it could have been in the circumstances, thanks to an extraordinary effort at coordination by the international donor community. Much of the organization was managed under programs established independently of ONUMOZ bureaucracy. In particular, the TU played a central role in providing a logistical framework for operations. Its work was strongly supported by a wide range of agencies and was complemented by the military observers and the CCF. The TU was both flexible and highly mobile, using an efficient communications system provided by Swed-Relief and about 80 percent of the helicopter capacity of ONUMOZ. The principal shortcoming of the demobilization process was the delay in collecting and disposing of weapons, although this could be largely attributed to the reluctance of the parties and the lack of priority given to the issue in the GPA.

There were recurring political uncertainties. On the one side, Renamo continued to resist the unification of territory and made an uncomfortable transition from military to political methods. On the other side, Frelimo used its incumbency and control of the national administration to erect numerous obstacles whenever it felt that its sovereignty was threatened by ONUMOZ, the SRSG, or the international members of the CSC. Attempts by ONUMOZ to maintain the balance between the two parties were regularly interpreted by the government as evidence of pro-Renamo sympathies in the international community.

The overlap between demobilization and the preparations for elections sometimes aggravated the tense political atmosphere. Ultimately, the government sought to recover from the humiliations it suffered during demobilization by resisting the formula of a postelection unity government, which international members of the CSC were openly canvassing. The acceleration of the peace process in fact highlighted the unreadiness of the rival political establishments for a complete change, and their old habits of confrontation were not replaced by reconciliation. Nevertheless, the accomplishment of demobilization did at least clear the way for electoral rather than military combat.

7.

ELECTIONS

Preparations, Crisis, and Success

$\mathbf{A}$s the last act of the peace process, Mozambique's elections were carefully prepared. They also attracted greater international media attention than did any other element of the ONUMOZ mandate. Progress toward elections was, however, necessarily influenced by other developments, including the assembly and demobilization of troops, the demining program, the return of refugees, and the integration of Renamo-controlled areas into the public administration.

From the outset, important lessons were learned from Angola, where demobilization and the creation of a single army were not concluded before elections were held. In Mozambique, as a result, there was some interdependence among the steps taken on the various fronts of the process. Moreover, the international community was prepared to invest in the establishment of a transparent system that would minimize the risk of disputed results.

As with demobilization, ONUMOZ had to face the fact that the parties—Renamo in particular—were scarcely ready to proceed with elections until the second year of the peace process. The first year's delay did, however, give the international community the advantage of time to lay the groundwork for an ambitiously comprehensive electoral process. Again, as in the case of demobilization, ONUMOZ benefited from close coordination among donors outside its own direct management. The essential logistics of voter registration and the elections were provided by a UNDP project financed primarily by the European Union and individual European governments. The National Elections Commission (CNE), which interpreted and enforced the electoral rules, was an entirely Mozambican body and, although established belatedly, it achieved an impressive degree of impartiality under the conciliatory leadership of its chairman, Brazao Mazula. The influence of the CNE was crucial in overcoming many of the problems that arose, particularly during the elections themselves.

Concerted efforts by members of the international community to force the government into forming a postelection pact with Renamo were unsuccessful. This failure was a further reflection of the continuing distrust and lack of real reconciliation between the parties, but did not ultimately threaten a peace process that had begun to take firm root. Despite a last-minute crisis on the eve of the elections, ordinary Mozambicans provided ample proof that a more substantial reconciliation was taking place throughout society as a whole, and that they were determined to exercise their first opportunity to declare their political preferences. The freeing up of the political atmosphere in the country was also greatly helped by the democratic advances made elsewhere in the region, especially the elections in South Africa and Malawi in April and May 1994.

A Complex Operation

Funding and organization of the entire electoral process was in the hands of UNDP, which first offered to play this role at meetings in Maputo of the international community's Aid for Democracy Group at the time of the signing of the GPA in October 1992. In a comprehensive agreement signed with the Mozambique government in May 1993, UNDP was charged with helping to "organize and carry out free and fair elections in Mozambique . . . and thus ensure one of the basic conditions for political stability and the reconstruction and development of the country."[1] The project was designed to provide assistance for the CNE and the Technical Secretariat for Electoral Administration, once both these bodies were established. The European Union was also involved at an early stage and helped the Mozambique government in revising and finalizing the draft electoral law.

The UNDP strategy was, essentially, to provide solutions to all potential problems. It took into account Mozambique's transportation and communications problems and anticipated the need for absolute transparency in the registration of voters and the counting and verification of the results. Starting with a small team of four advisers, the UNDP project developed during 1994 to become the electoral arm of ONUMOZ, employing a total of 154 international and 88 local staff members in the five months leading up to the elections. Its teams worked in a decentralized manner and those assigned to the provinces had considerable scope for initiative. Communications and computer systems were installed at the provincial and national level. Eventually more than 300 vehicles, 6 airplanes, and 26 large-capacity helicopters (12 from the South African Air Force) were deployed.

The budget for the electoral process, initially estimated at $66.9 million in December 1992, was kept under close review. From February 1994 onward it was revised and updated on a monthly basis, a method that UNDP found effective in persuading donors to fill a potential shortfall that threatened to arise in the last weeks before the elections. Donors' commitments covered slightly more than the final cost of $62.3 million, of which equipment, materials, and transportation accounted for the lion's share. The European Union met more than 40 percent of the cost with a contribution of $26.2 million; the largest bilateral contributions came from Italy ($9.2 million), the United States ($9.2 million), Sweden ($3.4 million), and Norway ($3.1 million).

Agreeing on the Electoral Commission

After the prolonged disagreements in the first year of the peace process about the electoral law and the composition of the CNE, Chissano and Dhlakama reached acceptable compromises in November 1993. The law was approved without significant changes from the draft that had been originally circulated. The structure of the CNE was, however, the result of negotiation. The government wanted the CNE to be composed in such a way that Renamo and the other parties would not have an overall majority, while Renamo and the smaller parties hoped to outweigh the influence of the government, proposing eight members from the government, seven from Renamo, and six from the minor parties. Eventually the government view prevailed and it was agreed that the government would provide ten, Renamo seven, and the small parties three. The chairman would be unaffiliated with any party.

One of the most propitious developments of early 1994 was the agreement between the government and Renamo to select as CNE chairman Brazao Mazula, a university lecturer who had experience as a civil servant in the Ministry of Education, but no obvious political affiliation.

Chosen during the CNE's first working sessions at the beginning of February, Mazula was formally appointed on February 11, along with two vice chairmen, Leonardo Simbine, nominated by the government, and Jose de Castro, named by Renamo. Mazula came to be respected equally by all sides and was praised as a genuinely nonpartisan consensus-builder, establishing himself, in the words of the British ambassador, Richard Edis, as "a calm, dignified, impartial and effective father figure of the electoral exercise."[2] Mazula ensured that all decisions of the CNE were reached by consensus and succeeded in defusing the issues that defied agreement. For example, the government was in favor of granting voting rights to Mozambicans living abroad, while Renamo was afraid of the risk of manipulation of foreign votes. Given the lack of consensus, the CNE decided not to grant such rights.

Under Mazula, the CNE received strong support from the donor community, which in April set up an electoral monitoring group to meet every two weeks (replacing the previous monthly meetings of the Aid for Democracy Group). The emphasis among donors was on providing effective coordination and reaching practical solutions. When the CNE was unable to secure UN funding to train its registration brigades, an Austrian agency provided the funding. Delays in the award of contracts for equipment and materials for the registration of voters were similarly overcome by effective collaboration among the donors.

Political Party Trust Funds

For ordinary Mozambicans, Renamo was clearly the only opposition party widely known throughout the country, but the fourteen smaller parties were determined to cash in on the special advantages being accorded to Renamo. They asked for their own funding, and Ajello announced in March that the United Nations was undertaking the legal work necessary to create a supplementary fund for these parties. The parties saw the opportunity to earn $200,000 each. The CNE was reluctant to become involved in the disbursement of this money, and in June ONUMOZ agreed to a proposal from the small parties for some of the money to be made available immediately. In August they each received an advance of $50,000, but all further disbursements were contingent upon proper accounting of their expenditures, a condition that few parties could fulfill. But the scramble for funding did nothing to enhance the smaller parties' standing in the eyes of the electorate. As the *Mozambique Peace*

Process Bulletin commented, "Out of the 15 parties officially registered, some remain little more than a front man and handful of cronies."[3] One abortive attempt was made to forge a common anti-Frelimo front, with the holding of a national congress of opposition parties in Xai-Xai at the end of April 1994. Renamo attended the congress in the hope that the smaller parties might agree to recognize Dhlakama as the single presidential candidate of the entire opposition. This was not the outcome, and the smaller parties remained remarkably unwilling to sink their differences before the elections.

ONUMOZ and Ajello remained engaged in pushing for larger contributions to the Renamo trust fund, which by June 1994 amounted to $8.2 million, of which Italy had provided $6.3 million, the Netherlands $1 million, Sweden $366,000, South Africa $290,000, and Switzerland $210,000. Commitments had also been made by the European Union ($1.5 million), the United States ($1 million), the United Kingdom ($750,000), Denmark ($500,000), and Portugal ($300,000).[4] Renamo leaders clearly had little difficulty spending their fund, which eventually took in contributions totalling $17.6 million, including transfers from the underspent UNOHAC trust fund.

Opening up Territory

As agreed by successive Security Council resolutions, the deployment of UN civilian police (Civpol) commenced in January 1994, with a gradual buildup to more than one thousand in September, in time for the election campaign. For Ajello, the main functions of Civpol were to help the reunification of Mozambique, to monitor the national police, and to help the national police deploy into Renamo-controlled areas.[5] The breakthrough in convincing the government to accept the presence of police observers took time to achieve, although the possibility had been persistently raised by Ajello and had won support from the CSC ambassadors, as well as from Amnesty International.

Civpol was in part insurance for Renamo against the risk of the government's transferring troops into the police. Its deployment in Renamo areas also helped to open access to those that remained closed at the beginning of 1994, despite the earlier agreements to bring about a unified territorial administration. The National Commission for Territorial Administration (CNAT) had been appointed in November 1993, with four members from each side and without UN participation. Renamo's advisers to the provincial governors were appointed in March and in May began to provide CNAT with lists of Renamo-controlled areas and of their nominees for administration of those areas. However, by June the lists covered only four provinces, Manica, Sofala, Nampula, and Gaza. Both sides were showing a clear reluctance to speed up reunification, and the government seemed unwilling to formalize the appointments of administrators even where agreement had been reached. Some of the more isolated Renamo areas remained inaccessible until the end of the peace process. By mid-1994, the CNAT was making little progress and in July its work ground to a halt when Renamo stopped attending its meetings. Before then, it had recognized Renamo control in five districts and forty-two administrative posts in different parts of the country, but this was a very incomplete picture. In reality, Renamo areas were gradually becoming more accessible for the United Nations, for international NGOs, and, in a significant number of districts, even for government-employed health and education workers. The opening up of Renamo areas was further eased following demobilization during July and August, whereupon Renamo's ability to control access was much reduced.

From the beginning of June, the voter registration program, with Civpol support, did much to improve access. The first UN police station was opened on May 30 and by the end of June there were eight Civpol posts in Renamo areas and sixteen in government areas. The Civpol presence filled the gaps where disagreements persisted between the two sides over territorial administration and where government police still refused to enter Renamo zones. Civpol deployment was timely and helped give ONUMOZ a visible presence in the remotest and most inaccessible districts in the country throughout the final months of the process, facilitating voter registration and the conduct of the elections themselves.[6]

Civpol police were not, however, always supported by the other arms of ONUMOZ and were often mocked for their lack of training and preparation for life in Mozambique. Civpol's monitoring of the government police was felt by some to be inadequate, and the quality of individual Civpol observers was heavily criticized by the international community. Civpol was, indeed, an ill-assorted group of 1,059 police officers from twenty-nine countries who did not share policing traditions, culture, or language. Few spoke Portuguese and some were even unable to drive the vehicles they were allocated. They had to confront operational and logistic hurdles for which they were ill prepared, despite some attempts at briefing them.[7] The Mozambican police resented their interference and, sometimes, their behavior. Civpol's difficulties in performing its mandated tasks could be attributed partly to its late deployment and partly to the wide differences in policing traditions in the countries that contributed officers. The force proved powerless to transform either systemic weaknesses in the Mozambican police or the country's human rights record. Equally, it could do little to improve the feeble performance of the National Police Affairs Commission (COMPOL), which took no action on the complaints that Civpol regularly referred to it. COMPOL's activities were apparently of little concern to the parties or to ONUMOZ, diverted as they were by the other priorities in the last months of the peace process.

Voter Registration

The CNE's technical body, the Mozambican-staffed Technical Secretariat for Electoral Administration (STAE), was assembled in February. Between March and May, STAE, with UNDP support, recruited 8,000 people as registration agents and appointed and trained more than 4,000 as civic education agents and members of the provincial and electoral commissions. Despite this impressive achievement, the lack of vehicles, buildings, and furniture in the provinces and districts, combined with the inexperience of the Mozambican electoral staff, ensured continuing uncertainty about how much could be achieved. Behind the scenes, UNDP maintained a central management role, providing logistics for STAE, putting pressure on the CNE to speed up its decisions, and keeping the donors, the SRSG, and the small electoral division of ONUMOZ closely informed of progress. The initial success of the training phase helped to persuade donors to release more funds, and by June UNDP had assembled its full complement of advisers and support staff for the electoral process.

From the outset, UNDP intended that all electoral procedures, including voter registration, would be as reassuring as possible to the parties and the electorate. Despite resistance from the DPKO's electoral assistance unit in New York, agreement was reached in early 1994 that each voter would receive an electoral identity card incorporating a photograph, effectively providing adult Mozambicans with proof of identity for the first time in their lives. (The funds for producing these identity cards were secured from the European Union.) Registration of the electorate had been planned to begin only after the assembly of soldiers had been completed, but pressure for elections to be held no later than the end of October meant that registration had to begin before the assembly and demobilization processes were finished.

Coordination among the donors and the close cooperation of the CNE made it possible for registration to start on time by June 1. Civpol helped to provide access and protection for electoral registration teams on the ground. CNE-STAE deployed 1,600 five-person brigades, although in some areas it was impossible to find enough people with six or more years of schooling—a requirement for membership in the brigades. To help ferry the brigades to all parts of the country, UNDP used a fleet of twenty-six helicopters, assisted by Portuguese air traffic controllers. These helicopters played a crucial role, as the STAE started out with only twenty cars. As more vehicles were purchased or hired, land access became easier during July and August; even so, helicopters provided the only practicable means of reaching the more remote Renamo-controlled areas in Sofala and Zambezia provinces. In all the more remote and war-damaged areas, camping equipment and food had to be provided; WFP allocated food rations for the brigades for a three-month period, although maintaining supplies to the most remote areas was a constant logistical challenge.

Registration started well in the south of the country but proceeded more slowly in the central provinces. The brigades prepared an electoral register for each group of one thousand voters, compiled a registration form for each voter, and issued the plastic-covered registration cards that contained each voter's photograph. Special days for registration were set aside in each area. As the brigades traveled through the country, they were widely praised for their seriousness, dedication, and willingness to endure uncomfortable conditions. The rate of registration rose from 260,000 in the first week (June 1–7) to a maximum of almost 700,000 in the seventh week (July 11-17). By August 5, the total registered reached 5.2 million. The CNE had to lower its initial estimate of 8.5 million eligible voters to 7.9 million; after a final extension of registration to September 2, the total registered was 6,363,311. Although below target, this total was far in excess of some pessimistic expectations that the brigades would not be able to reach more than 4 million, and it amounted to a creditable 81 percent of the CNE's own estimates of the number eligible.

On the basis of registration figures available in early September, the CNE assigned parliamentary seats by province, and the parties went ahead to propose their parliamentary candidates, again on a provincial basis.

The CNE checked and accepted twelve candidates for the presidency and registered fourteen political parties or coalitions seeking seats in the national assembly.

Pressures for a Coalition

Proposals for the formation of a postelection government of national unity had been quietly considered and discussed since the beginning of the peace process, and were favored by some diplomats as a means of avoiding the kind of postelection chaos that had engulfed Angola after 1992. The government in Maputo persistently rejected the idea, principally because it was not part of the deal reached in Rome. Moreover, members of the Frelimo old guard were appalled at the prospect of conferring respectability on Renamo by accepting it as a partner in government. To them, Frelimo was bound to win a resounding victory in the elections and had no need of a postelection deal. Having failed to defeat Renamo in war, their hearts were set on humiliating it at the ballot box.

The coalition concept was given a new validity by South Africa's inclusive power-sharing arrangements among its principal political antagonists, arrangements that were confirmed by the April 1994 elections that brought Nelson Mandela to power at the head of a government of national unity. Debates aired by the Mozambican media in the early months of 1994 provided an opportunity for further discreet pressure by the Western diplomats in Maputo who now saw a government of national unity ("GNU" was the English-language acronym, "GUN" the Portuguese) not only as insurance against postelection chaos in Mozambique but also as a formula that might be used to strengthen fragile nation-states throughout Africa. The issue was being raised bilaterally by some Western governments just as the international community and the Maputo government were increasingly at loggerheads over the speed of demobilization between April and July 1994. With some ambassadors on the CSC increasingly determined to pursue an aggressive style of diplomacy, it was only a matter of time before the discreet pressure became public knowledge. Indeed, the U.S. ambassador, Dennis Jett, raised no objection to having his name associated with the idea. After Jett accompanied Dhlakama on the latter's June 1994 visit to the United States, the Renamo leader felt sufficiently confident of international support to make his own public appeal for a GNU, suggesting that participation should be based on the percentage of votes each party obtained in the elections. Not surprisingly, the smaller parties responded favorably. As the private and public campaign mounted, there was much allusion to the "GUN being held to Frelimo's head." Elements in the Frelimo government were quick to air their suspicions of pro-Renamo sympathies among key Western ambassadors.

The pressure for a GNU also fueled government resentment at the increasingly assertive role of the international community in the handling of the peace process between April and July. During May and early June, Chissano refused to receive Ajello or any of the CSC ambassadors. In July, tension again heightened as the ambassadors debated issuing a joint condemnation of the government's progress on demobilization, a move that was only prevented by a passionate intervention from Italy's Manfredo di Camerana. Jett, however, was determined to put his criticisms of the government into the public domain and chose the opportunity of the annual U.S. Independence Day speech to make a direct comparison between the performance of the government and that of Renamo on the assembly and demobilization processes, linking the comparison to the kinds of choices that voters would make in the elections. "If a party does not fulfill its obligations under the general peace accord and its commitments to the international community, how will it fulfill its promises to the people?" he asked. "Has stability been ensured by making the arrangements necessary to share power or is stability threatened by those who only seek to accumulate power?" Intended as little more than a warning shot across the bows of the government, the speech was immediately interpreted by Frelimo and other commentators as a direct appeal to Mozambicans to vote for Renamo.

The speech went beyond pressure for a GNU and inflamed government opinion further, with the result that others in the international community now saw the need to backpedal on the issue. When President Mandela visited Mozambique from July 20 through 22, signing an agreement with Chissano to set up a joint cooperation commission to deal with relations between their two states, the South African president made it clear that he had no intention of dictating a South African formula for Mozambique. He told a press conference that he would not like to advise a country how to settle its own problems, unless expressly invited to do so. Of his brief meeting with Dhlakama, he commented that he was happy with Dhlakama's "conciliatory tone." Likewise, when U.S. Assistant Secretary of State George Moose visited on August 7 for meetings with both Chissano and Dhlakama, he did not push the GNU formula as such. He told reporters afterward that he thought the problems facing the peace process could be solved if everyone were committed to carrying out the agreed timetable. He said that the United States was interested in a process that did not end with elections but led to "the creation of circumstances that will ensure peace, stability, and development." Once elections were over, "a sense of participation" should prevail.

For the Security Council, the overriding issue during July and August was to ensure that delays in demobilization did not jeopardize the electoral schedule. The Security Council mission that visited in August was principally interested in establishing that the demobilization crisis had passed and that elections could now be held. The mission received assurances from Chissano, Dhlakama, and the parties that they were still committed to elections in October and was able to comment that "inasmuch as there is the political will to transcend problems, it is the view of the mission that the elections will be held and the results respected." The mission found a divide between those in the international community recommending an agreement on a political accommodation before the elections and those who preferred an understanding between the parties that democratic rules would continue to be observed after the elections. Opting for the latter, less prescriptive, formula, the mission recommended "an understanding that will promote post-electoral stability and harmony and respect for the rules of democracy."[8]

Chissano and Dhlakama held several face-to-face meetings in August to discuss the GNU issue. Some younger elements in Frelimo now openly favored an accommodation but the old guard strongly resisted. Observers noted that Chissano was having difficulty in keeping his party together over the issue.[9] The compromise government strategy that emerged was a general expression of willingness to reach agreements with individuals in the opposition parties, to consider formalizing the status of the parliamentary opposition, and to recognize the role of the leader of the main opposition party. Another idea put forward by the government was a national reconciliation council, to include high-level Renamo representatives, but this was rejected by Renamo. As the prospects for a GNU faded, Dhlakama's demands took on an ominous tone. On August 26, Dhlakama publicly demanded a unity agreement within a month, to which Chissano promptly replied, "He can make the agreement with himself."

The secretary-general's report to the Security Council on August 26 observed that the parties "might wish to explore, prior to elections, the possibility of concluding an arrangement that would enable opposition parties to play a legitimate and meaningful role in the post-electoral period."[10] This was misreported in the government daily newspaper, *Noticias,* as specifically stating that the opposition should be included in the postelection government. Frelimo hard-liners claimed interference and took the report as evidence of UN acquiescence to pressure from Western governments. The Mozambique government used diplomatic channels to insist that the subsequent statement of the president of the Security Council should not dictate any formula for a postelectoral dispensation in Mozambique. In the event, the Security Council merely gave bland encouragement to the parties to continue "their efforts in good faith to ensure post-electoral harmony on the basis of the observance of the democratic principles accepted by them in the General Peace Agreement."[11]

The last pre-election direct meetings between Dhlakama and Chissano were held in mid-September, in the lead-up to the election campaign. During one ten-hour session, Dhlakama demanded special status for the opposition, the right to name governors in provinces in which Renamo won a majority, and the status of vice president for himself. The first demand was accepted, the others were rejected. As Frelimo's intransigence over the GNU question increased, Dhlakama lost interest in the idea of accepting government posts at the whim of Frelimo and was increasingly determined to find ways to turn the electoral process to his and Renamo's advantage. Chissano reiterated the government's rejection of Western government pressure for a GNU. Having been pushed into a corner, he made his stand clear in a public statement on October 5. That battle lost, the donor community concentrated on persuading the government to recognize and strengthen the role of the parliamentary opposition.

Countdown to Elections

Official campaigning for the elections began on September 22 under the shadow of demands by Dhlakama that the international community furnish another $5 million to finance his party's campaign. His new threats of an election boycott produced a prompt response from the countries and organizations that had promised to contribute to the Renamo trust fund, including the United States, Denmark, Italy, and the European Union. Renamo's leaders were now handling ever-larger amounts of cash as they tried to bring in last-minute supplies of election campaign materials.

Both Chissano and Dhlakama traveled extensively in the politically contested north of the country. The parties held colorful and noisy rallies at which *capulanas* and T-shirts were handed out. The uncharismatic Chissano was helped by the unstinting support of the state-owned media and the services of Frelimo's public relations advisers, Afrovox, run by a Brazilian, Christiano Stein. Dhlakama, lacking a sophisticated political campaigning machine, could rely only on his fiery rhetoric, constantly repeating the claim that he was the "father of democracy" in Mozambique and that the war had been fought for no other purpose than to bring about these elections. In places regarded as Frelimo strongholds, he occasionally drew huge crowds. Knowing that the central provinces of Manica and Sofala were almost certain to provide victories for Renamo, his campaign focused on the northern provinces of Nampula and Zambezia, as well as Inhambane in the south. Dhlakama spiced his speeches with warnings against the possibility of fraud. In Nampula on October 4 he declared that if there were fraud and Renamo lost, "we will not return to war but we will not recognize the result." On October 7 in Ribaue, Nampula province, he formulated his threat more directly by claiming, "I have already won. Only by electoral fraud can Frelimo and Chissano win the elections."[12]

Amid understandable concern that the elections could end the peace and herald new conflict, ONUMOZ and the CSC were faced with a number of potential risks. The CCF was still discovering unreported armed groups and weapons, particularly on the Renamo side. Although most of these finds could be attributed to Renamo's poor control and record-keeping, the government was suspicious about Renamo's intentions and was particularly incensed by its failure to hand over to the CCF its military communication system, which Renamo claimed was needed for its electoral campaign. Renamo agreed to provide lists of its radio equipment but refused to surrender any of it. For its part, Renamo's leadership was determined to maintain its confrontational attitude toward the Frelimo establishment and loudly expressed its concerns about the possibilities of electoral fraud.

The overlap between the end of demobilization and the beginning of the electoral campaign raised the specter of the 1992 Angolan election disaster. At a CSC meeting on October 4, the British ambassador, Richard Edis, expressed concern that so late in the day the parties were still discussing questions related to demobilization and the handover of military equipment. The fact that most Renamo arms depots had not been found and that the government was denying access to some police and military depots "might indicate a deliberate policy of both parties to retain arms," he said, adding that it was "highly dangerous if anyone suggested that a military option was open during or after the elections." Edis was supported by the Portuguese ambassador, Manuel Lopes da Costa, who said it was clear that the parties still lacked mutual confidence.[13] Ajello suggested that, as on previous occasions when difficulties had arisen between the parties, this could be an appropriate time for another meeting between Chissano and Dhlakama. However, the opportunity was not taken by the two leaders. As the elections approached, the political tension was palpable. There were continuing isolated incidents during the campaign, including beatings of journalists and government supporters in Renamo areas, and allegations were made about intimidation by the PIR, all of which Civpol tried not very successfully to monitor. A group of Mozambican police who tried to set up a police station in the Renamo-controlled town of Inhaminga were forced to flee after threats from armed gangs. Frelimo supporters sometimes tried to disrupt opposition rallies and on one occasion threw stones at Dhlakama's helicopter and motorcade.

In addition to Frelimo and Renamo, there were now twelve minor parties or coalitions in the campaign (see page xvii for a list that covers all of the peace process), though with little organization behind them. Most claimed to represent a particular ideological position or to have the support of a religious community. During August, four of the parties, Palmo, Panade, PRD, and Panamo, had agreed to form the Democratic Union (UD), although PRD later dropped out and the remaining members could not agree on a presidential candidate. Other parties discussed joining this coalition or forming another, but by the time of the elections the only two coalitions were the UD and the Patriotic Alliance (AP) of Monamo, PSD, and FAP. In addition to Chissano and Dhlakama, ten presidential candidates were registered, of whom the best known were Maximo Dias (representing Monamo and PSD), Carlos dos Reis (Unamo), Domingos Arouca (Fumo and PCD), and Wehia Ripua (Pademo).

Electoral Education and Logistics

Civic education to inform people of the purpose and procedures of the elections was generally effective, especially where it was targeted at illiterate sectors of the population with no previous experience of voting.

Radio and television programs illustrating the process were popular in towns and cities, as were free newspapers that used comic strips to show the different stages of voting. In the countryside, teams of civic education workers used popular theater, mobile units, and simulated voting to convince people that they could influence the outcome. One of the greatest fears amongst many Mozambicans, that "sorcerers" would know how people would vote, was tackled by simple demonstrations showing that each ballot paper would be mixed up with hundreds of others and could not therefore be recognized by anyone during the counting. The idea that people would benefit from participation was emphasized by two principal slogans, "The Future of Mozambique Lies in Your Vote" and "Let's All Vote for Mozambique." In the final weeks, the message became, "Let's Make the Election the Great National Celebration."

The elections were not only full of political uncertainties but also a huge logistical challenge. "On many occasions we were on the edge of an abyss, both politically and organizationally," a UNDP official in charge of the electoral assistance project said later. Throughout the country, 7,417 polling stations were established; 2,600 electoral staff, 1,600 civic education agents, and 52,000 polling station officers were trained and deployed. In addition, 32,000 Mozambican party monitors were recruited and trained between September and October, and a further 25,000 were belatedly registered by CNE, although these were never trained or properly accounted for.

Preparations were in place for more than three thousand international observers to be deployed to all parts of the country. The observers were recruited from a variety of sources principally by the United Nations, the European Union, and the OAU, and they included UN volunteers, UN staff, and a number of the unarmed military observers already in the country. To manage the deployment of these observers, the strength of the ONUMOZ electoral division was boosted during September and October by the use of the 280 staff members of the TU. Transportation and communications were supplied by Civpol, which was required to ensure that each observer team could visit every polling station in the team's designated district at least once during the elections.

In a special project sponsored by USAID, IOM was called in at the last minute to deploy the Mozambican party monitors. In the eight weeks between September 19 and November 13, IOM registered the monitors, issued them with special travel cards, paid them an advance of their subsidy, transported them to their respective polling stations in locally hired vehicles, returned them home, and made final payments. Although criticized by Frelimo sympathizers on account of its U.S. sponsorship, IOM clearly possessed unique logistic advantages, including nationwide deployment and familiarity with the terrain as a result of its previous work transporting returnees and demobilized soldiers. At the outset, however, IOM found that all the political parties were too involved in their own campaigning to nominate their monitors. With time running out, the organization proposed recruiting "all available human resources" for the task, whereupon there was no shortage of recruits attracted by the prospect of earning 150,000 meticais (the equivalent of $25) for two days' work.

As the deadline of October 17 for the final registration of monitors approached, IOM found itself being undermined on the one side by the parties, which continued to promise payments to monitors who had not been registered, and on the other side by the CNE (apparently with ONUMOZ backing), which without warning on October 15 extended the deadline for registration to October 22. Unable to handle numbers greater than the thirty-two thousand it was already registering, IOM said it had no choice but to resist these last-minute changes to the agreed-upon procedures, even though this meant facing down protests from monitors recruited late. Some IOM staff were briefly held hostage in incidents in Nampula and Zambezia provinces, but the organization was determined to resist an uncontrolled rush that it felt could seriously disrupt the elections. Its staff were in any case fully stretched in organizing the deployment of the registered monitors to the polling stations by means of a shuttle system that ensured that the vast majority of stations around the country were reached.

Election Crisis

As the election approached, tension mounted. On October 21, the Security Council appealed to all concerned that the election campaign and subsequent voting be conducted calmly and responsibly. It asked the parties to ensure that there would be no violence or threat of violence during the election days and their aftermath.[14] In the last week before the elections, the demobilized soldiers' association, Amodeg, threatened the CNE president with a boycott of the elections unless the presidential candidates signed guarantees of support for the demobilized. Their fear was that the support being received from the international community would dry up after the withdrawal of ONUMOZ. Mazula responded by telling Amodeg that the CNE had no mandate to put such declarations to the presidential candidates, whereupon the association dropped the threat and agreed to join a peace march organized by religious leaders in Maputo for October 25, two days before the elections.

At the request of the Mozambique government, a summit meeting of frontline states was held in Harare, Zimbabwe, on October 25. The nine presidents and heads of government present included Chissano and Presidents Robert Mugabe of Zimbabwe and Ketumile Masire of Botswana; Dhlakama was invited to attend. Chissano succeeded in persuading his peers to issue a veiled warning of possible intervention if the outcome of the elections should be disputed, but Dhlakama was only perfunctorily consulted. The summit resolved "to be ready to take appropriate and timely action if the situation so demands."[15] Dhlakama left Harare for Beira feeling insulted and cheated. In Beira, while he was out of touch with the international community, his advisers fed him with new reports of alleged government preparations to rig the elections, including a document supposed to have been drafted by Frelimo's Brazilian electoral advisers. The principal allegations concerned the number of voter registration cards. The CNE had a surplus of more than 1 million such cards, and it was now suggested that the Brazilians had printed more for distribution to unregistered voters. Having already demanded that the CNE's surplus cards be destroyed (a demand that had yielded no response), Dhlakama felt that he had sufficient justification to order a boycott.

Late on October 26, Dhlakama made his move, announcing from Beira Renamo's withdrawal from the elections on the grounds of the potential for irregular voting. Ajello and other senior diplomats were at a dinner party at the home of the German ambassador, Helmut Rau, when news of Dhlakama's announcement reached them by telephone. U.S. deputy mission chief Mike McKinley soon confirmed the news, and the party broke up in confusion. Ajello and Ambassador Edis drove off to talk to Raul Domingos, while other diplomats tried to make direct contact with Dhlakama. The South African ambassador, John Sunde, flew directly to Beira to speak to Dhlakama, and Sant'Egidio's Matteo Zuppi also attempted to start negotiations through Archbishop Jaime Goncalves in Beira.

Although the Renamo leaders in Maputo quickly secured the support of three opposition parties (UD, Unamo, and PCN) and with them addressed a joint letter to the CNE president, Mazula, threatening to with-draw from the elections if the irregularities were not resolved before polling began, they felt vulnerable and isolated by their leader's action, realizing that they were an easy target if the crisis were to develop into confrontation. Renamo's South African adviser, André Thomashausen, persuaded both Domingos and Vicente Ululu not to try to leave the city; Renamo, Thomashausen pointed out, lacked the logistical capability to get all its people out and Frelimo would be well able to prevent such an exodus. His arguments helped to persuade them that they had an inter-est in getting Dhlakama to come to Maputo and reengage in the process. As a precautionary move, to allow time for the boycott to be called off, Domingos was persuaded to ask Mazula to extend the voting to a third day. At 5 A.M. on Thursday October 27, the day polling was to begin, the CNE issued a statement confirming that the elections would continue. Throughout the country, the polling stations opened and people started to vote. Dhlakama's call did not seem to have been heard or heeded. Only at a small number of polling stations in Renamo-controlled areas of Manica and Sofala did the voting not proceed smoothly.

Around 8:30 A.M., in his office at the Rovuma Hotel, Ajello asked Thomashausen to use his radio telephone to speak to Dhlakama. Dhlakama was in no mood to give any assurances or even to speak to Ajello, but the fact that contact had been made gave Ajello the confi-dence to tell the CSC ambassadors gathering in his office that it was worth talking to Dhlakama and that he might yet be persuaded to come to Maputo. While they discussed the options, ONUMOZ issued a state-ment that it was working with the CNE to find a formula with which to address the boycott. Ajello spoke to the UN secretary-general and to Portugal's president, Mario Soares, asking them to put pressure on Dhlakama to call off the boycott. From New York, the secretary-general and the Security Council issued statements urging that the elections should go ahead as planned.[16]

As the day wore on, increasing pressure was put on Dhlakama. Both Zimbabwe's President Mugabe and Sant'Egidio's Zuppi managed to make contact with him. His party leaders in Maputo were also pleading with him to join them in the capital. Domingos and Ululu, in their own discussions with U.S. diplomats, had by now been told that there was no chance that Washington would support either the boycott or a postponement of the elections. They were, however, assured by Jett that he would do all in his power to insist that the rights of the postelection opposition be respected.

The pressure from all sides eventually worked and Dhlakama flew into Maputo at 5:30 P.M. The very fact of his arrival made it likely that he would abandon the boycott, although he was showing that he was determined not to do so until he had wrung some advantage out of the situation. He was driven straight to his residence, where he locked himself away with his lieutenants, furiously accusing them of succumbing to the soft life of the city. All visitors were refused entry, and some calls from world leaders were put on hold. Eventually, some time after 7:30 P.M., he agreed to receive the senior U.S. diplomats Jett and McKinley, who stayed for nearly an hour. They repeated that Washington could not support the boycott, but they assured him that any alleged irregularities would be examined and that the United States would insist on a democratic order after the elections. Although still angry, Dhlakama was slowly becoming calmer and now began to look for ways to climb down without losing face. Closeted with Domingos and Ululu, he still refused to receive visitors, including Ajello.

After midnight, by which time he was clearly becoming tired, Dhlakama eventually agreed to Thomashausen's proposal that the CSC ambassadors be asked to give a guarantee that they would examine all Renamo's complaints before declaring the elections free and fair. Once this was agreed, by which time it was already 1:30 A.M., Thomashausen reached Ajello and Edis, who decided to leave the wording of a draft CSC statement to a group of three: Thomashausen, representing Renamo; Eric Lubin, on behalf of Ajello; and the British embassy's first secretary, Nick Busvine, for the international community. Staff of the Portuguese embassy were asked to be ready to translate the statement from English. At about 6 A.M., Edis reviewed the draft and then set about persuading each of the other CSC ambassadors to agree to sign it in Dhlakama's presence.

In the early hours, Dhlakama spoke again with Mugabe, whereupon the Renamo leader's mood lightened. In the opinion of di Camerana and several other CSC ambassadors, it was Mugabe's intervention that counted most with Dhlakama, although some observers attributed his about-face to the Western ambassadors' message that "he had put himself in a very dangerous situation and that if the boycott continued, the consequences could be catastrophic."[17] Ajello later said that Mugabe, Mandela, Portugal's Soares, and the White House had all played their part in pushing Dhlakama back into the elections.[18]

By 9:30 A.M., the second election day, Friday, October 28, was already many hours old, but the crisis finally passed as Dhlakama agreed to the final wording of the statement, and all the CSC ambassadors signed it in his presence. The joint declaration noted with concern the list of alleged irregularities submitted to the CNE by Renamo and undertook to make every effort to ensure that these complaints were fully investigated "and, where possible, resolved prior to the completion of polling." The key sentence read: "The CSC members wish to remind all parties concerned that any evidence of significant electoral fraud will prevent the elections from being declared free and fair by them."[19] At the same time, both the CSC and the CNE assured the Renamo leader that surplus registration cards and other materials, which Renamo suspected could be used by Frelimo to boost its total number of votes, would be destroyed by the election authorities in the presence of government and Renamo observers. Ajello also authorized the establishment of a special team to examine the results alongside the CNE, STAE, and UNDP, and to examine all Renamo complaints as they arose.

The CNE promptly extended the voting to a third day. Renamo agreed to tell its party monitors to return to their polling stations, which they did during the morning. At 11:20 A.M., Dhlakama went on Radio Mozambique to announce Renamo's return to the elections, using the broadcast to urge people to vote for him. He cast his own vote at a polling station in the Polana primary school near his residence. At a press conference, he tried to put a brave face on his actions, saying: "There are elections in this country because I, Dhlakama, personally with the people and my brothers during 16 years struggled so that there could be this celebration. So the celebration is of the people. President Dhlakama saved the nation." Overcome by the extravagant absurdity of these words, the journalists could not restrain their laughter.[20]

An Impressive Turnout

More than 5.4 million people voted; in other words, at least two-thirds of all Mozambicans over eighteen years old cast a ballot. The atmosphere was calm and good humored. Long lines had formed on the first day, several hours before the polling stations opened. By 2:30 P.M. UN monitors had reported a large turnout and no major voting irregularities and had seen Renamo party monitors at a large number of stations. In many stations, more than 60 percent of the registered voters turned out on the first day, making the second day calmer and the third day almost unnecessary.[21] The extension of the voting caused inevitable logistical difficulties, and polling station staff and party monitors alike demanded additional pay. After last-minute negotiations, IOM was instructed to increase the subsidy for each monitor to 200,000 meticais ($33). IOM was also subsequently ordered to settle the demands of an estimated 25,000 individuals whom the CNE had unilaterally registered in addition to the 32,000 registered by IOM. Money for this purpose had to be diverted from the unused portions of the trust fund for the political parties. IOM's final report on its electoral support noted that holders of CNE forms and stamps were freely issuing credentials and that there was no record of how many monitors the CNE did eventually register.

Politically, the extension was unexpectedly useful in establishing the transparency and effectiveness of the elections, allowing the closest possible monitoring by national and international observers. The checking procedures in the polling stations proved simple and manageable and prevented any voting by ineligible people. The counting and immediate publication of results at each polling station, in front of the polling staff, also contributed greatly to the credibility of the elections. The principal technical snag derived from the late decision to allow polling station staff, police, and monitors to be included as voters at their stations, with the result that the number of actual voters often exceeded the number registered at each station. This caused the computer software at the provincial and central offices of the technical secretariat to reject many results, and meant that much of the process had to be conducted manually rather than electronically. Further delay was caused by the new safeguards insisted upon by the CNE, in particular the requirement that the ballots from each station be taken under escort to the provincial offices for counting within seven days, followed by their dispatch to CNE-STAE headquarters in Maputo for the national count within a further seven days.

Ajello put out a preliminary statement on November 2 saying that the elections were peaceful, well organized, and free of major irregularities, and that UN observation did not support any claim of fraud or intimidation or any pattern of incidents that could affect the credibility of the elections. He noted that more than 90 percent of the registered electorate voted in some provinces. Counting was under way and ONUMOZ would "maintain its vigilance."[22] A statement by the observers from the European Union issued on the same day expressed satisfaction that the elections had been conducted in "a calm, peaceful, and effective manner" and that irregularities had proved to be minor and "of no significant effect." Most diplomatic and media commentaries were full of praise for the orderly conduct of the elections and the strong participation of Mozambicans, a theme taken up by press reports in neighboring South Africa, where a much less well-organized election had taken place six months earlier. Observers commented on the calm and patience of Mozambicans throughout the country as the two-week period of counting stretched into a third week. The security situation was stable and improved significantly in those parts of the country that had only recently been affected by disturbances during the periods of demobilization and the election campaign. Mazula was widely commended for his persuasive insistence that the parties should rise above politics for the sake of the nation.

The CNE's decision not to use faxed messages from the provincial centers, but instead to collect all individual polling station returns by land and by air for counting centrally, meant that even educated guessing was hazardous. The first real indications of the results came in a piecemeal fashion after Frelimo released partial figures on November 7 showing that, although the government party was heading for defeat in the five central provinces of Sofala, Manica, Tete, Nampula, and Zambezia, it had scored substantial success in the southern provinces of Maputo, Gaza, and Inhambane, as well as in the far northern provinces of Cabo Delgado and Niassa. These results, based on nearly 77 percent of the ballots, suggested that although Chissano led Dhlakama by 54 to 32 percent, the positions were far closer in the parliamentary vote, where Frelimo had scored 45 percent to Renamo's 40 percent. These figures were to prove close to the final tally.

The prospect of Renamo majorities in five out of Mozambique's eleven provinces was important in helping Dhlakama reconcile himself to an overall defeat. There was also consolation in the fact that he would be nationally and internationally recognized as the leader of the opposition, and that there would be opportunities to return to the electoral fray, because local government elections were planned for 1996 and national elections for 1999. Uncertainty about how Dhlakama would react to the results was dispelled by a message he sent to the UN secretary-general on November 14, in which Dhlakama stated that he would accept the results and was "prepared to cooperate with the government."

The CNE's prolonged delay in cross-checking the results nevertheless created endless speculation and rumors in the capital. The physical collection of all polling station results by the central STAE took at least a week, and even more time was taken up by the reappraisal of invalid or contested votes, a procedure for which no criteria had been laid down beforehand and which was conducted twice to satisfy the parties. Public concern about the delay reached a high pitch by November 18, when the final results were realistically expected but did not appear. A day later, the results were announced by Mazula in the presence of all the party leaders, as well as the diplomatic corps and other representatives of the international community. Mazula said that the CNE had taken action to correct inadequacies and avert potential irregularities but that there was no reason to annul any of the results.

Frelimo's Victory

In the presidential race, Chissano won 53.3 percent of the votes to Dhlakama's 33.7 percent. In parliament, Frelimo won 44.3 percent to 37.8 percent for Renamo. Translated into seats, the parliamentary vote gave Frelimo a small majority of 129 seats against 112 for Renamo and 9 for the UD. The unexpected number of votes for the UD, 5.1 percent of the total, was attributed to the fact that it was listed at the bottom of the ballot paper, in the same position as Chissano on the presidential ballot paper, where illiterate Frelimo voters were told to place their cross. No other political parties received more than 2 percent of the votes and in the presidential vote only three of the candidates received more than 2 percent—Wehia Ripua, 2.9 percent; Carlos dos Reis, 2.4 percent; and Maximo Dias, 2.3 percent. (Table 2 provides complete results.)

The CNE declared that 5.4 million votes were cast, of which 4.9 million of the votes for presidential candidates were valid, and 4.8 million of the votes for parties were valid. Of registered voters, 12.6 percent did not participate at all. The distribution of seats among the provinces (see table 3) followed the adopted system of proportional representation, which required a party to achieve a minimum national threshold of 5 percent of the valid votes to qualify for seats in parliament.

The results by province gave Renamo the greatest comfort, even if the message of the voting in these provinces was often interpreted as one of disillusionment with Frelimo rather than one of confidence in Renamo. Frelimo's undisputed hold was maintained only in the far north and the far south. The north-central regions were shown to be loyal to Renamo. Nearly sweeping the board in its home province of Sofala, Renamo also maintained a strong lead over Frelimo in Mozambique's two most populous provinces, Nampula and Zambezia, and was clearly the dominant party in both Manica and Tete.

Table 2. Results of Presidential and Party Elections.

Presidential Candidates	Number of Votes	Percentage of Votes
Joaquim Chissano	2.63 million	53.30
Afonso Dhlakama	1.67 million	33.73
Wehia Ripua	141,905	2.87
Carlos dos Reis	120,708	2.44
Maximo Dias	115,442	2.34
Vasco Alfazema	58,848	1.19
Jacob Sibindy	51,070	1.03
Domingos Arouca	37,767	0.76
Carlos Jeque	34,588	0.70
Casimiro Nhamitambo	32,036	0.65
Mario Machele	24,238	0.49
Padimbe Andrea	24,208	0.49
Parties		
Frelimo	2.12 million	44.33
Renamo	1.80 million	37.78
UD	245,793	5.15
AP	93,031	1.95
SOL	79,622	1.67
Fumo/PCD	66,527	1.39
PCN	60,635	1.27
Pimo	58,590	1.23
Pacode	52,446	1.10
PPPM	50,793	1.06
PRD	48,030	1.01
Pademo	36,689	0.77
Unamo	34,809	0.73
PT	26,961	0.56

Source: United Nations Development Programme, "Assistance to the Electoral Process in Mozambique, Final Report," MOZ/93/016, April 1995.

The announcement of the results was accompanied by a statement from Ajello officially declaring the elections free and fair, and affirming that the outcome reflected the will of the Mozambican voters. He admitted that problems had occurred, that irregularities were recorded, and disruptions had taken place, but he emphasized that "throughout the entire process there has been no event or series of events which could affect the credibility of the elections." Ajello praised the "high degree of professionalism displayed by the electoral authorities," the "strong commitment

Table 3. Distribution of Seats in the National Assembly.

Province	Total Number of Seats	Frelimo	Renamo	UD
Maputo City	18	17	1	0
Maputo Province	13	12	1	0
Gaza	16	15	0	1
Inhambane	18	13	3	2
Sofala	21	3	18	0
Manica	13	4	9	0
Tete	15	5	9	1
Zambezia	49	18	29	2
Nampula	54	20	32	2
Niassa	11	7	4	0
Cabo Delgado	22	15	6	1
Total	250	129	112	9

Source: United Nations Development Programme, "Assistance to the Electoral Process in Mozambique, Final Report," MOZ/93/016, April 1995.

of the political players to let the principles of democracy prevail," and the "will of the Mozambican people to live in peace and harmony."[23]

The international members of the CSC put out a terse statement that was an uncomfortable compromise between the doves who felt that Frelimo had won a fair fight and the hawks who were still pushing for Renamo to be given stronger guarantees. It accepted that any irregularities in the elections were insufficient to alter the outcome, but it also set out a series of demands to the government that strongly implied that the main donors' future relationship with Mozambique would have a political component. In particular, they stressed that they wanted to see independence for the legislature and the judiciary to ensure that the power of the executive branch of government would not be abused, as well as a truly free press. Distancing himself from these demands, the OAU representative, Ahcene Fzeri, was far more conciliatory, thanking the Mozambican people for "the victory they have just given to the African continent and all peace-loving nations" and congratulating Chissano on his victory.

With the international CSC members setting a sour tone, the official reactions from Chissano and Dhlakama were similarly grim. Speaking as the undisputed victor of Mozambique's first free elections, Chissano reserved his congratulations for the Mozambican people, the CNE, and Mazula, while merely acknowledging the roles of ONUMOZ, UNDP, the European Union, the OAU, and Ajello. He stressed that he was not considering power sharing with Renamo ("government and opposition have their own places which should not be confused") and said that celebrations were inappropriate ("rather than speeches, it is time to get down to work"). In an equally barbed statement, Dhlakama repeated his accusations that there had been discrimination against Renamo and that the elections were "not fair," although he stressed that the party accepted the results "as a basis for it to exercise its democratic rights of opposition."

The announced results were proof that elections could be held in Mozambique and that it was possible to collect, count, and double-check results that would be accepted by all concerned. There was no reason to doubt the general accuracy of the announced results, but some of those involved felt that the discrepancies deserved further examination, not least a gap of more than 200,000 between the number of registered voters given at the end of the registration process (6,363,311) and the number given as registered in the final table of results published by the CNE in November (6,148,842). Inconsistencies of this kind would clearly have to be examined with a view to avoiding any breakdown in confidence in future elections.

Aftermath

In accordance with the wishes of the Security Council, the task of ONUMOZ was now to withdraw as rapidly as possible. The last meetings of the peace process commissions were held on December 5 and 6. Final reports of the peace commissions were compiled for the last meeting of the CSC on December 6 and were handed over to Chissano on December 7. The ONUMOZ mandate came to an end with the swearing in of Chissano as president on December 9. Before his departure on December 13, Ajello said that it had been difficult to build trust between the parties at the leadership level, although confidence had been built at the community level. To the local press he said that, if he had the chance to do the job again, he would do the same, but with a different approach to demobilization. He admitted that the unfinished tasks were the verification of the arms caches and the clearance of landmines.[24]

The phased but rapid withdrawal of ONUMOZ saw the departure of nearly all its military, police, and civilian personnel by the end of January

1995. Responsibility for security now reverted to the Mozambican police, backed by the underfunded and understrength FADM, several units of which were still not operational. Although weakened by the familiar problems of inadequate resources and inefficient delivery of services, the government was eager to reestablish its authority. The departure of ONUMOZ punctured the all-too-temporary economic boom that it had brought in its train. The problems left in the wake of ONUMOZ caused one commentator to observe that "ONUMOZ did not seem to have an exit strategy other than 'vote and forget.'"[25] The German ambassador, Helmut Rau, similarly regretted the lack of an "after-sales service."[26] Several thousand Mozambicans had directly or indirectly come to depend on the UN operation for a living, and they now swelled the ranks of the unemployed or underemployed.

In delivering humanitarian aid and organizing projects for future development, the international community was set to remain dominant. Few of the ongoing emergency and rehabilitation activities were incorporated into national plans, leaving donors the choice of whether or not to support them. UNOHAC's sudden departure meant that a number of vital programs, including demining, experienced a management hiatus while DHA in New York negotiated arrangements for them to continue. Antonio Donini commented that "UNOHAC's lifespan was so short that its more durable activities were exceedingly vulnerable to its abrupt termination." "It might have been wiser," he added, "to maintain a UNOHAC presence post-ONUMOZ, or at least to ensure that whichever UN body would take over its residual functions had a proper strategy and capacity."[27]

One of the last events of the ONUMOZ mandate was the seating of the new parliament on December 8, but it was no sooner seated than disrupted by an argument over the rules of election for the assembly chairman. Frelimo nominated Eduardo Mulembwe and Renamo nominated Raul Domingos. Frelimo called for an open vote, according to accepted parliamentary procedure; Renamo wanted the vote to be held in secret. Chissano, sitting in the chair, ruled that the vote be by a show of hands, prompting Renamo to walk out. The resulting boycott of the new parliament lasted for three weeks. Eventually, Dhlakama agreed to climb down, seeing that Renamo's absence from parliament would give Frelimo the opportunity to do what it wanted, unchallenged.

Chissano appointed a government drawn entirely from the ranks of Frelimo and consisting of people who had held high rank for some time, although a few hard-liners were replaced by pragmatists and the Ministry of Defense passed from military to civilian leadership under Aguiar Mazula. Deputy ministers became ministers and the average age of ministers dropped only slightly. The appointments showed that Frelimo was in no hurry to change its style and methods. All the provincial governorships, too, went to Frelimo members, despite Chissano's earlier indications that he would consider naming governors from other parties.

Renamo continued to refuse to give up its control of several areas of territory, particularly in Sofala province. It boycotted schools, health centers, and shops that it believed to be funded by Chissano's government and on occasions also blocked free movement. In June 1995, a number of chiefs who supported Renamo chiefs prevented the opening of a government police station at Dombe, Manica province. There were also continuing allegations of heavy-handed government policing and intimidation of Renamo supporters by the PIR.[28] The government's relationship with the outside world was now to be at least partly determined by its democratic practice, although different countries soon proved to have different expectations. Not all went along with the continuing pressure from the U.S. embassy for the government to enter a power-sharing arrangement with Renamo. The principal emphasis of the international community as a whole was on the need for ongoing economic reforms, transparent budgetary procedures, controls on corruption, and reduced military expenditure.

Conclusions

The determination to make the elections a success resulted in an elaborate and expensive program that had to take into account the lack of mutual trust between the parties and the logistic difficulties of operating in a country with damaged infrastructure and strewn with landmines, as well as the vital need for transparency and confidence in the technical aspects of the elections. It was considered essential that the results should not be open to serious challenge, hence the complex arrangements for extensive national and international monitoring. UNDP later noted that its strategy of providing the machinery to solve all possible problems produced "an excessively heavy electoral apparatus, with complex and time-consuming decision making processes, . . . increased costs and subsequent dependence on the donor community."[29]

Although Dhlakama drew international attention to himself at the moment of the elections, after they were over and ONUMOZ began to depart he had little choice but to accept the loss of power and influence that he had enjoyed during the peace process. His role, and that of Renamo, was now to criticize, if possible constructively, but only from the sidelines. One of the new risks to stability was that the spirit of dialogue and reconciliation was insufficiently well rooted; even so, over the course of the following year Renamo's performance in parliament remained generally constructive. Dhlakama himself was vulnerable and unpredictable but his commitment not to restart the war proved genuine. An unknown factor was the extent of the pacification of Mozambican society as a whole.

8.

ONUMOZ

Achievements, Weaknesses, and Legacy

Peace was consolidated in Mozambique by the Mozambicans themselves and by a collaborative and active commitment from a wide range of foreign interests, with the United Nations playing an unusually flexible political role. Although ONUMOZ was a cumbersome construct, slow to be brought into being and often ineffective in delivery, the dynamic leadership of the SRSG and the support he mustered in the supervisory commission created a generally productive interplay between the international community and the conflicting parties. The government and Renamo were never entirely reconciled, but the transparent electoral outcome to the peace process laid a strong foundation for a new democratic order in this key Southern African country, in sharp contrast to the problems that still beset its sister-state, Angola.

In retrospect, much of the machinery of ONUMOZ could be deemed to have been superfluous, but this overloading was inherited from the original mandate in 1992, which established it as a multifunctional peacekeeping operation almost on the scale of the simultaneous UN operation in Cambodia. Where a lightweight and flexible operation would have been more appropriate, the international determination to avoid the kind of failure experienced in Angola burdened ONUMOZ with substantial managerial and technical responsibilities. As a side effect, the activities and operations of both the United Nations and the international community as a whole tended to be invasive and destabilizing to, rather than creative and supportive of, the shaky structures of the Mozambican state and society.

The success of the peace operation can be attributed to several factors, chief among them the commitment to peace of all Mozambicans; the importance placed on the political functions of the leading peace commission; the skill, patience, and flexibility of the SRSG; strong financial and logistic support from the international community; and the political support of neighboring states. The weaknesses of ONUMOZ derived in part from unrealistic procedures laid down by the GPA, and in part from an overambitious mandate that, in turn, generated lapses in focus and coordination. Opportunities were missed to contribute to the country's long-term recovery and to take practical measures to achieve important objectives (such as disarmament, demining, and human rights monitoring).

The Credit for Success

In achieving the political targets of the Mozambican peace agreement, ONUMOZ was a remarkable success. As a logistic operation, it had weaknesses, which were compensated for by a consortium of donor countries. The consistent view among international representatives in Maputo has been that peace was achieved through a collaborative effort rather than through the workings of ONUMOZ alone, and that in several respects the operation was badly flawed. "Success was achieved despite ONUMOZ and not because of ONUMOZ," was the categorical conclusion of a senior UN agency official in Maputo. "Nothing bad happened, but it is politically wrong to give ONUMOZ the credit for it," concurred a representative of the "like-minded" group of donors. "Donors worked hard to ensure that things worked. There was good coordination in the donor community, high-quality participation, and a conviction that the peace process could and would work," said the UNDP resident representative, Erick de Mul.[1]

Donor nations and independent UN agencies proved more able than the ONUMOZ management hierarchy to provide the quick responses that kept the peace process moving forward. They also were keenly committed to achieving the aims of the GPA and supportive of Ajello, who came to depend more heavily upon the most active multilateral and bilateral agencies than upon the UN Secretariat. The SRSG's success was in the political arena, in his handling of Dhlakama, and in his understanding of, and ability to sustain some level of dialogue with, the government. He was less skilled at making the UN bureaucracy work, although he was helped toward the end of the process by the appointment, as deputy SRSG, of Behrooz Sadry, who was well acquainted with the UN Secretariat and who had acquired valuable experience in the comparable operation in Cambodia.

Ajello himself attributed the successes of ONUMOZ to three main factors: a strong will for peace by the people and the parties; consistent support from the international community; and a flexible approach in implementation of the mandate. His assessment of the GPA was that it provided an effective political management structure but that it had weaknesses: no police monitoring component; no provision for the impartiality of the media; and no power-sharing arrangement for the post-election period. He emphasized the need for flexibility in the implementation schedule in view of the unrealistic calendar of the GPA, the two parties' reluctance to implement the GPA, and the fact that the ONUMOZ mission was not ready in time for implementation. Pragmatism was not applied indiscriminately. "When it was necessary we gave them time. When the parties were dragging their feet we pushed them."[2]

Donors rallied around the peace process and, by working together, brought about the two miracles of the process, demobilization and elections. The "like-minded" donors laid the groundwork for the Technical Unit for Demobilization and then pressed for the Reintegration Support Scheme. USAID provided valuable inputs at different stages of demobilization, funding much of the work of IOM, which provided essential transport and logistics. The European Union and individual European nations led the financial and management support for the elections. WFP supplied the food that kept both the demobilization and election processes going. UNDP, although temporarily displaced by ONUMOZ as the leading UN agency in Mozambique, was a primary instrument in the success of both demobilization and the elections.

Coordination was made possible largely by the presence on the Supervision and Control Commission (CSC) of the ambassadors of the principal donor countries, but also by the long-established relationships among a large number of bilateral and multilateral agencies. The various donor groups had different historical motives for their involvement, but they were prepared to pull together in the interests of consolidating peace. The UN system had long been involved in providing humanitarian relief; the European Union had played an important role in supporting the Southern African Development Community of which Mozambique was a founding member; and the international financial institutions had, since 1985, encouraged reform in the Mozambican state and economy. Donor involvement also had political and diplomatic origins. The "like-minded" donors had stood by the Mozambican government when it was threatened by South African destabilization. Italy hoped to reap benefits from its long-standing aid program in Mozambique and worked hard to build on its connections with both the government and Renamo that eventually helped produce the GPA. Portugal was looking for ways to recover its influence so disastrously lost in Mozambique's rapid decolonization in 1974 and 1975. The United States had in the 1980s involved Mozambique in its policy of "constructive engagement" with South Africa. Once South Africa's own reform process was under way after 1990, the United States remained committed to promoting dialogue in the region. The United Kingdom had helped train the Mozambique armed forces in the interests of preserving stability, particularly in neighboring Zimbabwe, and also saw the opportunity to recruit Mozambique as a member of the Commonwealth. The political support for the process from Southern African governments 'was crucial. These positive political dynamics at the national, regional, and international levels gave the donor community the necessary confidence to make its vital contributions.

Political Outcomes

The principal political achievement was the conversion of Renamo from an almost entirely military force and an instrument of destruction into a credible political organization. Such a conversion was, indeed, the primary goal of the GPA, and it was achieved through patient engagement with the Renamo leadership, both by Ajello and by the international community as a whole. The defusing of the military threat had to be accompanied by inducements, including the controversial Renamo trust fund, which became an effective insurance policy against failure. But the international community's efforts to keep Renamo in play, and its efforts on occasion to treat the government and Renamo as equivalents, provoked considerable resentment on the part of the government and the Frelimo leadership, especially in the second year of the process. This sentiment was fueled by the apparent ease with which Renamo managed to compensate for the loss of its support from South Africa with funding from a wide range of Western governments.

By the second year, the United Nations came to be perceived as a parallel administration. At times it almost had the features of a colonial operation, fulfilling a foreign agenda rather than a domestic one, although the rapid scaling-down of ONUMOZ after the elections showed that the United Nations had no long-term political intentions. It did use interventionist diplomacy but only to ensure the completion of the steps laid down by the GPA. Between December 1993 and December 1994, ONUMOZ and the international community effectively displaced the normal functions of government. The short-term priorities of that period diverted attention from Mozambique's longer-term requirements for social and economic reconstruction and ironically—and perhaps inadvertently—derailed the government's own efforts to reform and restructure the state and economy. The undermining of the already weak authority of the state spurred corruption and further weakened the capacities of state agencies.

The proposal to establish a government of national unity at the end of the peace process was favored by many in the international community as a way to restore the state's authority, but all attempts to pressure Frelimo to accept the idea backfired. Frelimo was quick to interpret any form of pressure as an attempt to lever Renamo into power. Although Ajello tried to avoid becoming too closely associated with the concept and the UN Security Council resisted recommending the establishment of a unity government, the Frelimo old guard blamed the United Nations for attempting to infringe Mozambique's sovereignty beyond the life of ONUMOZ. "Once there was pressure from outside, there was a tendency to resist," said Zimbabwe's ambassador in Maputo, John Mayowe. "The government detested being patronized and wanted to be treated as a government."[3] Eventually, Ajello and the CSC had to switch their emphasis to trying to ensure that the postelection parliament would prove durable, and in the process the international community seemed compelled to make a postelection commitment to sustain democratic development.

The conversion of Renamo into a political force was in several respects artificial. Although the movement did attract support from some members of the middle class and the business community, it could not break Frelimo's hold on the core elite. Renamo's electoral support was strongest in the rural areas of those provinces where it had been most active militarily and among remote communities that had been neglected or alienated by Frelimo's policies and practices. It earned some new support during the peace process in the urban areas of the central and northern provinces but did not in general succeed in weaning the intelligentsia away from Frelimo. Many Mozambicans perceived Renamo as dependent on international support, an impression that was reinforced by international pressure on its opponent, Frelimo, to dismantle Mozambique's socialist state.

At the end of the process, a leading Frelimo member, Teodato Hunguana, attributed success to the will for peace on the part of the population; the role of the international community in general; the Security Council, which remained "impartial and balanced"; the role of ONUMOZ in verifying and controlling the agreements; and the influence of developments elsewhere in Southern Africa. For him, the failures of ONUMOZ were its inadequate responses to Renamo violations; its tendency to side with Renamo; and its infringements of sovereignty. Hunguana felt that the role of the United Nations should have been restricted and that the CSC should have been chaired rather than directed by the SRSG. The jobs that ONUMOZ did not complete, said Hunguana, included the collection of arms; the formation of the new army; demining; the reintegration of demobilized soldiers; and the integration of Renamo zones into the state administration.[4]

Renamo's critique was less trenchant. The party's general secretary, Francisco Marcelino (alias Jose de Castro), blamed the government for what he claimed were frequent violations of the cease-fire and for failing to provide accommodation to Renamo in Maputo. He confined his criticism of ONUMOZ to its inability to ensure the impartiality of the police. He praised the SRSG for his formula for the composition of the National Elections Commission.[5]

The small size of the new joint army was a point of concern but it turned out not to be a major weakness of the peace process. Even the postelection government accepted the reality. The new defense minister, Aguiar Mazula, declared that he had no intention of increasing the number of troops. His higher priorities were the need to complete the basic training that had been undertaken and to develop the capacity of the police to work effectively.

Costs and Consequences

The cost of ONUMOZ and its peacekeeping-related operations was in the region of $700 million, although a complete reconciliation of accounts has proved an elusive and inconclusive task. The largest single national contribution to the peacekeeping budget was made by the United States, which, under the prevailing agreements covering UN peacekeeping, was obliged to meet 31.4 percent of the ONUMOZ budget, and which made substantial bilateral and multilateral contributions to operations that in general supported the work of ONUMOZ. The individual and collective contributions of European countries also comprised a substantial part of the funding of the peacekeeping and its related components. In addition, there was a substantial budget for emergency humanitarian and rehabilitation programs throughout the peace process; total commitments to this budget between October 1992 and December 1994 reached $633 million, somewhat short of the notional requirement of $775 million. Ongoing development funding and debt relief were coordinated by the World Bank.[6]

Money was sometimes spent sometimes excessively, but more often just inefficiently. The complicated financial bureaucracy within the UN system interfered with any rapid execution of emergency programs. The United Nations's trust funds and its elaborate procurement procedures do not allow for quick responses, and some agencies decided that funding vital activities independently was a more efficient and accountable way to contribute to the peace process. The ONUMOZ structure found it hard to harmonize the disparate elements of the operation, each of which had its own headquarters office. In this respect, UNOHAC was the unit that attracted the most persistent charges of incompetence. For instance, a U.S. embassy cable of July 15, 1994, stated that the SRSG would have been better served by working directly with donors rather than trying to coordinate activities through UNOHAC. The TU, which cooperated more closely with the SRSG, was, however, commended.

In any peacekeeping operation, the SRSG has special powers that override or interfere with the established powers of the UN resident representative. Distinctions between the two powers are not clearly defined, and the United Nations's independent agencies are in any case instinctively wary of yielding authority. In such situations, the SRSG is under time constraints and may find it hard to engage full support from the different agencies. Much depends on the personalities involved. In Mozambique, the powers of the permanent and temporary forms of the UN presence came into conflict. The relationship between ONUMOZ and UNDP was especially complex and competitive but, with the foremost exception of the demining issue, it worked. A sense of necessity and mutual dependence prevailed.

Unusually for a peacekeeping operation, UN personnel suffered no deaths from acts of war, although some were held hostage or sustained injuries during demobilization. Two UN staff members were killed when a light plane crashed; illness and road accidents claimed the lives of a few others.

The presence of the United Nations provided a brief, although entirely artificial, boost to Mozambique's stagnant and collapsing economy, especially for property rents and services such as hotels and restaurants. This boost neither alleviated the widespread economic hardship in the country nor enhanced the image of the United Nations, which often came to represent wealth and waste amid poverty and scarcity. The provisioning of ONUMOZ itself seemed extravagant to ordinary Mozambicans, as was shown all too clearly when bottled water was flown in by helicopter for the military contingents or when UN officials drove around in empty vehicles while Mozambicans were lining up for hours to find standing room on overcrowded buses.

ONUMOZ was remote from Mozambican society in general. Although there was no reason for the operation to share the ethos of the long-term development community, Mozambicans understandably complained that ONUMOZ staff could have made more effort to understand Mozambique and that more use could have been made of locally available sources for the operation's equipment needs. (UN procurement rules, it should be noted, do not encourage such an approach.) Faced with the United Nations's superior resources, the government administration suffered a severe loss of morale, and whole departments began to abdicate their responsibilities. Many government officials developed an acute sense of how to use the UN presence to their advantage and how to extract money from the system. This was an area in which Renamo could not compete, causing some resentment among the Renamo leadership and fueling the movement's tendency to make ludicrously overstated demands for money.

Ajello and the Ambassadors

As SRSG, Aldo Ajello's energy was remarkable and his informality was very useful. He tried to get to know everyone of importance personally and to find out all he could about them. He had no compunction about calling people at midnight to overcome problems as they arose. Operating in an ad hoc manner, he called meetings at short notice to resolve issues swiftly and worked hard to gauge the value and acceptability of every move before advancing proposals or making formal decisions. He was adept at assessing the political will of the parties and tried to maintain a degree of political balance, although not always successfully. The time he spent winning over Dhlakama was time lost in keeping the government in step with the process.

At the beginning, when he still felt somewhat insecure about his position, Ajello chose to form an alliance with the Western ambassadors that paid dividends in assuring their continued support for him. As well as remaining in close contact with the parties, he would consult the international members of the CSC every Monday and planned carefully for the formal CSC meetings. Ajello built his credibility brick by brick. His network of informal contacts helped to sustain the pressure for action in the formal processes. He had a knack for turning setbacks to his advantage and was adept at staging what one ONUMOZ staff member called "theatrical performances." His skill at "doing things by bluff" (as one CSC ambassador put it) was complemented by his openness toward the Mozambican press, which was impressed by the frequency of his briefings and the honesty with which he explained both his problems and his priorities. Ajello was not afraid to criticize either party publicly, although in private he was often more conciliatory and always pragmatic.

Ajello's performance as SRSG earned conflicting assessments, but there was no doubting his courage and commitment to making a success of the peace process. His principal strength was his ability to act as a politician rather than as a UN bureaucrat—a role for which he was unsuited. "As an organizer and manager he left a lot to be desired," remarked a senior UN agency official later. "His treatment of his staff in ONUMOZ was rough and rude and there were many temperamental explosions." Some described Ajello as a "lousy manager" who was "unable to understand technical matters," but those who saw the larger picture regarded him as "talented," "energetic, with a lot of technical knowledge," and "brave enough to extend his own mandate."

At the most important stages, and particularly throughout the second year of the process, the CSC was effectively in almost constant session. "We had meetings every day and I was on call twenty-four hours a day," Ajello said later. "This way we had the right answers at the right time." The ambassadors in the CSC (representing France, Germany, Italy, Portugal, the United Kingdom, and the United States) constituted a mini–Security Council and most problems were could be solved through debate among the ambassadors without excessive consultation with their respective capitals. The same applied to Ajello's relationship with the UN Secretariat, where his regular contact was with DPKO. Ajello noted later that it was only after each problem was solved that New York would be informed simultaneously of the problem and its solution.[7] As a result of this close coordination and management on the ground, the members of the Security Council in New York appeared, on the whole, to feel comfortable with developments in Maputo, on which they were briefed every two weeks or so. The African group of ambassadors in New York was continually informed and consulted.

The fact that "everybody played the same game," as Ajello put it, kept the CSC broadly united. At the end of the peace process, Ajello described the CSC as "instrumental in the implementation of the GPA, giving the United Nations strong leverage in driving the process." In the search for consensus, the role of the United Nations became highly political. "The secret of success," according to Ajello, was the legitimacy conferred by the CSC on all the important decisions.[8] The inclusion in the CSC of an OAU representative, Ahcene Fzeri of Tunisia, helped to provide a counterpart to the Western group and to resolve issues when there were splits among the Western ambassadors. The work of the CSC was also helped by close coordination with the leading subsidiary commissions, particularly the Cease-Fire Commission (CCF), the Commission for the Joint Armed Forces for the Defense of Mozambique (CCFADM), and the National Elections Commission (CNE).

The Subsidiary Peace Commissions

The CCF was an essential mechanism to prevent minor incidents and misunderstandings from escalating and it performed this function successfully from an early stage in the process. It kept the parties talking, sometimes more actively and effectively than in the forum of the CSC, and it ensured that the military observers were able to move relatively quickly in cases of reported cease-fire violations. Its importance increased significantly during the assembly and demobilization process, when it became a focal point for the resolution of actual and potential difficulties.

The responsibilities of the CCF covered not only the initial cease-fire procedures and mine clearance but also, subsequently, various other activities, including analyzing and verifying data on troop strength and weapons, monitoring and verifying the disbanding of irregular and private armed groups, and implementing demobilization. Having been directly responsible for approving the assembly areas, the CCF approved the rules of conduct for the assembly areas and the non-assembled locations, and the procedures for registration and demobilization.

Chaired for the United Nations by Colonel Segala of Italy, the CCF brought together the government and Renamo with representatives of

Botswana, Egypt, France, Italy, Kenya, Nigeria, Portugal, the United Kingdom, the United States, and Zimbabwe. It had three regional sub-commissions with headquarters in Nampula, Beira, and Matola. Like the CSC, the CCF maintained formal and informal processes in tandem. At the end of the peace process, Segala calculated that the CCF had held 2,200 hours of meetings, consisting of 75 plenary sessions, 324 tripartite meetings, and numerous bilateral contacts. Segala's final report described the process: "The tripartite meetings were an informal forum in which an open and frank dialogue between the parties could take place. This allowed the parties to find technical solutions to most of the problems which arose during the process. The solutions found in these informal fora were presented at the plenary sessions of the CCF for formal approval." He added that the bilateral contacts between himself and each party allowed him to learn about the concerns of each and subsequently to find acceptable compromises.

The CCF was hampered from the outset by the parties' inability to provide reliable information on their respective troop strength, arms, and equipment or on the physical positions held. This, compounded by the high level of mistrust between the two parties, made CCF arbitration difficult and caused a series of delays that affected the entire peace process. The CCF did, however, claim success in solving a total of ninety-five formal cease-fire complaints and hundreds of incidents in the assembly areas. It collected registered weapons from the assembly and non-assembly areas, and it verified a total of 744 declared and undeclared arms caches.

Segala characterized most of the difficulties confronting the commission, apart from the CCF's day-to-day challenges, as stemming from the two parties' political strategies, their mutual lack of trust, and the absence of a basic infrastructure in the country. In his final report he recommended that attention be paid to mine clearance and to the destruction of the large quantities of weapons that were obviously surplus to the requirements of the new army.[9] Segala also recommended that in future PKOs the United Nations should insist on complete access to all military installations from the start of an operation, beginning with the collection and storage of all military equipment independently of demobilization, and that the United Nations should be allowed to destroy excess military equipment.[10]

The CCFADM became active only as the peace process began to mature, once assembly had begun. When the United Nations agreed to take the chair, the commission held its first plenary meeting on July 22, 1993, bringing together the government, Renamo, and the three nations that were to provide training, France, Portugal, and the United Kingdom. In all, the CCFADM held twenty-seven plenary meetings, most of them in 1994 under the chairmanship of the deputy SRSG, Behrooz Sadry, whose experience of Cambodia proved helpful in integrating the commission's work with that of the leading peace commissions, the CSC and the CCF. At the end of the process, the British representative, Lieutenant Colonel John Wyatt, observed that it would have been beneficial to establish the new army's high command much earlier in the process, as its absence made training difficult.[11]

Exclusively Mozambican, the CNE provided coherent and credible political oversight of the electoral operation, and thus played the vital role of finally securing the peace process. As the final arbiter concerning the future government of Mozambique, it laid down and monitored the fundamental democratic rules. By operating flexibly and with a degree of transparency and by accommodating complaints, it promoted the reconciliation of Mozambique's fiercely opposed political positions. Nominally, it managed the elections through its Mozambican-staffed technical secretariat, the STAE, but actual operations were usually performed by the international community in support of the ONUMOZ mandate to provide technical assistance and monitoring for elections.

The creation of the CNE, delayed until the two major parties could agree on its composition, was not accomplished until the secretary-general's visit to Mozambique in October 1993. A balance was kept between Frelimo, with ten representatives, and the ten allocated to all the other parties, of which Renamo fielded seven. The same balance ran through its implementing arm, the STAE. With most of the electoral organization dependent upon the UN system, there was close consultation between its president, Brazao Mazula, and the SRSG. Mazula's knack of generating confidence enabled the donors to provide strong support to the CNE and to help with the early identification of needs and the effective solution of problems. There was, however, periodic tension between the Mozambican and foreign electoral staff. An official UNDP report pointed out the contradiction between the need to support an electoral process run by Mozambicans and the obligation to contribute toward the holding of the elections. The report added: "It was not always possible to obtain the right balance between 'adviser' and 'executor,' since the pressure of events and the practical ineffectiveness of some structures sometimes forced the team to intervene decisively."[12] Both the CNE and the

STAE were accused of lax management of resources and overrecruitment of electoral support staff and party monitors. In confirmation of this perception, one of the CNE's conclusions was that provincial- and district-level staff should have been trained, as part of the UNDP's support project, to manage financial resources more efficiently and rigorously.[13]

The CNE worked with all political forces, with the other commissions, and with the international community. The civic education program was in general effective in explaining the electoral process to ordinary Mozambicans. Last, the CNE helped to make the electoral process acceptable to the people, ensured a balance of political forces, acted as an impartial referee, and, most importantly, gave credibility to the elections.[14]

The other peace commissions were of minor importance. The Reintegration Commission (CORE) was undermined by the delay in starting demobilization and by donors' outright rejection of the joint UNOHAC-CORE formula for reintegrating the soldiers. Many of the projects for the demobilized were formalized under the auspices of bilateral programs and so fell outside CORE's mandate or control. It even remained dependent upon other units for information on the demobilized.

The territorial, police, and secret services commissions—CNAT, COMPOL, and COMINFO—were generally inactive and ineffective. CNAT fell victim to the two parties' deep political differences over the terms of territorial control. Once its membership was agreed, it held only a few inconclusive sessions until Renamo withdrew its representatives for the remainder of the peace process. For its part, COMPOL took no action in pursuing the complaints about the behavior of the police and the civil rights abuses that were referred to it by Civpol, which initiated investigations into 505 different cases, 61 of which were related to complaints against the Mozambique police about human rights violations. Neither the government nor Renamo considered COMPOL important. The same can be said about COMINFO, the least active of the all the commissions, which held its first meeting only in December 1993 and received funds only in June 1994, whereupon it deployed four brigades to try to ensure that the secret police did not abuse its powers and to investigate cases in which political prisoners were alleged to be held. The COMINFO chairman, Manuel Fonseca, said that members of the secret police (SISE) regarded the commission as a threat to their existence and were openly hostile to it, and that they disturbed the electoral registration process in Manica and disrupted political meetings in Cabo Delgado.[15] Although these points were recorded, no action was taken.

Contingents, Observers, and Civpol

The 350 military observers played a vital role throughout the peace process, monitoring cease-fire violations, staffing assembly areas, assisting demobilization, collecting arms caches, and verifying weapons deposits. Most of the six thousand troops in the UN military contingents spent their time patrolling the transportation corridors without any severe risk of attack or disruption. In the first year, the arrival of the contingents was useful in demonstrating the will and capability of the United Nations but, once the process of demobilization had begun, there was little need for large battalions. There could have been a more flexible deployment and a more rapid withdrawal. Drawn principally from Bangladesh, Italy, India, Zambia, Uruguay, Botswana, and Portugal, the contingents played a more symbolic than practical role in assisting the peace process. Of the individual battalions, those from Bangladesh and Botswana were commended for their professionalism and willingness to adapt to local conditions. The well-equipped Italian battalion patrolled the key Beira corridor in the first ten months of deployment until it was withdrawn with its reputation marred by reports of sexual exploitation of young girls. Similar accusations were made against the Uruguayan battalion on the north-south highway. The contribution of the poorly equipped Zambian battalion was uncontroversial, but probably unnecessary. By contrast, important contributions to military operations were made by specialist units from India (logistics), Portugal (communications), and Argentina (a field hospital).

The team of military observers, headed by Egypt's Colonel Ghobashi, provided the manpower and operational capacity for monitoring the cease-fire and the subsequent activities of troop assembly and demobilization. Its efficient logistics enabled rapid responses to situations as they arose. The observers' monitoring was, however, also greatly facilitated by the comprehensive preparation and management of the civilian Technical Unit for Demobilization.

The civilian police (Civpol) contingent was fully deployed only during the last five months of the ONUMOZ mandate. Although the principle of introducing a human rights observation element into peacekeeping operations was integral to the original mandate, this was initially obstructed by the government. By the time Civpol was fully deployed in May 1994, it numbered 1,095 police officers drawn from twenty-nine nations, but its functions were largely diverted from investigating infringements of human rights to supporting other priorities of the peace process. It established itself in ninety-seven locations throughout Mozambique and its principal achievements were the opening of access to Renamo areas and the facilitation of the international observation of the elections. The wide variety of training and approaches among contributing police forces created difficulties in Civpol's management and organization, and there was a feeling in the international community as a whole that recruitment had been on the basis of maintaining numbers rather than providing skills in human rights monitoring. The government delayed Civpol's access to some training centers, to the facilities of the Rapid Intervention Police, and to those of the presidential guard until early October 1994. Although Civpol was able to enter Renamo areas, the government police remained unwelcome and were unwilling to enter many areas. At the end of the peace process, the departure of Civpol often resulted in a return to the status quo ante.

The Achievement of Demobilization

Demobilization of the two sides' armed forces was very slow to begin and, once under way, fraught with risks and danger, but it was ultimately successful. This can be attributed to the considerable care that went into achieving balance and providing incentives. ONUMOZ assembled, disarmed, and demobilized practically all the identifiable combatants from both sides. Although the parties tried to delay, it was the demobilizing soldiers themselves who drove the process to conclusion, rioting in order to be allowed to go home. The crisis in the assembly areas broke in June and July 1994. Once the parties had agreed to an almost entirely voluntary recruitment into the new army and to let non-volunteers return home, they could not realistically keep any troops in reserve. Over several months, demobilization created serious and widespread unrest, and there was a risk that the protests could threaten security at the time of elections. In the event, the election campaign ran its course in a relatively stable environment.

A challenge facing ONUMOZ throughout assembly and demobilization was the lack of reliable information about the numbers of troops on both sides, and the risk that substantial numbers might not be declared. There may be some significance in the fact that the very last groups to come forward were Renamo fighters. However, after July 1994, any carefully planned strategy either side may have had for keeping troops back was collapsing, along with the morale of the assembled troops. The troops already registered loudly demanded their benefits, and those held back from assembly became determined not to miss out. With the help of the Reintegration Support Scheme (RSS), demobilization succeeded in flushing out most of the organized combatants in the country.

The key to providing the logistics of demobilization was the Technical Unit for Demobilization (TU), the military observers' civilian support unit, which developed an impressive logistic capability under Swiss management. The head of the TU concluded that part of the recipe for success was the presence of non-UN staff members in the unit. Things were achieved that would not have been possible entirely within the UN system. The unit was animated by a spirit of shared responsibility and a determination to find solutions to all the difficulties that arose. Different donors brought different skills. The TU was also asked to provide logistical support for the elections, and UN volunteers attached to it were put on electoral duty.

Of those demobilized, nearly 90,000 were transported home, along with 95,000 dependents; the new army, however, was only 12,000-strong by the end of 1994.[16] The convincing success of demobilization created some risk that the new army could not guarantee security after the departure of the United Nations, and that the poor results in collecting weapons could aggravate security conditions. The reintegration strategy would also be tested in the future. "Problems raised by reintegration transcend the ambit of a UN peacekeeping mission," wrote J-P. B. Coelho and Alex Vines, who, in their study of the subject, argued for a continued effort to ensure employment of ex-combatants, particularly in farming.[17]

The Failures of Disarmament and Demining

The soldiers were eventually demobilized, but very few of their weapons were collected or destroyed. Disarmament in Mozambique as a national priority was never addressed seriously by the GPA, by the ONUMOZ mandate, or by the international donor community. It was common knowledge that millions of AK-47s were at large in the country, in the possession of soldiers and civilians alike. The rare opportunity that the ONUMOZ period provided for a comprehensive disarmament was missed entirely. As a result, there is continuing concern about the effects of the proliferation of Mozambican weapons on the stability of the wider Southern African region and of South Africa in particular. Only 180,000 weapons were collected under CCF monitoring and all these were handed over to the new army, with the exception of 24,000 that were destroyed.

Another missed opportunity was the failure to start a comprehensive demining program until the ONUMOZ mandate was ending. Although the number and location of landmines planted throughout Mozambique over nearly thirty years of conflict could only be guessed at, there was a general consensus in 1992 that mine clearance should begin along priority roads, to permit the distribution of food relief and to improve the safety of returning refugees. UNOHAC and UNDP controlled the largest budgets for this work but failed to authorize programs or projects until mid-1994, leaving the bulk of mine clearance during the ONUMOZ mandate to the actions of individual agencies. The failure of UNOHAC to provide either leadership or coordination in demining came to be seen as one of the greatest weaknesses of the ONUMOZ operation.

The Achievement of Elections

The elections were managed by the CNE and STAE with the support of the electoral unit run by UNDP, which raised $60 million for the purpose from the international community. ONUMOZ provided the political framework and some logistical support. Electoral observation was by blanket coverage, with sufficient numbers from the United Nations alone for two observers to visit each polling station, and supplementary observer groups were provided by the European Union, the OAU, the Christian Council, the Episcopal Conference, and AWEPA, the Association of West European Parliamentarians for Southern Africa. The total number of international observers was 3,090, considerably more than the numbers usually deployed for African elections.

Although ostensibly supervised by a Mozambican commission, the elections, because they provided a signposted exit from the overall peace process, were strongly driven by the international community. The elections showed that a democratic exercise in Mozambique was possible, but the electoral campaign focused on issues of resources and security and hardly touched upon matters of ideology or development policy. Nevertheless, the leading positions in national politics of both Frelimo and Renamo were convincingly confirmed. These two parties would therefore between them establish the pattern of democratic debate in the future. Attention would henceforth turn to the issue of providing some kind of democracy at the local level.

The involvement of large numbers of Mozambicans in the electoral process was important in establishing the credibility of the elections. The payments for electoral monitors during the elections put the financial control of the process under some strain, creating a certain amount of petty corruption and extortion at the end of spending line. But there is little evidence that this amounted to a direct form of political corruption.

The Failures of UNOHAC

As the humanitarian arm of ONUMOZ, UNOHAC faced great resistance and criticism from international donors and other UN agencies throughout the peace process, at the end of which its director, Felix Downes-Thomas, described it as a "unique experiment"—implying that important lessons were learned but that it is unlikely to be repeated. UNOHAC's problems resulted largely from its creation as an apparently convenient way for the United Nations to continue coordinating emergency relief programs and to bring humanitarian affairs under political management for the duration of the peace process. But satisfying the convenience of the UN Secretariat and the Security Council did not necessarily provide solutions on the ground. The major UN relief agencies such as UNHCR, Unicef, and WFP like to be self-reliant; they know how to do their own work, they have their own networks in place, they coordinate with others when they want to, and they tend to resent the passing fads foisted on them by New York. In late 1992, the bigger UN agencies were more interested in resolving the food crises affecting Mozambique and the Southern African region as a whole than in undertaking an experiment in which they clearly had little confidence.

Integration of humanitarian work within the overall mandate of ONUMOZ was made difficult by the slow start of the UN operation as a whole. When ONUMOZ was being planned, military protection was assumed to be necessary for the delivery of humanitarian aid. In the event, most of the troops were deployed along the main transportation corridors serving neighboring countries rather than over the internal road network. UNOHAC tried to urge greater protection but this issue never became sufficiently pressing, partly because the cease-fire was holding, partly because the contingents arrived so late. Had the military contingents been mobilized more promptly, better coordination between the military and humanitarian components of the operation could have avoided duplication and waste in logistical and management resources.

At the planning stage, the deployment of troops in the transportation corridors took precedence over the distribution of humanitarian aid within Mozambique and over the military's possible contribution to de-mining operations. This was despite observations in September 1992 by DPKO's own technical adviser, Noel François, that the distribution of humanitarian aid to military and civilians was inextricably linked and that the military could lead the way in opening up access to displaced persons and refugees returning voluntarily, as well as protect food convoys from disaffected soldiers, hungry civilians, and bandits. Problems in the rela-tionship between DHA and DPKO in New York seem to have prevented the use of the military contingents from becoming a pivotal part of the SRSG's management in Mozambique. The ONUMOZ military and UNO-HAC were established as separate and distinct operations and they never tried to work together on the ground. As it turned out, the military con-tingents arrived too late to make much impact on either the overall Southern African drought relief operation or the provision of relief to Renamo areas. Access to the latter was negotiated by a variety of agen-cies, including WFP and UNOHAC officials at the provincial level. Before the peace agreement, food convoys were susceptible to armed attacks by Renamo or other soldiers; afterward, they were relatively safe. The mili-tary contingents' presence on the main roads became a routine precau-tion rather than a necessity.

For Ajello, the first problem for coordinating humanitarian aid in Mozambique was revealed in the complexity of the United Nations's operational rules and procedures in a situation where "timeliness can make the difference between success and failure." The slow implemen-tation of the mine-clearance plan tarnished the image of the United Nations. The second problem was the variety and inconsistency of rules and procedures in the United Nations and its agencies. The third prob-lem was the conflict between what Ajello called the "culture of devel-opment" and the "culture of peacekeeping." UN peacekeepers "must ensure that things move as fast as possible and, thus, they must under-take many of the tasks which under normal circumstances would be car-ried out by the government or the local people." He added that "UNO-HAC's staff were mainly development people and they acted according to their culture."[18]

The UNOHAC mandate was not clear. Other donors disagreed about UNOHAC's attempts to link short-term humanitarian assistance to the longer-term programs of development after the completion of the peace process. The authority of the SRSG over UNOHAC was constrained. The problem of interaction between the UN resident coordinator and an ad hoc structure like UNOHAC was not resolved. The conclusion that many reached was that the resident coordinator should have been in charge of UNOHAC. The U.S. embassy in Maputo considered UNOHAC an unmitigated disaster, duplicating the efforts of other UN agencies and blocking donors' efforts to deal with problems promptly. The embassy felt that UNOHAC's approach to mine clearance and demobilization could have jeopardized the entire process.[19]

For Ajello, the solutions to problems raised by UNOHAC lay in reform of the rules and procedures and in giving the SRSG the authority to decide how operations should be harmonized. At the end of the peace process, Ajello continued to argue that the imperatives of peacekeeping should take priority over humanitarian action. In his view, assistance had to be prioritized to take care of the needs of those who could make trouble during a peace process. Food had to be distributed to the soldiers first, overriding the normal requirement of attending to the most needy. He added that ONUMOZ had to ensure that the armed groups were "not demoted in society."[20] The establishment of UNOHAC under the overall authority of the SRSG was "the correct decision," and "equally correct was the concept of coordination linked to the provision of valuable services." The failure to provide such services in Mozambique did not mean, Ajello argued, that the concept is wrong. He urged that efforts should be coordinated to provide the various organizations delivering humanitarian assistance with "a valuable support structure."[21]

In the view of Larry Minear and Thomas Weiss, "interventions need to be approached with a longer-term and more comprehensive view of what is required to put war-torn societies back on their feet. . . . The dual persona of the United Nations—humanitarian and political—should be acknowledged, but with the former insulated as tightly as possible from the latter."[22] On the evidence provided by ONUMOZ and UNOHAC, there needed to be some interaction between the humanitarian and the political, but the work of coordination could have been left to the professionals with experience of the country rather than to a hastily assembled bureaucracy that did not command respect or deliver its services efficiently. "In the humanitarian enterprise today, there is no alternative to greater professionalism, and no way of getting there apart from clearer objectives, methods, and accountability."[23]

The Achievement of Resettlement

Reconciliation at the community level and a common desire for peace among Mozambicans everywhere facilitated possibly the most important single achievement of the peace process, namely, the resettlement of refugees and citizens who had been displaced within the country. The energy and enterprise of the returnees themselves ran far ahead of the efforts of most humanitarian agencies. At least 4 million people returned home, of whom more than 1 million returned spontaneously from neighboring countries. UNHCR, WFP, and IOM all came to play important roles in the process. They and other agencies found themselves having to address the challenge of helping to rebuild the social, economic, and administrative structures of a society shattered by war, a challenge that would persist long beyond the lifetime of ONUMOZ.

The End Result

Mozambique regained control of its own affairs in December 1994 but will probably take years to recover, painfully, from the destructive effects of its long years of war. The presence of ONUMOZ at least facilitated the solution of the country's most important political problems but it was not the comprehensive solution that its original planners had intended. Without doubt, too much was expected of a mission whose original mandate was for only one year and that could only start to address its principal objectives in its second year. Outside the arenas of demobilization and elections, where ONUMOZ scored remarkable success, a sense of perspective was lost and opportunities were missed.

For Mozambique and Mozambicans, the presence of ONUMOZ put the seal on the peace process, facilitating the return of civilians and soldiers to their homes and starting the country on a road to normality. Having first benefited from the remarkable peace agreement forged, with the help of Sant'Egidio and the Italian government, between its two warring parties in Rome, Mozambique was fortunate to have attracted the attention of the wider international community, which was motivated not least by concern to protect the parallel process of reconciliation in South Africa. But such attention is double-edged. At the end of the process, Mozambique had increased rather than shaken off its dependence on international financial and humanitarian assistance, and the voices of ordinary Mozambicans were in danger of being drowned out by the agendas of international development agencies. Above all, much still needed to be done: landmines cleared from the fields so that agriculture could resume; the beginnings of an economy of exchange developed; health and educational facilities provided; and weapons removed from a society that had no more need of them.

According to Ajello, the achievements of ONUMOZ lay in letting the international members of the commissions become active players, in helping Renamo to become a real partner, in the fact that the TU was integrated in the office of the SRSG, and in the role of the RSS in ensuring successful demobilization. For him, the TU and the RSS "made the difference." Demobilization would never have been as efficient had this task been left exclusively to the military observers. The military component was too big and inefficient; it did not assure security of the main roads or the free circulation of aid, people, and goods or the return of refugees.[24]

The U.S. embassy's assessment of the performance of ONUMOZ was contained in a cable of January 11, 1995, that was circulated to the international community and the United Nations. "The achievements in Mozambique are real, but many materialized despite, not because of the UN's supervision of the peace process. . . . Many of the things that have gone wrong in other UN operations also went wrong in Mozambique. Timetables slipped. The local parties delayed compliance. Budgets soared. Parent UN agencies engaged in obstructionism, and UN resources on the ground were underutilized and worse. What did work was an unexpected mix of strong leadership, donor coordination, and aggressive diplomacy which provided the critical underpinning for continued forward movement throughout the process." The U.S. cable recommended that the military terms of any peace agreement should be "subject to aggressive, intrusive, outside oversight," and that the local actors need to be "constantly prodded and not allowed to claim national sovereignty as a reason for delay or failure to implement."[25]

ONUMOZ was not a perfect peacekeeping operation. Its mandate was too ambitious and tended to make it an invasive force that tried to perform tasks beyond its capacity. Only a common desire, among Mozambicans and the international community as whole, for peace helped to bring the mandate to a satisfactory conclusion. In other circumstances, the United Nations would have been highly vulnerable to manipulation and military challenge. It was a rare kind of peacekeeping operation, one that helped to extinguish a dying conflict. In the less predictable era ahead in Africa and elsewhere, the United Nations will face sterner challenges from complex emergencies, disasters, and wars. It will be called upon to exercise much greater professionalism in managing humanitarian aid, to ensure that those who infringe human rights are held accountable, and to secure a democratic basis for the survival and development of nations.

9.

LESSONS FOR PEACEKEEPING AND PEACEBUILDING IN AFRICA

$\mathbf{M}$ozambique won a level of international support for its peacekeeping requirements that few African states with comparable problems can expect to enjoy in the future. The geopolitical importance of Southern Africa and South Africa's new readiness to cooperate with (rather than to interfere in) neighboring states combined to create a positive dynamic of collaborative international support for peace from which Mozambique, as a country drained of the will to fight, was the primary beneficiary. The same dynamic may yet benefit Angola, even if the precise formula for success in that country has been extraordinarily elusive. Elsewhere in Africa, however, the international community sees fewer of its interests at stake and may abandon conflict-ridden states to their fate. As the crisis in Central Africa of the mid- and late 1990s has shown, new conflicts may run unchecked, without a clear response from either the regional or the international community.

The collapse of states such as Liberia, Rwanda, and Somalia—where armed conflicts have grown out of domestic competition for power or deep-rooted antagonisms that are poorly understood by the outside world—has tended to result in indecision and disagreement among the international players and to encourage a hands-off approach that has at times left the humanitarian community operating in a dangerous and destructive political vacuum. It can only be hoped that "crisis management" does not have to give way to "chaos management" in any more of Africa's ongoing political crises and that the elusive skills of preventive diplomacy, peacemaking, and peacebuilding can evolve alongside, and in support of, genuine local efforts to rebuild civil society. The marshalling of timely and appropriate international action depends upon effective monitoring by a combination of resident UN and other agencies.

The lessons of Mozambique relate less to incipient or ongoing conflicts than to those that are ripe for resolution, where there is a strong will among warring parties to bring their conflict to an end. As Mozambique's experience showed, every peace process has to be constructed individually, in accordance with the political and humanitarian realities prevailing in each state and region. Not every situation can generate an overarching peace agreement as solid as the one signed by the Mozambican parties on October 4, 1992, but their GPA stands as a useful model for bringing resolution to other such conflicts. A similar formula was followed for Sierra Leone in largely successful peace talks held during 1996. In negotiations in Abidjan, the Sierra Leone government and rebels of the Revolutionary United Front (RUF) were able to agree on the terms of a cease-fire, the formation of two supervisory bodies (a Commission for the Consolidation of the Peace and a Joint Monitoring Group, both with international community representation) and other reconciliation forums, the encampment of rebel fighters in designated assembly areas, and the integration of RUF elements into the national armed forces, as well as immunity for members of the RUF and measures for their reintegration into civil and political life. The negotiations leading to these agreements were a direct result of cooperative efforts among an NGO based in the United Kingdom, International Alert, the OAU, the United Nations, the ICRC, the Commonwealth, and the government of Côte d'Ivoire. Although the cease-fire was later violated, by early 1997 the agreement was seen to have provided a basis for further progress toward peace.

A peace agreement that comprehensively represents the commitments of parties in conflict with guarantees provided by the international community is the best grounding for success. It does not, of course, ensure success, not least because the original signatories may press for subsequent renegotiation or because other parties may arise, either as splinter groups from the original signatories or as new, opportunistic elements with access to arms and the means of coercion. The experience of ONU-MOZ showed that the organization managing the agreement has to carry substantial authority, command general respect, and display political discretion. The role of subsidiary peace commissions was also shown to be important, particularly for military verification and observation and in helping to achieve reconciliation at different levels of society. Equally, however, ONUMOZ demonstrated that the establishment of too many such commissions could impede progress.

Peacekeeping operations must be answerable to both national and international expectations, but they also depend on quick reaction and on good logistics for the rapid delivery of humanitarian and other assistance directly related to the peace process they support. In a succinct assessment of the lessons that the U.S. mission in Maputo learned from ONUMOZ, the U.S. embassy, in the cable it distributed on January 11, 1995, proposed that PKOs should be small, self-supporting, and quick to react, and that police contingents should be fully integrated with the military command. The leadership of an operation "must not only be capable, but have the authority, responsibility, and accountability to apply the mandate in a flexible and dynamic way in order to adjust to a country's shifting political realities." At the same time, the mandate should not be overly inclusive. "In some areas, [such as] humanitarian assistance, the less the PKO attempts to do, the better." The United Nations's "creaky and leaky logistical and procurement support structure" was recommended for overhaul.[1]

The U.S. embassy cable went on to suggest that a UN operation does not have to be big to work, that NGOs should be engaged as full partners, that the United Nations must be prepared to assume the burden of leading and orchestrating all peace commissions, that the military terms should be subject to outside oversight, and that peacekeeping forces need a robust military observer presence. The cable stressed what it saw as the need for flexibility in interpreting the mandate and for permanently active diplomacy. It also highlighted the important role of local UN agencies and the possibilities offered by close coordination among donors, but doubted that the United Nations itself would be able to overcome its tendency to try to dominate rather than facilitate.

The U.S. embassy's conclusions are appropriate for the kind of well-supported PKO that was staged in Mozambique, where the international community was already present through a large number of official and nongovernmental agencies. But in most states in Africa the international community is thinly represented, and the leading roles in any necessary conflict-resolution efforts would tend to be played by a small group of interested parties, with the OAU perhaps playing the leading diplomatic role. In such situations, any attempt to mount an appropriate PKO would likely be frustrated by insufficient resources.

Member-states of the UN Security Council have tended to shy away from making commitments in situations where there is little confidence that the parties to the conflict will abide by the agreements they have negotiated and less certainty about the outcome. This suggests that regional African groupings will often have to improvise without the support of troops trained or equipped to NATO standards and without substantial resources to underwrite the more politically risky operations, particularly the demobilization of combatants and the holding of elections. Repeated failures in Liberia have shown that, without adequate resources, such improvisation is unproductive or, worse, counterproductive. On their own, poorly equipped African contingents may be no match for determined rebels and insurgents and may be unable to protect deliveries of humanitarian aid. However, with international logistical support, African peacekeeping contingents have often shown themselves best able to adapt to local conditions and to win support from local populations.

A substantial and multifunctional PKO on the scale of ONUMOZ should be attempted in Africa only where there is both sufficient international concern about the problem and substantial confidence in the outcome. There is, however, a pressing need for efficient, less cumbersome PKOs mounted by concerned regional political leaderships who would be more prepared to offer their armed forces if they could count on strong logistic support from the wider international donor community, as well as on the provision of resources for peacebuilding if and when the prospects for a successful conclusion to the peace process seem encouraging. An appropriate balance between African and non-African components has to be found. Circumstances such as those in Zaire (now Congo) in late 1996 and early 1997 prompted negotiations about the composition of a potential humanitarian intervention. They also raised the possibility of the deployment of South African forces, although it might not serve South Africa's interests to assume the leading role in African PKOs.[2] Peacekeeping contingents should normally be provided by a balanced group of nations; otherwise, the contingents run the risk of being seen as agents of their own nation's strategic interests.

Whatever the agreed military component, the political leadership for operations should be derived as much as possible from a regional, continental, and international consensus, however difficult this may be to bring about and sustain. A top priority for this political leadership must be to sustain whatever agreements have been achieved between the parties and to clarify and refine the agreements if necessary. Equally important is the maintenance of international support, both political and material.

Elements That Favor Success

The experience of ONUMOZ suggests six elements that are likely to increase the prospects for a successful outcome to peacekeeping and peacebuilding interventions in Africa.

1. *A credible formula.* A peace process that derives its legitimacy from a credible agreement between the warring parties is the essential starting point for any peace process. If such an agreement is then endorsed by outside powers (for instance, by a subregional organization, the OAU, or the United Nations), political management of the process can be enhanced by a strong peace commission, led where appropriate by a representative of the international community and supported by a small number of subsidiary commissions. Agreed procedures for the verification of progress and resolution of disputes must be firmly established from the outset; timetables, however, may need to be interpreted flexibly in the light of overall progress.

2. *Manageable components.* The composition and functions of the military element must be clear from the outset, but deployment should be made on an as-needed and, where possible, short-term basis. Legitimacy has to be derived from the predominant political commission, and its leadership requires resources, but the overall operation should be streamlined without sacrificing effectiveness or accountability.

3. *A closely monitored cease-fire.* Where demobilization has been agreed upon, effective measures and credible verification are needed for assembling and disarming combatants. Procedures may also be required for the early collection and disposal of weaponry, the removal of landmines, and prompt response to threats that can derail an agreed-upon process. Convincing and acceptable provision has to be made for the immediate needs of demobilized combatants as they return to civilian life. Such measures require professional management, by civilian as well as military planners, and strong donor support.

4. *Outside support.* Formal and informal cooperation with the peace process from the bilateral and multilateral donor community and from neighboring states has to be visible and sustained, especially to facilitate the delivery of essential assistance, to support local consensus-

building efforts, and to put the seal on the last act of the process (for instance, elections).

5. *Clear rules*. There is room for greater professionalism in all areas of peacekeeping activity, political, administrative, military, and humanitarian. Humanitarian and military operations should be mutually supportive but separately managed. (Where peacekeeping forces are themselves militarily engaged, all attempts must be made to ensure that humanitarian operations work, and are seen to work, independently from the PKO.) Tasks should be shared among the agencies present on the ground before new and essentially short-term institutions are introduced. The humanitarian and NGO community will increasingly be required to observe agreed-upon codes of conduct. Responsible and timely reporting of human rights abuses by any party, including the PKO itself, must be expected and an international procedure for responding to such abuses established.

6. *Capacity building*. A general policy of support for key government structures, rather than one of displacement, should help to provide sustainable management capacity for the political and administrative authorities at the end of the process.

In Mozambique, the peace process was generally successful in providing elements 1, 3, and 4 but performed less creditably in terms of elements 2, 5, and 6. As detailed in chapter 8, success was greatly facilitated by the power and flexibility of the leading commissions, while the measures for assembling and demobilizing combatants were subject to effective overall management—although opportunities were missed in disarmament with potential implications for future stability. The high level of international cooperation with the peace process was impressive—although ONUMOZ was ineffective as a coordinator. The humanitarian community, for its part, was generally efficient—although it was largely unaccountable. Among the failings were the operation's insensitivity to local conditions and a lack of professionalism in PKO staff at all levels. Human rights questions were not satisfactorily resolved because inadequate provision was made to call violators to account, either from the earlier period of war or during the peace process itself. In addition, the sheer weight of the international presence weakened the structures of national administration in Mozambique. The country was left poorly equipped to manage its own affairs or to begin to compete in the regional or world economy. Such issues will require close consideration in other peacekeeping or peacebuilding operations in Africa.

❖ ❖ ❖

ONUMOZ was formulated with the benefit of lessons learned from Angola's UNAVEM II operation, which during 1991 and 1992 proved to have inadequate powers either to hold the rival armies to their commitments or to force a renegotiation of the terms or timing of the peace process when it was undermined. These weaknesses helped to persuade the United Nations to insist on taking the chair on the leading peace commissions in Mozambique and to recommend a multifunctional operation with comprehensive military, electoral, and humanitarian components. The mandate given to ONUMOZ provided it with political flexibility and considerable discretionary powers that were important assets in holding the Mozambican parties to their commitments, but that same mandate also created an overweight operational entity. Such a mandate was, in retrospect, more appropriate to Angola before 1992 than to Mozambique after 1992. (It might be noted that the mandate would probably be no more appropriate to post-1992 Angola, where conditions have rendered conventional peacekeeping increasingly irrelevant.) Mozambique gained in some respects but not in all. What Frelimo and Renamo needed was constant persuasion and peacebrokering, accompanied by practical logistics for assembly, demobilization, disarmament, and elections. All these were delivered. What the Mozambican people needed was an effective rehabilitation of their divided and devastated land, a job that would have been best left to the donor and NGO community on the ground.

In Angola, as John Prendergast and David Smock have pointed out, "the usual international responses to emergencies—seeking peace agreements between warring parties, providing humanitarian aid, inserting peacekeeping troops, supporting elections—are strikingly inadequate." The elements of the more comprehensive response they recommend include "support for the rebuilding or creation of institutions and cultures of broader participation."[3] It is in this connection that some of the weaknesses in the ONUMOZ formula—the areas of long-term capacity building and training and education for a more transparent political order, including accountability for human rights violations—also provide lessons for Angola.

The lessons of ONUMOZ may not apply directly to the kind of crisis unfolding in Central Africa in the later 1990s, but once the parties in a conflict are ready to bury their grievances and to alter their priorities from "winning everything to salvaging something" in a peace process, operations like ONUMOZ have a clear role to play.[4] When the time is ripe for similar settlements in Africa—whether in Liberia, Rwanda, Sierra Leone, Somalia, or Sudan—the lessons of ONUMOZ will be a helpful guide to action.

There is no simple model for those who seek to construct effective bridges between war and peace, but ONUMOZ shows, as clearly as any blueprint can, that the basic foundations have to be laid by the leading parties to the conflict, with the support of their people. The appropriate role for the international community is to accept political challenges while maintaining close communication with the leading parties. When conflicts are ripe for resolution, outsiders can help promote dialogue and sustain the momentum toward resolution. Opportunities for peace can be convincingly seized and managed. The evidence of Mozambique is that, by building upon a nationwide mood of reconciliation, refugees can be encouraged to return, soldiers can be persuaded to lay down their arms, and peace can be convincingly consolidated.

APPENDIX I

Report of the Secretary-General on ONUMOZ (S/24892, 3 December 1992, and S/24892/Add.1, 9 December 1992)

Introduction

1. In my report of 9 October 1992 (S/24642), I conveyed to the Security Council the principal features of the general peace agreement for Mozambique, which is contained in document S/24635, and brought to its attention the role proposed for the United Nations in relation to the peace process. I recommended an immediate plan of action. On 13 October 1992, the Security Council adopted resolution 782 (1992), by which it welcomed the signature of a general peace agreement between the Government of the Republic of Mozambique and the Resistência Nacional Moçambicana (RENAMO), approved the appointment by the Secretary-General of an interim Special Representative and the dispatch to Mozambique of a team of up to 25 military observers, and requested the Secretary-General to report on the establishment of a United Nations Operation in Mozambique (ONUMOZ), including in particular a detailed estimate of the cost of that operation.

I. The current status of the peace process

2. In pursuance of that resolution, I took action the same day to appoint Mr. Aldo Ajello, a national of Italy and a staff member of the United Nations Development Programme (UNDP), as my interim Special Representative for Mozambique, and asked him to proceed to Maputo to assist the parties in setting up the joint machinery, which was to be chaired by the United Nations, in finalizing the modalities and conditions for the military arrangements and in carrying out the various other actions that were required of them at the very beginning of the process. I also entrusted him with the functions described in paragraphs 14 and 15 of my report of 9 October 1992 to the Security Council (S/24642). At the same time, I made arrangements to send to Mozambique a military team whose personnel had been drawn from existing peace-keeping missions and whose limited tasks were described in paragraph 16 of the above-mentioned report.

3. The interim Special Representative and the team of 21 military observers arrived in Mozambique on 15 October 1992, the day when the general peace agreement (hereinafter referred to as "the agreement") came into force, following publication in the *Official Gazette* of the legal instruments adopted by the Assembly of the Republic of Mozambique. On 20 October 1992, two teams of military observers were also deployed to Nampula and Beira.

4. Since his arrival, the interim Special Representative has met on several occasions with the President of Mozambique, Mr. Chissano, as well as with Mr. Dhlakama, President of RENAMO, and has had extensive exchanges with both leaders on various matters related to the early start of implementation of the agreement. He has also met with members of the Mozambican Government and representatives of RENAMO, representatives of the Organization of African Unity (OAU), and the ambassadors of the mediator State (Italy) and of the observer States at the Rome talks (France, Portugal, United Kingdom of Great Britain and Northern Ireland and United States of America), as well as with other members of the diplomatic community in Maputo. He has, in addition, discussed aspects relating to the implementation of the agreement with representatives of United Nations agencies and programmes and major non-governmental organizations that are currently involved in humanitarian relief effort in Mozambique and that are called upon to assist in carrying out related aspects of the agreement.

5. I am pleased to report that both the Government of Mozambique and the leadership of RENAMO, as well as representatives of the diplomatic community in Mozambique, have expressed their appreciation for the prompt action taken by the Security Council and the Secretary-General.

6. Both parties have committed themselves to undertake immediately after, and in some instances before, the entry into effect of the agreement, specific action to set in motion the joint mechanisms to monitor and verify its implementation. However, no such action had been initiated at the time when the interim Special Representative arrived in Mozambique. Nor had the parties been in direct contact since the signature of the agreement, and RENAMO had no official delegation in the capital. The RENAMO delegation did not wish to move from its headquarters in Gorongosa to Maputo until the Government had provided adequate logistic support, i.e. appropriate housing, transport and communication facilities as foreseen in the agreement. This logistic problem, seemingly marginal, turned out to be a major impediment to the early establishment of the monitoring and verification machinery. Meanwhile, major violations of the cease-fire were reported in various areas of the country, and the parties presented official complaints to the interim Special Representative. A large military operation was reportedly undertaken by RENAMO, which occupied one major town, Angoche, and the villages of Maganja da Costa, Memba and Lugela.

7. In the absence of the machinery foreseen in the agreement for the verification of alleged violations, the interim Special Representative has not been in a position to investigate these incidents. He offered to send United Nations military observers into the areas where military operations had taken place, but this was not possible for lack of agreement between the two parties. I brought these matters to the attention of the Security Council in my letter of 23 October 1992 to its President. The President, in a statement dated 27 October 1992 (S/24719), expressed the Council's deep concern about the reports of major violations of the cease-fire, called upon the parties to halt such violations immediately and urged them to cooperate fully with the interim Special Representative.

8. In order to avoid the escalation of violations, the interim Special Representative called for an informal meeting of the two parties. In a personal letter, he urged Mr. Dhlakama to attend such a meeting, the unsolved logistics problems notwithstanding. He also made a public appeal to both parties. The initiative was successful, and both the Government and RENAMO sent high-level delegations to attend their first meeting in Maputo.

9. Thereafter, the two delegations met on numerous occasions, both bilaterally and together with the interim Special Representative. All conditions and modalities for the establishment of the Commissions foreseen under the agreement were reviewed. The composition of each Commission was extensively discussed and agreement was finally reached. On 4 November 1992, one month after the signature of the agreement, the interim Special Representative was able to appoint the Supervisory and Monitoring Commission, which held its first meeting the same day and appointed the three main subsidiary commissions, the Cease-fire Commission, the Reintegration Commission and the Joint Commission for the Formation of the Mozambican Defence Forces.

10. The Supervisory and Monitoring Commission is composed of government and RENAMO delegations, with representatives of France, Italy, Portugal, the United Kingdom of Great Britain and Northern Ireland, the United States of America and the Organization of African Unity. This Commission is chaired by the United Nations. The Cease-fire Commission is composed of government and RENAMO delegations, with representatives of Botswana, Egypt, France, Italy, Nigeria, Portugal, the United Kingdom and the United States, and is also chaired by the United Nations. The Cease-fire Commission will have subordinate subcommissions in three regional headquarters and also monitoring groups at the assembly areas. The Reintegration Commission is composed of government and RENAMO delegations, with representatives of Denmark, France, Germany, Italy, the Netherlands, Norway, Portugal, South Africa, Spain, Sweden, Switzerland, the United Kingdom, the United States and the European Community (EC) and is chaired by the United Nations. The Joint Commission for the Formation of the Mozambican Defence Forces is composed of government and RENAMO delegations, with representatives of France, Portugal and the United Kingdom. The United Nations has not been requested to take part in this commission.

11. The Supervisory and Monitoring Commission will guarantee the implementation of the agreement, assume responsibility for authentic interpretation of it, settle any disputes that may arise between the parties and guide and coordinate the activities of the other Commissions. The Cease-fire Commission is responsible for supervising the cease-fire and demobilization. The Reintegration Commission is responsible for the economic and social reintegration of demobilized military personnel. The Joint Commission for the Formation of the Mozambican Defence Forces is responsible for supervising the formation of the new unified armed forces.

12. All Commissions and their subordinate bodies have been established and have begun their work. However, they will require some technical support, including an impartial secretariat, which could best be provided by ONUMOZ. Legal services will also be necessary in order to ensure that the working procedures of the commissions meet international standards and to resolve possible legal disputes. As the composition of the main commissions is multinational and all decisions need to be recorded, translation, secretarial and information services will be required. As for the regional offices of the Cease-fire Commission, transport facilities will be necessary to enable the commissions to carry out their duties on the spot.

13. Meanwhile, the Government has undertaken military operations to retake the four places seized by RENAMO in mid-October (see para. 6 above). The interim Special Representative has continued to urge the two parties to refrain from any type of military operation and to discuss and settle all disputes in the appropriate commissions.

II. Basic assumptions for the United Nations Operation in Mozambique

14. In formulating my recommendations to the Security Council on the establishment of a United Nations Operation in Mozambique (ONUMOZ), I have been guided by three fundamental considerations. The first relates to the trust placed in the United Nations by both parties, as well as by the people of Mozambique. The agreement envisages that the United Nations will provide an impartial and supportive structure to help both parties to break the vicious cycle of violence that has caused so much suffering to Mozambique over the years.

15. The second consideration derives from the breadth of the responsibilities entrusted to the United Nations under the agreement. These will require the involvement of the entire international community, especially United Nations programmes and specialized agencies, and also bilateral entities, intergovernmental agencies and non-governmental organizations, all of which can contribute to the rebuilding and development of a peaceful Mozambique.

16. The third consideration relates to the geography of Mozambique and the country's current condition after 14 years of civil war. It covers an area of 800,000 square kilometres. It is elongated in shape, extending about 1,800 km from north to south, 600 km from east to west in the north and 300 km in the south. Its communications have been devastated by the war. It has been afflicted by the worst drought in decades and food is in short supply. There is an abundance of arms and many armed bandits operate outside the control of the armed forces of either side. Several million Mozambicans are internally displaced or are refugees in neighbouring countries.

17. All these factors have to be taken into account in assessing the human and material resources that ONUMOZ will require. An additional factor is the existence of four transport corridors (the Beira, Limpopo, Nacala and Tete corridors, each providing road, rail and/or pipeline links), which run across Mozambique from the Indian Ocean to land-locked countries to the north and west. These corridors are of critical importance to Mozambique itself, to United Nations humanitarian and other operations in southern Africa and to neighbouring countries. As the civil war intensified, Malawi and Zimbabwe, with the Government of Mozambique's agreement, deployed troops in some of the corridors to assist the Government's forces in keeping them open. With the implementation of the agreement's provisions on the assembly and demobilization of the two sides' forces and on the withdrawal of foreign forces, ONUMOZ will have to assume transitional responsibility for the security of the corridors in order to avoid any vacuum that could be exploited by bandits, pending the formation of the new unified armed forces.

III. Overall framework for the operation

18. In accordance with the agreement, the mandate of ONUMOZ would, if the Security Council agrees, be as follows:

(a) *Political*: to facilitate impartially the implementation of the agreement, in particular by chairing the Supervisory and Monitoring Commission and its subordinate commissions;

(b) *Military*:

(i) To monitor and verify the cease-fire, the separation and concentration of forces, their demobilization and the collection, storage and destruction of weapons;

(ii) To monitor and verify the complete withdrawal of foreign forces;

(iii) To monitor and verify the disbanding of private and irregular armed groups;

(iv) To authorize security arrangements for vital infrastructures; and

(v) To provide security for United Nations and other international activities in support of the peace process, especially in the corridors;

(c) *Electoral*: to provide technical assistance and monitor the entire electoral process;

(d) *Humanitarian*: to coordinate and monitor all humanitarian assistance operations, in particular those relating to refugees, internally displaced persons, demobilized military personnel and the affected local population, and, in this context, to chair the Humanitarian Assistance Committee.

19. The operational concept of ONUMOZ is based on the strong interrelationship between the four components of its mandate. Without sufficient humanitarian aid, and especially food supplies, the security situation in the country may deteriorate and the demobilization process might stall. Without adequate military protection, the humanitarian aid would not reach its destination. Without sufficient progress in the political area, the confidence required for the disarmament and rehabilitation process would not exist. The electoral process, in turn, requires prompt demobilization and formation of the new armed forces, without which the conditions would not exist for successful elections.

20. These strong linkages require a fully integrated approach and strong coordination by the interim Special Representative. The following description of the activities proposed for ONUMOZ in each of its four areas of responsibility should, therefore, be seen as an indivisible and interdependent operational plan.

IV. Operational plan for United Nations observation of military aspects of the agreement

21. The arrangements for the cease-fire and other military aspects of the peace process are set out in detail in Protocol IV to the agreement and were highlighted in my report to the Council of 9 October 1992 (S/24642). This role is similar to that entrusted to the United Nations in other recent cases where the Organization has monitored the implementation of a cease-fire, the separation and concentration of forces, their demobilization and the collection and storage of weapons. In addition, the Cease-fire Commission would also approve plans for dealing with other armed groups, including irregulars, and would authorize security arrangements for vital infrastructure, including the corridors.

22. To ensure credible verification, it would be necessary to obtain from the parties lists of all troops and paramilitary forces, assembled or unassembled, together with details of weapons and ammunition held by them. There would have to be an agreement on the categories of troops that would be temporarily exempted from the requirement to assemble. Their numbers should be strictly limited and regularly verified. The demobilization process would be initiated and vigorously pursued as soon as troops started to assemble. Arrangements would also be needed for ONUMOZ to control weapons and ammunition in possession of the Government and RENAMO. All arms and ammunition not required for the new armed forces would be destroyed under close supervision of the United Nations. A systematic programme for removal of weapons from the civilian population would also be required from the outset.

23. ONUMOZ's verification function would be carried out mainly by teams of United Nations military observers at the 49 assembly areas in 3 military regions and elsewhere in the field. They would work with, but would remain separate from, the monitoring groups composed of representatives of the two parties at each location. They would observe the manner in which those groups were carrying out their functions in order to verify that the joint monitoring machinery was working effectively. They would respond to requests for assistance and would use their good offices to resolve any problems that might arise within the monitoring groups, conducting their own investigations and patrolling the whole extent of their assembly areas. Teams would also be deployed at airports, ports and other critical areas, including RENAMO headquarters. The security of United Nations personnel would primarily be the responsibility of the parties that controlled the zone where they were present, although in some cases the military observers would be collocated with armed United Nations troops.

24. The military aspects of the United Nations operation in Mozambique would be inescapably linked with the humanitarian effort. The approximately 110,000 soldiers who come to the assembly areas will be disarmed, demobilized and reintegrated into civil society. They will need food and other support as soon as the assembly areas are established, and there should be special provision in the ONUMOZ budget to cover these costs. The refugees and displaced persons who will inevitably gather around the assembly areas will also require food assistance, which will be provided as part of the humanitarian programme. The relief programmes for assembled soldiers and civil populations in the vicinity will need to be closely coordinated, and it will be desirable to avoid population movements towards the assembly areas. Improved accessibility, the de-mining of roads and the organization of secure transport will be important in this context.

25. An ONUMOZ technical unit, staffed by civilian personnel, will assist the interim Special Representative in the implementation of the demobilization programme and will collaborate closely with a United Nations Office for the Coordination of Humanitarian Assistance (UNOHAC) (see para. 44 below) on its humanitarian aspects. These will include:

> (a) The distribution of food, medicine, health care and other essential services to the assembly areas;

> (b) The organization of a database, as well as the issue of personal documents for the demobilized;

> (c) The supply of civilian clothing and the organization of transport for the ex-combatants when they leave the assembly areas for their homes;

> (d) The establishment of a solid link with the provincial and district authorities responsible for the civilian dimension of the demobilization process.

26. The agreement provides for the withdrawal of foreign troops to be initiated following the entry into force of the cease-fire. Simultaneously, the Supervisory and Monitoring Commission, through the Cease-fire Commission, would assume immediate responsibility "for verifying and ensuring security of strategic and trading routes", of which the most important are the corridors described in paragraph 17 above. The withdrawal of foreign troops started after the agreement's entry into force, and two teams of United Nations military observers have been deployed to monitor it. The withdrawal of the remaining foreign troops before alternative security arrangements were in place would leave the corridors at the mercy of roaming groups of heavily armed irregulars. My interim Special Representative has explored several options, but for political and legal reasons, including the clear provisions of the agreement, it would be extremely difficult to extend the presence of the Malawian and Zimbabwean troops.

27. I have given this question much thought. There is an imperative need to continue to ensure the security of the corridors and other key routes and to protect humanitarian convoys using them. There seems to be no alternative but for ONUMOZ to assume this responsibility. For this function it will be necessary to deploy five logistically self-sufficient infantry battalions. In addition, three logistically self-sufficient engineer companies will be needed, supported, as necessary, by mine-clearing and engineering contractors in order to assist in de-mining and road repair and in the destruction of arms and ammunition not required for the new armed forces. These units must be deployed as rapidly as possible in order to permit early completion of the withdrawal of foreign forces.

28. The following additional elements would be part of ONUMOZ's military component and would provide support to the other components of the mission:

(a) A Headquarters company, including a military police platoon;

(b) A military communications unit to ensure secure communications within the entire mission area for all components of ONUMOZ;

(c) A substantial aviation unit to provide a high degree of air mobility in a devastated country where many of the roads have been made impassable. The aviation unit would be responsible for command and liaison, reconnaissance, investigations, medical evacuation and resupply. It would probably be obtained from commercial sources and would consist of up to 24 rotary and fixed-wing aircraft (utility helicopters, light passenger aircraft, medium passenger/cargo aircraft); additional heavy cargo capacity would be obtained, if needed, on a local charter basis;

(d) A military medical unit to support all ONUMOZ components, including a field hospital and medical evacuation capability. The infantry battalions would include integral medical support;

(e) Three logistic companies, as the conditions in Mozambique make it impossible to rely on a civilian resupply system. Each company would consist of a transport platoon, a supply platoon, a fuel, oil and lubricant platoon and a workshop platoon. One would be located at each of the three regional headquarters;

(f) A movement control company.

V. Possible monitoring of the police

29. While the agreement does not provide a specific role for United Nations civilian police in monitoring the neutrality of the Mozambican police, experience elsewhere suggests that this could be desirable in order to inspire confidence that violations of civil liberties, human rights and political freedom will be avoided. Throughout the peace process, but particularly during the electoral campaign, the presence of a United Nations police component could be most useful, although agreement on this point was not reached in the Rome negotiations. If agreed by the two sides, such a component could be headed by an Inspector General, and consist of up to 128 police officers, deployed in the regions and provincial capitals. It would work in close cooperation with the National Police Affairs Commission and provide technical advice to this body as required. I believe that such a unit would be a valuable addition to ONUMOZ and I therefore intend to ask my interim Special Representative to reopen this matter with the parties and seek their concurrence.

VI. Monitoring of the electoral process and the provision of technical assistance for the elections

30. Under the terms of the agreement, legislative and presidential elections will be held simultaneously one year after the date of signature of the agreement. This period may be extended if it is determined that circumstances exist that preclude its observance. In the light of recent experience in Angola, I believe it to be of critical importance that the elections should not take place until the military aspects of the agreement have been fully implemented. It is also important that the peace process should not be drawn out indefinitely. I have therefore asked the interim Special Representative to give the highest priority to timely implementation of the cease-fire, the assembly, disarmament and demobilization of troops, and the formation of the new armed forces.

31. In the agreement, the parties agreed to invite the United Nations and other organizations and private individuals to observe the elections from the start of the electoral campaign until the new Government's assumption of office. They also agreed to seek technical and material assistance from the United Nations. On the day the agreement was signed, President Chissano formally addressed appropriate requests to me on these matters (S/24635).

32. The terms of reference of ONUMOZ's electoral component would be as follows:

(a) To verify the impartiality of the National Elections Commission and its organs in all aspects and stages of the electoral process;

(b) To verify that political parties and alliances enjoy complete freedom of organization, movement, assembly and expression, without hindrance and intimidation;

(c) To verify that all political parties and alliances have fair access to State mass media and that there is fairness in the allocation of both the hour and duration of radio and television broadcasts;

(d) To verify that the electoral rolls are properly drawn up and that qualified voters are not denied identification and registration cards or the right to vote;

(e) To report to the electoral authorities on complaints, irregularities and interferences reported or observed, and, if necessary, to request the electoral authorities to take action to resolve and rectify them, as well as conducting its own independent investigation of irregularities;

(f) To observe all activities related to the registration of voters, the organization of the poll, the electoral campaign, the poll itself and the counting, computation and announcement of the results;

(g) To participate in the electoral education campaign;

(h) To prepare periodic reports on the evolution of the electoral process, that will be submitted to the Secretary-General through his interim Special Representative.

33. The electoral component would prepare independent reports about the conduct of the elections. It would establish a special relationship with the National Elections Commission.

34. In carrying out its mandate to verify the impartiality of the National Elections Commission and its organs, the electoral component would evaluate the criteria for the appointment of electoral authorities at the regional and provincial levels. The fairness of challenged actions or significant decisions at both the national and the provincial levels would be similarly evaluated.

35. In order to verify that political parties and alliances enjoy complete freedom of organization, movement, assembly and expression without hindrance and intimidation, the electoral component would establish offices in each provincial capital, with an adequate number of observer teams at each of them. The latter would establish contact with political parties and social organizations at the national and local levels and would visit villages and municipalities throughout the country. They would attend all important political rallies and other relevant activities, and verify the observance by all parties of the electoral law and any code of conduct that might be agreed between the parties or established by the electoral authorities. This activity would be reinforced by a public information campaign about electoral activities, ONUMOZ's objectives and the mechanisms established.

36. To verify that all political parties and alliances have fair access to State mass media, the electoral component would verify the distribution of broadcasting time between parties, the content of news broadcasts and the fairness of tariffs. It would also evaluate complaints received on the use of other public resources for political purposes.

37. In carrying out its mandate to verify that the electoral rolls were properly drawn up, the teams would periodically visit registration centres and evaluate complaints received or irregularities observed. The electoral component would accordingly have to be deployed before the beginning of registration.

38. In order to follow up complaints, irregularities and interferences reported or observed, provincial offices would receive complaints and requests presented by political parties or relevant social organizations, analyse their relevance, compile the information on the issues in question and transmit them to the electoral authorities and/or appropriate parties. Significant threats to the fairness of the elections would be carefully investigated and, if necessary, independently reported. A data bank would record the complaints received and analyses of trends would be produced periodically.

39. ONUMOZ would need to include an Electoral Division headed by a Director, with a total of up to 148 international electoral officers (including two consultants), supported by an appropriate number of United Nations volunteers and international and local support staff. It should have the following structure:

>(a) The Office of the Director (Maputo): a unit that would provide overall direction to the Electoral Division. It would maintain contacts with the Government of Mozambique, RENAMO and the National Elections Commission and the main political parties;

>(b) Three Regional Offices, each headed by a Regional Coordinator in the southern, central and northern regions;

>(c) Provincial Offices each headed by a provincial coordinator assisted by a team of up to 10 Electoral Officers.

40. During the polling itself, the Electoral Division would require the services of up to 1,200 international observers. I have asked the interim Special Representative to seek the cooperation of regional organizations, governments and non-governmental organizations who intend to send election observers to Mozambique, in order to minimize the number of additional observers who will have to be deployed by the United Nations. It should also be possible to draw on United Nations and other international personnel who will already be in Mozambique for non-electoral purposes. All observers would have to have full access to all stages of the poll. With their help, the Electoral Division would develop a projection of results for internal purposes.

41. When a country for the first time prepares for multi-party elections, it is crucial that its electoral authorities have adequate access to technical assistance and material support. The planning and execution of voter registration and polling presents a formidable challenge to national electoral authorities. In Mozambique adequate legal advice, logistical planning and support would be as important as political commitment of the two parties to ensure free and fair elections. A major national as well as international effort would be required. This would encompass a broad range of needs: vehicles, aircraft, communications, voting booths and material, food, tents, salary for registration and electoral brigades. Legal advice on the drafting of an electoral law and technical guidance on the conduct of elections would be especially essential. Technical assistance, if timely, would help to create an orderly and coherent process. In anticipation of the request from the Government referred to in paragraph 31 above, a United Nations technical mission on electoral matters visited Mozambique in September 1992 and established contacts with the Government. It is envisaged that United Nations consultants will continue to cooperate closely with the national electoral authorities.

42. Specific activities of the United Nations in this area will largely occur outside the immediate mandate of ONUMOZ, albeit in close coordination with its electoral component. It is my intention to provide technical assistance to the electoral authorities through the United Nations Development Programme and other existing mechanisms of the United Nations system. These United Nations activities will have to be coordinated closely by my interim Special Representative with those of other intergovernmental bodies, in particular OAU and the European Community, and with bilateral donors. Some of the donors have already sent preparatory teams to the country with a view to elaborating a comprehensive document on electoral support which would be presented to the forthcoming pledging conference in Rome. The United Nations would be ready to play the main coordinating role for the provision of technical assistance to the whole electoral process in Mozambique.

VII. Plan for the United Nations coordination of the humanitarian aspects of the agreement

43. The character and scope of the United Nations ongoing humanitarian assistance programmes in Mozambique require adjustment following the signing of the agreement, in which the parties undertook to facilitate significantly the provision of humanitarian aid to previously inaccessible areas and called on the United Nations to coordinate the provision of all such assistance. Immediately after the signing of the agreement, I accordingly dispatched a humanitarian assistance mission to Mozambique to assess existing United Nations operations in this area and to devise a more effective United Nations response to the intended expansion of humanitarian activities, with emphasis on the development of an appropriate coordination mechanism.

44. As a result, it is my recommendation that ONUMOZ should have a humanitarian component in the form of a United Nations Office for the Coordination of Humanitarian Assistance, which would be established in Maputo, with suboffices at the regional and provincial levels. It would replace the present office of the United Nations Special Coordinator for Emergency Relief Operations. Headed by the Humanitarian Affairs Coordinator, and under the overall authority of my interim Special Representative, it would function as an integrated component of ONUMOZ. To ensure the proper provision and delivery of relief assistance to an expanded beneficiary population in Mozambique, UNOHAC would coordinate the various humanitarian assistance programmes. Operational agencies and the non-governmental aid community would be asked to provide representatives to work within the United Nations Office for the Coordination of Humanitarian Assistance.

45. It is estimated that, as a result of both the war and the continuing drought, the internally displaced population in Mozambique totals some 3 to

4 million people. At present, about 3 million Mozambicans living in accessible areas are receiving humanitarian assistance. The signing of the agreement has already created access to additional affected areas, many of which are controlled by RENAMO. As a consequence, nearly 270,000 additional beneficiaries are being provided with humanitarian assistance by the United Nations and by the International Committee of the Red Cross (ICRC), under the terms of the Declaration of Rome on the Principles of Humanitarian Assistance of 15 July 1992. Indications are that the number of additional beneficiaries may reach 500,000 in a matter of months.

46. While 1.4 million of the estimated 1.8 million Mozambican refugees living in neighbouring countries receive assistance, the drought is reported to have caused many other Mozambicans to seek refuge there during the past three months. The expected returnee population can thus be estimated at not less than 1.8 million.

47. The United Nations Office for the Coordination of Humanitarian Assistance will also make available food and other relief for distribution to the soldiers in the assembly areas by a technical unit of ONUMOZ, as described in section IV above. Subsequently, humanitarian aid would be required for the reintegration of demobilized troops into their communities.

VIII. Organizational structure of ONUMOZ

48. The organizational structure of ONUMOZ would be as follows:

(a) Mission headquarters and the Office of the interim Special Representative of the Secretary-General, Maputo. The Office will consist of an Executive Director, a Special Assistant, a Political Adviser, an Information Officer, a Planning and Analysis Officer, a Legal Adviser and both international and locally recruited support staff;

(b) A Military Component with headquarters in Maputo, which would include a Military Observer group, five infantry battalions, one engineer battalion, three logistic companies, a Headquarters company, a movement control company, a communications unit, a medical unit and an air unit (probably from commercial sources). The military component would be headed by a Force Commander with the rank of Major General. There would be three regional offices, as set out in section IV above;

(c) If the parties agree, a police component in Maputo, headed by a Chief Police Observer, who would hold the rank of Chief Superintendent or its equivalent, with three regional offices and staff outposted in provincial towns, as set out in section V above;

(d) An electoral component in Maputo, with three regional offices and provincial offices, as set out in section VI above;

(e) An Office for the Coordination of Humanitarian Assistance in Maputo, with 3 regional offices and 10 provincial offices, as set out in section VII above;

(f) An administrative component in Maputo, with three regional offices, providing support in the areas of finance, personnel, procurement, communication, travel, compensation, building management, property control, translation and interpretation, electronic data processing and security.

IX. Observations and recommendations

49. It is a matter of great satisfaction that an end is at last in sight to the cruel war that has ravaged Mozambique for 14 years. Both the Government and RENAMO deserve to be commended for their statesmanship and diplomatic skill and, above all, for their commitment to their people and their country. I very much hope that in the months ahead they will be guided in their actions by the same spirit of national reconciliation and unity. As the people of Mozambique prepare for democratic multi-party elections, they are starting out on a road that can be either divisive or constructive. It is my fervent hope that the spirit of national unity will also shape the electoral process, and that this will be an opportunity for the people of Mozambique to choose freely the leaders who will jointly work for a better future.

50. The mediators and the observers who have so patiently helped to bring about the agreement also deserve the highest praise. I trust that I can count on their continued political and material support as the peace process evolves.

51. The task which the Government and RENAMO have agreed to ask the United Nations to assume is a large and difficult one. The difficulties derive from the size of the country, the devastated state of its infrastructure, the disruption of its economy by war and drought, the limited capacity of the Government to cope with the new tasks arising from the general peace agreement and the complexity of the processes enshrined in the agreement. An additional dimension derives from the critical importance of the Mozambican corridors for so much of southern Africa. To achieve in one year (of which a month and a half have already passed) the assembly, disarmament and demobilization of the two sides' troops, the formation of new armed forces, the resettlement of 5 to 6 million refugees and displaced persons, the provision of humanitarian relief to all parts of the country and the organization and conduct of elections will require a huge and cooperative effort by the Government and RENAMO and by the international community, with the United Nations in the lead.

52. As will be evident from the present report, I feel obliged to recommend that very substantial resources should be made available for this purpose, especially on the military side. This reflects my conviction that it will not be possible in Mozambique to create the conditions for a successful election unless the military situation has been brought fully under control. If the United Nations is to undertake the responsibilities entrusted to it by the Mozambicans, what has to be done must be done well, and quickly. But however great the resources the United Nations decides to devote to Mozambique, the general peace agreement will not be implemented unless the Mozambican parties make a determined effort in good faith to honour their commitments. The efforts of the United Nations can only be in support of theirs. In the light of recent experiences elsewhere, the recommendations in the present report may be thought to invite the international community to take a risk. I believe that the risk is worth taking; but I cannot disguise that it exists.

53. On this basis, I recommend to the Security Council that it approve the establishment and deployment of ONUMOZ as set out in the present report, and in particular that it agree to:

(a) The establishment of an Office of the interim Special Representative for Mozambique, with up to 12 international Professional staff, 8 international support staff and an adequate number of locally recruited staff;

(b) The deployment of a military component consisting of a Headquarters company and military police platoon; 354 military observers; 5 logistically self-sufficient infantry battalions, each composed of up to 850 personnel; 1 engineer battalion, with contracted assistance as needed; 3 logistic companies; and air, communications, medical and movement control support units;

(c) The deployment of a civilian technical unit to support the logistic tasks relating to the demobilization programme in the assembly areas, with adequate resources;

(d) The deployment, subject to the concurrence of the parties, of 128 police officers to monitor civil liberties and to provide technical advice to the National Police Affairs Commission;

(e) The deployment of an Electoral Division consisting of up to 148 international electoral officers and support staff, from the start of the electoral component of the peace process, followed by the deployment of up to 1,200 international observers for the elections themselves and the periods immediately preceding and following them;

(f) The deployment of 16 international Professional staff to enable the United Nations Office for the Coordination of Humanitarian Assistance to coordinate and monitor all humanitarian assistance within the regions and provinces of Mozambique;

(g) The deployment of up to 28 international Professional staff, up to 100 United Nations Volunteers, up to 124 international support staff and an adequate number of local staff to provide secretariat functions and administrative support to the military, police (if confirmed), electoral and humanitarian components of ONUMOZ, as well as to the commissions chaired by the United Nations.

54. Preliminary cost estimates for ONUMOZ are contained in an addendum to the present report which is being circulated separately.

Addendum (S/24892/Add.1)

1. As stated in paragraph 54 of my main report (S/24892), I indicated that an addendum to the report would be issued which would contain preliminary cost estimates related to the establishment and deployment of a United Nations Operation in Mozambique (ONUMOZ).

2. Based on the operational plan and general assumptions outlined in my main report, it is estimated that an amount of $331.8 million would be required for the period from inception to 31 October 1993. This amount includes the costs of start-up and acquisition of capital equipment. A breakdown of the estimated cost by main objects of expenditure is provided for information purposes in the annex to the present addendum.

3. It would be my recommendation to the General Assembly that, should the Security Council agree to the establishment and deployment of ONUMOZ, the cost relating thereto should be considered as an expense of the Organization to be borne by Member States in accordance with Article 17, paragraph 2, of the Charter of the United Nations and that the assessment to be levied on Member States be credited to a special account to be established for this purpose.

Annex

Cost estimates by objects of expenditure
(For the period from inception to 31 October 1993)
(Thousands of United States dollars)

Objects of expenditure

1.	Military component	
	(a) Observers	19 900
	(b) Contingent personnel	97 000
	(c) Other costs pertaining to contingents	41 100
2.	Civilian police	6 900
3.	Civilian staff costs	59 700
4.	Premises, rental and maintenance	35 200
5.	Vehicle operations	11 000
6.	Air operations	26 900
7.	Communications and other equipment	11 900
8.	Miscellaneous supplies, services, freight and support costs	11 200
9.	Programme related to former combatants in the assembly areas	11 000
	TOTAL	331 800

Appendix II

Security Council Resolution Establishing ONUMOZ (S/RES/797 [1992], 16 December 1992)

The Security Council,

Recalling its resolution 782 (1992) of 13 October 1992,

Recalling also the statement of the President of the Security Council of 27 October 1992, 1/

Having considered the report of the Secretary-General of 3 December 1992 on the United Nations Operation in Mozambique, 2/

Stressing the importance it attaches to the General Peace Agreement for Mozambique 3/ and to the fulfilment by the parties in good faith of the obligations contained therein,

Noting the efforts made so far by the Government of Mozambique and the Resistência Nacional Moçambicana to maintain the cease-fire, and expressing concern over the delays in initiating some of the major tasks arising from the Agreement,

Welcoming the appointment by the Secretary-General of an interim Special Representative for Mozambique who will be in overall charge of United Nations activities in support of the Agreement, as well as the dispatch to Mozambique of a team of twenty-five military observers, as approved by resolution 782 (1992),

Noting the intention of the Secretary-General, in this as in other peace-keeping operations, to monitor expenditures carefully during this period of increasing demands on peace-keeping resources,

1. *Approves* the report of the Secretary-General of 3 December 1992 on the United Nations Operation in Mozambique 2/ and the recommendations contained therein;

2. *Decides* to establish a United Nations Operation in Mozambique as proposed by the Secretary-General and in line with the General Peace Agreement for Mozambique, 3/ and requests the Secretary-General in planning

and executing the deployment of the Operation to seek economies through, *inter alia*, phased deployment and to report regularly to the Council on what is achieved in this regard;

3. *Also decides* that the Operation is established for a period until 31 October 1993 in order to accomplish the objectives described in the report of the Secretary-General;

4. *Calls upon* the Government of Mozambique and the Resistência Nacional Moçambicana to cooperate fully with the interim Special Representative of the Secretary-General for Mozambique and with the Operation and to respect scrupulously the cease-fire and all the commitments entered into under the Agreement, and stresses that the full respect of these commitments constitutes a necessary condition for the fulfilment by the Operation of its mandate;

5. *Demands* that all parties and others concerned in Mozambique take all measures necessary to ensure the safety of United Nations and all other personnel deployed pursuant to the present and prior resolutions;

6. *Endorses* the approach in paragraphs 30 and 51 of the report of the Secretary-General as regards the timetable for the electoral process, and invites the Secretary-General to consult closely with all the parties on the precise timing of and preparations for the presidential and legislative elections, as well as on a precise timetable for the implementation of the other major aspects of the Agreement, and to report back to the Council on this as soon as possible, and in any event not later than 31 March 1993;

7. *Calls upon* the Government of Mozambique and the Resistência Nacional Moçambicana to finalize as soon as possible, in close coordination with the interim Special Representative of the Secretary-General, organizational and logistical preparations for the demobilization process;

8. *Encourages* Member States to respond positively to requests made to them by the Secretary-General to contribute personnel and equipment to the Operation;

9. *Also encourages* Member States to contribute voluntarily to United Nations activities in support of the Agreement, and requests United Nations programmes and specialized agencies to provide appropriate assistance and support for the implementation of the major tasks arising from the Agreement;

10. *Requests* the Secretary-General to keep the Security Council informed of developments and to submit a further report to the Council by 31 March 1993;

11. *Decides* to remain actively seized of the matter.

1/ S/24719.
2/ *Official Records of the Security Council, Forty-seventh Year, Supplement for October, November and December 1992*, documents S/24892 and Add.1 and Corr.1.
3/ Ibid., document S/24635 and Corr.1, annex.

NOTES

1. Mozambique and the Challenges of Peacekeeping in Africa

1. Lori Damrosch, introduction, in Lori Damrosch, ed., *Enforcing Restraint: Collective Intervention in Internal Conflicts* (New York: Council on Foreign Relations Press, 1993); and James Rosenau, "Security in a Turbulent World," in Gene Lyons and Michael Mastanduno, eds., *Beyond Westphalia? State Sovereignty and International Intervention* (Baltimore and London: Johns Hopkins University Press, 1995).

2. Larry Minear and Thomas G. Weiss, *Mercy under Fire: War and the Global Humanitarian Community* (Boulder, Colo.: Westview, 1995), 199–226.

3. I. William Zartman, *Ripe for Resolution: Conflict and Intervention in Africa* (New York: Council on Foreign Relations Press, 1984, updated 1989).

4. William J. Durch, introduction, in William J. Durch, ed., *The Evolution of UN Peacekeeping: Case Studies and Comparative Analysis* (New York: St. Martin's Press, 1993; and Basingstoke, United Kingdom: Macmillan, 1994), 12.

5. Fen Osler Hampson, *Nurturing Peace: Why Peace Settlements Succeed or Fail* (Washington, D.C.: United States Institute of Peace Press, 1996), 125.

6. See, for example, Paul F. Diehl, *International Peacekeeping* (Baltimore and London: Johns Hopkins University Press, 1993), 33–40.

7. Durch, introduction, *Evolution of UN Peacekeeping,* 12.

8. Michael Doyle and Nishkala Suntharalingam, "The UN in Cambodia: Lessons for Complex Peacekeeping," *International Peacekeeping* (Plymouth, United Kingdom) 1, no. 2 (summer 1995): 143–144.

9. Gareth Evans, *Cooperating for Peace: The Global Agenda for the 1990s and Beyond* (London: Allen and Unwin, 1993), 109–114.

10. Yasushi Akashi, "The Challenge of Peacekeeping in Cambodia," *International Peacekeeping* (Plymouth, United Kingdom) 1, no. 2 (summer 1995): 213.

11. Meryl A. Kessler and Thomas G. Weiss, "The United Nations and Third World Security in the 1990s," in Thomas G. Weiss and Meryl A. Kessler, eds.,

Third World Security in the Post–Cold War Era (Boulder, Colo.: Lynne Rienner, 1991), 112–116; and Evans, *Cooperating for Peace,* 120–129.

2. The Spirit of Rome

1. The most detailed accounts of the negotiations are contained in Cameron Hume, *Ending Mozambique's War: The Role of Mediation and Good Offices* (Washington, D.C.: United States Institute of Peace Press, 1994); and Alex Vines, *Renamo: From Terrorism to Democracy in Mozambique?* 2d ed. (London: James Currey, 1996).

2. Evidence collected during the ONUMOZ period showed that, by 1992, Renamo controlled more than half the territory of the provinces of Sofala and Zambezia, more than 40 percent of Manica, and more than 30 percent of Nampula. In all other provinces of the country Renamo was present, occupying pockets of territory from which it could undertake hit-and-run operations and paralyze normal economic activity. Its presence in the southernmost province of Maputo was particularly strong although not concentrated. A map showing these areas is published in Joseph Hanlon, *Peace without Profit: How the IMF Blocks Rebuilding in Mozambique* (London: International African Institute, 1996), 20–21.

3. Objective assessments of the performance and methods of Renamo and the government are given by Vines, *Renamo*; William Finnegan, *A Complicated War: The Harrowing of Mozambique* (Berkeley, Calif.: University of California Press, 1992); and Human Rights Watch, *Conspicuous Destruction: War, Famine, and the Reform Process in Mozambique* (New York: Human Rights Watch, 1992).

4. United Nations, "Report of the Secretary-General on Special Programmes of Economic Assistance to Mozambique," A/47/539, October 22, 1992; reprinted as document 18 in United Nations, *The United Nations and Mozambique, 1992–1995* (New York: United Nations, 1995), 133.

5. United Nations, *Mozambique: Out of the Ruins of War,* Africa Recovery Briefing Paper no. 8 (New York: United Nations, 1993), 20.

6. The GPA is reprinted as document 12 in *The United Nations and Mozambique,* 105–126.

7. Hume, *Ending Mozambique's War,* 51–71.

8. Eric Berman, *Managing Arms in Peace Processes: Mozambique* (Geneva: United Nations Institute for Disarmament Research [UNIDIR], 1996), 49–52.

9. Statement by Pascoal Mocumbi, Mozambique's foreign minister, during a visit to Lisbon in May 1992, quoted in *SouthScan* (London) 7, no. 19 (May 15, 1992): 143.

10. Tayeb Merchoug, interview by author, New York, November 14, 1994.

11. The secretary-general's letter is reprinted as document 10 in *The United Nations and Mozambique,* 102–104.

12. Alex Vines, *No Democracy without Money,* CIIR Briefing Paper (London: Catholic Institute for International Relations, April 1994), 32.

13. United Nations, press release, SG/SM/4829; reprinted as document 11 in *The United Nations and Mozambique,* 104.

14. Hume, *Ending Mozambique's War,* 138.

15. See the GPA; reprinted as document 12 in *The United Nations and Mozambique,* 105–126.

3. The Launch of ONUMOZ

1. United Nations, "Report of the Secretary-General on the UN Operation in Mozambique," S/24642, October 9, 1992, reprinted as document 13 in *The United Nations and Mozambique,* 126–128; and Security Council Resolution S/RES/782 (1992), October 13, 1992, reprinted as document 16 in *The United Nations and Mozambique,* 130.

2. See Hampson, *Nurturing Peace,* 103–108.

3. Ibid., 125; Alex Vines, *One Hand Tied: Angola and the UN,* CIIR Briefing Paper (London, Catholic Institute for International Relations, June 1993), 18; and Karl Maier, *Angola: Promises and Lies* (London: Serif, 1996), 58–59.

4. Hampson, *Nurturing Peace,* 120.

5. Vines, *One Hand Tied,* 19–20.

6. As quoted in Maier, *Promises and Lies,* 177, 141.

7. Aldo Ajello, interview by author, Rome, July 19, 1995.

8. Berman, *Managing Arms in Peace Processes,* 39.

9. United Nations, "Report of the Secretary-General on ONUMOZ," S/24892, December 3, 1992, reprinted as appendix I in this volume and as document 26 in *The United Nations and Mozambique,* 149–157; and Security Council Resolution S/RES/797 (1992), December 16, 1992, reprinted as appendix II in this volume and as document 27 in *The United Nations and Mozambique,* 158.

10. *Mozambique Peace Process Bulletin,* no. 1 (January 1993): 4.

11. Letter from Afonso Dhlakama to Boutros Boutros-Ghali; reprinted as document 29 in *The United Nations and Mozambique,* 170–171.

12. See *SouthScan* 8, no. 1 (January 8, 1993): 6.

13. Ibid.

14. Vicente Ululu, interview by author, Maputo, February 11, 1993.

15. Richard Edis, interview by author, Maputo, February 11, 1993.

16. Ajello, interview by author (Rome).

17. Aldo Ajello, interview by UN Department of Public Information, March 13, 1993.

18. Dirk Solomons (Ajello's interim deputy in Maputo 1992–93), interview by author, New York, October 6, 1994.

19. *Mozambique Peace Process Bulletin,* no. 3 (May 1993): 4.

20. Ajello, interview by UN Department of Public Information.

21. Ibid.

22. Ibid.

23. *Mozambique Peace Process Bulletin,* no. 3 (May 1993): 1.

24. *Mozambique Peace Process Bulletin,* no. 4 (June 1993): 5.

25. United Nations, "Secretary-General's Report on UN Support for Democratization," AG/50/332, August 7, 1995.

26. UN Department of Public Information, press release, SG/1994, May 20, 1993.

27. *Guardian* (London), June 10, 1993.

28. Ajello, interview by author (Rome).

29. *Mozambique Peace Process Bulletin,* no. 5 (August 1993): 3–4.

30. Ibid., 1.

31. Ibid., 3.

32. Ibid., 1–6.

33. Ibid., 5–6.

34. The agencies in the coordinating group included the UN Children's Fund, the World Food Programme, the World Health Organization, and the European Union.

35. Security Council Resolution S/RES/850 (1993), July 9, 1993; reprinted as document 38 in *The United Nations and Mozambique,* 189–190.

36. *Mozambique Peace Process Bulletin,* no. 6 (October 1993): 4.

4. Assembling the Parties and Their Armies

1. United Nations, "Final Document of the Meeting between President Chissano and Mr. Dhlakama," S/26432, September 13, 1993; reprinted as document 41 in *The United Nations and Mozambique,* 196–198.

2. Security Council Resolution S/RES/863 (1993), September 13, 1993; reprinted as document 43 in *The United Nations and Mozambique,* 199–200.

3. Amnesty International, "Peacekeeping and Human Rights" (report issued January 1994, AI Index IOR 40/01/94).

4. Andrea Bartoli, "For a Peaceful Mozambique," *CROSSLINES Global Report* (Geneva) 1, no. 4 (September 1993).

5. Ajello, interview by author (Rome).

6. *Mozambique Peace Process Bulletin,* no. 7 (December 1993): 4.

7. Ibid.

8. United Nations, "Secretary-General's Report on ONUMOZ," S/26666, November 1, 1993; reprinted as document 48 in *The United Nations and Mozambique,* 205–212.

9. Ajello, interview by author (Rome).

10. Security Council Resolution S/RES/882 (1993); reprinted as document 49 in *The United Nations and Mozambique,* 212–213.

11. United Nations, letters from the secretary-general to Chissano and Dhlakama; reprinted as documents 50 and 51 in *The United Nations and Mozambique,* 214.

12. *Noticias* (Maputo), December 4, 1993.

13. United Nations, Supervision and Control Commission, "Minutes of Meetings of December 14 and 23, 1993," CSC/MIN/020, ONUMOZ, Maputo.

14. Ibid.

15. *Mozambique Peace Process Bulletin,* no. 8 (February 1994): 6.

5. Landmines in the Peace Process

1. Chester Crocker, foreword to John L. Hirsch and Robert B. Oakley, *Somalia and Operation Restore Hope: Reflections on Peacemaking and Peace-keeping* (Washington, D.C.: United States Institute of Peace Press, 1995), xvi.

2. United Nations, "Report of the Secretary General on ONUMOZ," S/24892, December 3, 1992; reprinted as document 26 in *The United Nations and Mozambique,* 155.

3. Aldo Ajello, "The Coordination of Humanitarian Assistance in Mozambique in the Context of ONUMOZ," in Jim Whitman and David Pocock, eds., *After Rwanda: The Coordination of United Nations Humanitarian Assistance* (Basingstoke, United Kingdom: Macmillan, 1996), 196.

4. United Nations, "Consolidated Humanitarian Assistance Programme, 1993–94" (report issued by UNOHAC in Maputo, May 1993).

5. Aldo Ajello, interview by author, New York, July 25, 1995.

6. Toby Lanzer, *The UN Department of Humanitarian Affairs in Angola: A Model for the Coordination of Humanitarian Assistance?* Report no. 5, SIDA Studies on Emergencies and Disaster Relief (Uppsala, Sweden: Nordiska Afrikainstitutet, 1996), 8–9.

7. Joseph Hanlon, *Mozambique: Who Calls the Shots?* (London: James Currey; and Bloomington, Ind.: Indiana University Press, 1991).

8. United Nations, "Declaration on the Guiding Principles for Humanitarian Assistance, Rome, July 16, 1992, Appendix to the General Peace Agreement for Mozambique"; reprinted as document 12 in *The United Nations and Mozambique,* 124–125.

9. *SouthScan* 7, no. 36 (September 25, 1992): 279.

10. United Nations, "Consolidated Humanitarian Assistance Programme, 1992–94, Final Report" (report issued by UNOHAC in Maputo, December 1994).

11. World Food Programme, *Mozambique in War and Peace* (Maputo: World Food Programme, 1995).

12. United Nations, "Consolidated Humanitarian Assistance Programme, 1992–94, Final Report."

13. Information supplied to author by UNDP Plans Office, Maputo, October 1995.

14. Shawn Roberts and Jody Williams, "After the Guns Fall Silent: The Enduring Legacy of Landmines" (a report issued by the Vietnam Veterans of America Foundation, Washington, D.C., May 1995); and information supplied to the author by Handicap International, Maputo, October 1995.

15. Information supplied to the author by Handicap International, Maputo, October 1995.

16. UNHCR registered the following numbers of refugees: Malawi, 1.1 million; Zimbabwe, 138,000; Zambia, 25,000; Swaziland, 24,000; and Tanzania, 20,000. UNHCR's estimates of unregistered refugees were South Africa, 250,000; Zimbabwe, 100,000; and Tanzania, 50,000.

17. K. B. Wilson, *Internally Displaced, Refugees, and Returnees from and in Mozambique,* Report no. 1, SIDA Studies on Emergencies and Disaster Relief (Uppsala, Sweden: Nordiska Afrikainstitutet, 1992).

18. U.S. Committee for Refugees, *No Place Like Home: Mozambican Refugees Begin Africa's Largest Repatriation* (Washington, D.C.: USCR, December 1993).

19. Jeff Crisp, "From Social Disarticulation to Social Reconstitution" (paper presented to the Second International Conference on Displacement and Resettlement, Refugee Studies Programme, Oxford, September 1996), 3.

20. Ibid., 23–25.

21. Refugees returning from Malawi numbered 1.35 million; from Zimbabwe, nearly 242,000; from South Africa, 67,000; from, Tanzania 32,000; from Zambia, nearly 23,000; and from Swaziland, nearly 17,000. Information from UNHCR Mozambique, September 1995.

22. Crisp, "Social Disarticulation," 10–11.

23. U.S. Committee for Refugees, *No Place Like Home.*

24. International Organization for Migration, "Assistance Programme for Internally Displaced Persons" (IOM internal report, Maputo, August 1995).

25. United Nations, "Workshop on Reintegration Programmes for Demobilized Soldiers in Mozambique, October 13–14, 1994, Final Report" (issued by UNOHAC, Maputo, 1994).

26. Friedrich Ebert Foundation, "International Workshop on the Successful Conclusion of ONUMOZ, March 27, 1995" (report issued by the Friedrich Ebert Foundation, Ebenhausen, Germany, 1995).

27. United Nations, Reintegration Committee, "Final Address of the Chairman of CORE, December 5, 1995, ONUMOZ, Maputo."

28. Minear and Weiss, *Mercy under Fire*, 202–203.

29. Antonio Donini, *The Policies of Mercy: UN Coordination in Afghanistan, Mozambique, and Rwanda,* Occasional Paper no. 22 (Providence, R.I.: Thomas J. Watson Jr. Institute for International Studies, Brown University), 66–67.

30. Roger Carlson, interview by author, Maputo, October 13, 1995.

31. Ajello, "Coordination of Humanitarian Assistance," 199.

32. United Nations, "Consolidated Humanitarian Assistance Programme, 1992–94, Final Report."

33. Ibid.

34. Ibid.

35. Donini, *Policies of Mercy,* 83.

6. Demobilization

1. Security Council Resolution S/RES/898 (1994); reprinted as document 57 in *The United Nations and Mozambique,* 228–229.

2. United Nations, "Report of the Secretary-General on ONUMOZ, April 28, 1994"; reprinted as document 63 in *The United Nations and Mozambique,* 232–240.

3. Berman, *Managing Arms in Peace Processes,* 72–75.

4. United Nations, Cease-Fire Commission, "Memorandum from CCF chairman to CSC chairman, May 25, 1995."

5. The scheme required the TU to issue ex-combatants with demobilization cards and RSS checkbooks, each containing nine checks, worth a minimum of 150,000 meticais each for the lowest ranks, and redeemable every two months over an eighteen-month period.

6. AIM (Mozambican Information Agency), *Mozambiquefile* (Maputo), no. 216 (July 1994).

7. "Mozambique Government to the President of the Security Council, July 7, 1994," S/1994/803, July 9, 1994; reprinted as document 66 in *The United Nations and Mozambique,* 249.

8. United Nations, "Statement by the President of the Security Council," S/PRST/1994/35, July 19, 1994; reprinted as document 67 in *The United Nations and Mozambique,* 250.

9. United Nations, "Report of the Secretary General on ONUMOZ," S/1994/803, July 7, 1994; reprinted as document 65 in *The United Nations in Mozambique,* 248.

10. United Nations, Cease-Fire Commission, "Report of CCF Chairman to CSC Meeting of July 18, 1994," CSC/MIN/033, annex 1.

11. United Nations, "Statement by the President of the Security Council," S/PRST/1994/35, July 19, 1994; reprinted as document 67 in *The United Nations and Mozambique,* 250.

12. United Nations, Supervision and Control Commission, "Minutes of CSC Meeting of July 20, 1994," CSC/MIN/034.

13. Ibid.

14. United Nations, Supervision and Control Commission, "Minutes of CSC meeting of July 25, 1994," CSC/MIN/035.

15. John Wyatt, "Report on UK Assistance to Formation of FADM" (Commission for the Joint Armed Forces for the Defense of Mozambique, Maputo, October 31, 1994).

16. *Mozambique Peace Process Bulletin,* no. 13 (October 1994): 3.

17. An analysis by UNOHAC of the assembly and demobilization process between January and November 1994 produced figures of 371 incidents and 34 related deaths. Serious injuries were sustained by 111 persons; there were many cases of rape and beating. A breakdown of the types of incidents showed that 123 involved either seizure of buildings or blocking of roads and 74 involved damage to UN property. In 178 incidents, the dispute was resolved by intervention of staff involved in demobilization or reintegration, mainly from ONUMOZ. In a number of important cases, top ONUMOZ staff intervened personally. The Mozambique police intervened in 76 cases; government and Renamo representatives personally resolved 25 and 22 incidents, respectively; and NGOs resolved 8. In the remaining cases, solutions were reached by various parties, including the staff of other UN organizations, or by the local population. The provinces of Zambezia, Nampula, and Sofala accounted for more than 60 percent of all incidents. The months in which the greatest number of incidents occurred were April and August, with exceptional peaks occurring in Zambezia province in July, and in Maputo city during May and July. The UNOHAC study concluded that there were three main reasons for the unrest: (1) demands for food; (2) demands for payments and subsidies; (3) demands for immediate demobilization.

18. Of the TU budget, $15 million was for demobilization subsidies, excluding the RSS; $15 million was for transportation of the soldiers and their dependents to their home areas; $8 million was for food in the assembly areas; $4 million was for health care; and $3 million was for nonfood items and accommodation.

19. Ton Pardoel, "Demobilization Programme in Mozambique, Summary Report" (Maputo, October 4, 1995; privately distributed).

20. In 1993, IOM transported 27,106 former soldiers and dependents, and in the much larger operation during 1994, it transported 156,617 individuals (75,169 demobilized soldiers and 81,448 dependents).

21. United Nations, "Workshop on Reintegration Programmes for Demobilized Soldiers in Mozambique, October 13–14, 1994, Final Report."

22. United Nations, Cease-Fire Commission, "Report of CCF Chairman to CSC Meeting of July 18, 1994," CSC/MIN/033, annex 1.

23. United Nations, Supervision and Control Commission, "Minutes of CSC meeting of September 19, 1994," CSC/MIN/042.

24. Ajello, interview by author (New York).

25. Berman, *Managing Arms in Peace Processes,* 74–75.

26. GPA, reprinted as document 12 in *The United Nations and Mozambique,* 122.

27. United Nations, "Report of the Secretary General on ONUMOZ," S/24892, December 3, 1992; reprinted as document 26 in *The United Nations and Mozambique,* 151.

28. Berman, *Managing Arms in Peace Processes,* 84.

29. Ton Pardoel, interview by author, Maputo, October 23, 1995.

30. Alex Vines, "Light Weapons Transfers, Human Rights Violations, and Armed Banditry in Southern Africa" (paper prepared for a workshop on light weapons proliferation, London, June 30–July 2, 1996), 9–15.

7. Elections

1. United Nations Development Programme, "Assistance to the Electoral Process in Mozambique, Final Report," UNDP Project MOZ/93/016, April 1995, 1.

2. Richard Edis, "Mozambique's Successful Peace Process: An Insider's View," *Cambridge Review of International Affairs* 9, no. 2 (1995): 10.

3. *Mozambique Peace Process Bulletin,* no. 10 (July 1994): 13.

4. By August, Renamo had spent $13.6 million, according to the Security Council mission report, and there was only a further $1 million pledged. In September, after a further $6 million was paid into the fund, including $3 million transferred from Italy's allocation to the UNOHAC trust fund, the contributions reached a final total of $17.6 million. See document 72 in *The United Nations and Mozambique,* 268.

5. Ajello, quoted in *Mozambique Peace Process Bulletin,* no. 9 (April 1994): 5.

6. By September, the numbers of Civpol stations reached sixty-eight in government areas and fifteen in Renamo areas, and the government police had opened seven of its own stations in Renamo areas.

7. Amnesty International, "Mozambique: Monitoring Human Rights— The Task of UN Police Observers" (report issued June 1994, AI Index AFR 41/03/94).

8. United Nations, "Report of the Security Council Mission to Mozambique of August 7–12, 1994," S/1994/1009, August 29, 1994; reprinted as document 70 in *The United Nations and Mozambique,* 258–267.

9. *Mozambique Peace Process Bulletin,* no. 12 (September 1994): 5–6.

10. United Nations, "Further Report of the Secretary-General on ONUMOZ," S/1994/1002, August 26, 1994; reprinted as document 69 in *The United Nations and Mozambique,* 257.

11. United Nations, "Statement by the President of the Security Council," S/PRST/1994/51, September 7, 1994; reprinted as document 71 in *The United Nations and Mozambique,* 267–268.

12. *Mozambique Peace Process Bulletin,* no. 13 (October 1994): 1.

13. United Nations, Supervision and Control Commission, "Minutes of CSC meeting of October 4, 1994," CSC/MIN/043.

14. United Nations, "Statement by the President of the Security Council," S/PRST/1994/61; reprinted as document 75 in *The United Nations and Mozambique,* 283.

15. "Final Communiqué of the Summit Meeting of the Frontline States, October 25, 1994"; reprinted as document 76 in *The United Nations and Mozambique,* 284–285.

16. UN press releases SG/SM/5456 and SC/5922, October 27, 1994; reprinted as documents 77 and 78 in *The United Nations and Mozambique,* 285.

17. As reported in *The Independent* (London), October 29, 1994.

18. AIM, Maputo, December 12, 1994.

19. United Nations, "Joint Declaration by the International Members of the CSC"; reprinted as document 79 in *The United Nations and Mozambique,* 286.

20. *Independent,* October 29, 1994.

21. United Nations Development Programme, "Assistance to the Electoral Process in Mozambique, Final Report," UNDP Project MOZ/93/016, April 1995, 21.

22. United Nations, "Letter from the Secretary-General to the Security Council," S/1994/1282, November 11, 1994; reprinted as document 80 in *The United Nations and Mozambique,* 288.

23. United Nations, "Statement by the Special Representative of the Secretary-General," UN press release SG/SM/5488, November 19, 1994; reprinted as document 82 in *The United Nations and Mozambique,* 289–290.

24. AIM, Maputo, December 11 and 12, 1994.

25. Donini, *Policies of Mercy,* 81.

26. Friedrich Ebert Foundation, "International Workshop on the Successful Conclusion of ONUMOZ, March 27, 1995."

27. Donini, *Policies of Mercy,* 82–86.

28. Human Rights Watch, *Human Rights Watch World Report, 1996* (New York: Human Rights Watch, 1995), 30–33.

29. United Nations Development Programme, "Assistance to the Electoral Process in Mozambique, Final Report," UNDP Project MOZ/93/016, April 1995, 8.

8. ONUMOZ

1. Erick de Mul, interview by author, Maputo, October 18, 1995.

2. Friedrich Ebert Foundation, "International Workshop on the Successful Conclusion of ONUMOZ, March 27, 1995."

3. John Mayowe, interview by author, Maputo, October 20, 1995.

4. Friedrich Ebert Foundation, "International Workshop on the Successful Conclusion of ONUMOZ, March 27, 1995."

5. Ibid.

6. United Nations, "Consolidated Humanitarian Assistance Programme, 1992–94, Final Report."

7. Ajello, interview by author (Rome).

8. Aldo Ajello, interview by author, Maputo, December 8, 1994.

9. United Nations, Cease-Fire Commission, "Final Report of the Chairman, December 5, 1994" (issued by ONUMOZ in Maputo).

10. Friedrich Ebert Foundation, "International Workshop on the Successful Conclusion of ONUMOZ, March 27, 1995."

11. Wyatt, "Report on UK Assistance to Formation of FADM."

12. United Nations Development Programme, "Assistance to the Electoral Process in Mozambique, Final Report," UNDP Project MOZ/93/016, April 1995.

13. United Nations, National Elections Commission, "Final Report" (issued by CNE in Maputo in 1995).

14. Friedrich Ebert Foundation, "International Workshop on the Successful Conclusion of ONUMOZ, March 27, 1995."

15. United Nations, Supervision and Control Commission, "Minutes of CSC meeting of September 19, 1994," CSC/MIN/042.

16. United Nations, Cease-Fire Commission, "Final Report of the Chairman, December 5, 1994" (issued by ONUMOZ in Maputo).

17. João Paulo Borges Coelho and Alex Vines, "Demobilization and Reintegration of Ex-Combatants in Mozambique" (a pilot study, Refugee Studies Programme, Oxford, 1995).

18. Ajello, "The Coordination of Humanitarian Assistance in Mozambique."

19. U.S. embassy cable, January 11, 1995, circulated to the international community as a non-paper.

20. Ajello, interview by author (New York).

21. Ajello, "The Coordination of Humanitarian Assistance in Mozambique."

22. Minear and Weiss, *Mercy under Fire,* 200.

23. Ibid., 197.

24. Friedrich Ebert Foundation, "International Workshop on the Successful Conclusion of ONUMOZ, March 27, 1995."

25. U.S. embassy cable, January 11, 1995.

9. Lessons for Peacekeeping and Peacebuilding in Africa

1. U.S. embassy cable, January 11, 1995.

2. Jakkie Cilliers and Mark Malan, *South African and Regional Peacekeeping,* CSIS Africa Notes, no. 187 (Washington, D.C.: Center for Strategic and International Studies, August 1996), 8–9.

3. John Prendergast and David Smock, *Angola's Elusive Peace,* CSIS Africa Notes, no. 182 (Washington, D.C.: Center for Strategic and International Studies, March 1996), 2.

4. Durch, *Evolution of UN Peacekeeping,* 12.

INDEX

United States Institute of Peace

The United States Institute of Peace is an independent, nonpartisan federal institution created and funded by Congress to promote research, education, and training on the peaceful resolution of international conflicts. Established in 1984, the Institute meets its congressional mandate through an array of programs, including research grants, fellowships, professional training programs, conferences and workshops, library services, publications, and other educational activities. The Institute's board of directors is appointed by the President of the United States and confirmed by the Senate.

Chairman of the Board: Chester A. Crocker
Vice Chairman: Max M. Kampelman
President: Richard H. Solomon
Executive Vice President: Harriet Hentges

Board of Directors

Chester A. Crocker (Chairman), Research Professor of Diplomacy, School of Foreign Service, Georgetown University

Max M. Kampelman, Esq. (Vice Chairman), Fried, Frank, Harris, Shriver and Jacobson, Washington, D.C.

Dennis L. Bark, Senior Fellow, Hoover Institution on War, Revolution and Peace, Stanford University

Theodore M. Hesburgh, President Emeritus, University of Notre Dame

Seymour Martin Lipset, Hazel Professor of Public Policy, George Mason University

Mary Louise Smith, civic activist; former chairman, Republican National Committee

W. Scott Thompson, Professor of International Politics, Fletcher School of Law and Diplomacy, Tufts University

Allen Weinstein, President, Center for Democracy, Washington, D.C.

Harriet Zimmerman, Vice President, American Israel Public Affairs Committee, Washington, D.C.

Members ex officio

Madeleine K. Albright, Secretary of State

Richard A. Chilcoat, Lieutenant General, U.S. Army; President, National Defense University

Ralph Earle II, Deputy Director, U.S. Arms Control and Disarmament Agency

Walter B. Slocombe, Under Secretary of Defense for Policy

Richard H. Solomon, President, United States Institute of Peace (nonvoting)

Richard Synge is a writer on African political and economic issues. Formerly editor of leading specialist journals, reference works, and magazines—including *Africa Research Bulletin, Africa Contemporary Record, Africa Economic Digest,* and *Africa Analysis*—he is now an associate of the African Studies Centre at the University of Cambridge, a consultant to the United Nations, and a contributor to many publications on Africa. Synge also writes regularly in the *International Herald Tribune.* He undertook research and editing for *The United Nations and Apartheid, 1948–1994* and *The United Nations and Mozambique, 1992–1995* (published by the United Nations in 1994 and 1995, respectively). Other recent books include *Nigeria: The Way Forward* (Euromoney Books, 1993) and *Issues in African Development* (Heinemann Nigeria, 1995).

Mozambique: UN Peacekeeping in Action

This book is set in Garamond Light. Cover design by Hasten Design Studio; interior design by Joan Engelhardt. Page makeup by Helene Y. Redmond. Computer cartography by Ken Allen. Editing by Nigel Quinney, Frances Bowles, and Wesley Palmer.